Creation of a Novel Class:
The Oxazolidinone Antibiotics

Editors

Donald H. Batts, MD, FACP

Marin H. Kollef, MD

Benjamin A. Lipsky, MD, FACP, FIDSA

David P. Nicolau, PharmD, FCCP

John A. Weigelt, MD, DVM

Medical Writer
Laurel Ranger

This program is made possible by an unrestricted educational grant from

 U.S. Pharmaceuticals

Supported by

UNIVERSITY OF KENTUCKY

INSTITUTE FOR MEDICAL EDUCATION

Creation of a Novel Class: The Oxazolidinone Antibiotics

Editors
Donald H. Batts, MD, FACP
Marin H. Kollef, MD
Benjamin A. Lipsky, MD, FACP, FIDSA
David P. Nicolau, PharmD, FCCP
John A. Weigelt, MD, DVM

Printed in the United States of America

ISBN 0-9748338-0-0

Innova Institute for Medical Education
7857 Woodland Center Blvd.
Tampa, FL 33614-2410

Editors
Wilma M. Guerra, ELS
Mary K. Osterbrock

Editorial Assistant
Trudy Grenon

Clinical Content Director
Isabelle V. Tate, RN

Senior Editor
Maria B. Uravich, ELS

Graphic Design
Charles Fair
Denyse Lyons
John Pelerossi

Production
Nilsa Ortiz

Medicine is an ever-changing field. As new research and clinical experience widen our knowledge, changes in treatment and drug therapy are required. The writer, editors, and publisher of this work have used sources believed to be reliable in their efforts to provide information that is complete and accurate and generally matching accepted standards at the time of publication. However, in view of the possibility of human error and changes in the field of medicine, neither the writer, editors, nor the publisher, nor any other party involved in the preparation or publication of this work, warrants that the information contained in this work is in every respect accurate or complete, and they are not responsible for the use of such information or the results obtained. Readers are encouraged to confirm the information in this work with other sources.

The publisher has made every effort to trace the copyright holders for borrowed material. If any copyright holders have been over-looked, the necessary arrangements will be made at the first opportunity.

Acknowledgements

This book is dedicated to all of those, named and unnamed, who have contributed to the discovery and development of antibiotics, thereby saving and improving the lives of millions. Every effort has been made to unearth and accurately record the events in the development of linezolid and the oxazolidinones and to credit the efforts of all major contributors.

Steven Brickner provided much of the information on the early development of linezolid and the oxazolidinones at The Upjohn Company and gave invaluable technical help in reviewing portions of this manuscript. Without his contribution, this would have been a much shorter and less accurate book. Thanks are due to Christopher Demos, Walter Gregory, and Patricia Bartholomew for providing details on the discovery of the oxazolidinones at DuPont. Their contributions have enriched our understanding of the development of this class of drugs considerably. Additionally, Michael Barbachyn, Charles Ford, and Gary Zurenko reviewed portions of the manuscript and made important additions. Robert Moellering also provided invaluable assistance. Thanks are also due to Gudrun Hibberd, Iris Gonzalez, Julie Noe, ELS, and all those who assisted in editing, fact checking, and preparing the manuscript.

Supported through an unrestricted educational grant from

 **U.S. Pharmaceuticals**

Jointly sponsored by the University of Kentucky Colleges of Pharmacy and Medicine and Innova Institute for Medical Education.

This content was edited by:
Robert P. Rapp, PharmD, FCCP
Professor of Pharmacy and Surgery
University of Kentucky Chandler Medical Center
Lexington, KY

Overview

This history is meant to provide an understanding of the context in which linezolid and the oxazolidinones were developed during the last decades of the 20th century and to give credit to those who were most instrumental in the development of these valuable antimicrobials. It charts the early preclinical and regulatory history, as well as the postmarketing experience. This work also explores those pathogens and illnesses for which linezolid is the most appropriate treatment, and it is intended to promote a better understanding of the agent's pharmacology.

Target Audience

This continuing medical education offering is intended to meet the needs of physicians who care for critically ill patients.

Learning Objectives

Learning objectives are listed at the beginning of each chapter.

Physician Accreditation

This activity has been planned and implemented in accordance with the Essential Areas and Policies of the Accreditation Council for Continuing Medical Education through the joint sponsorship of the University of Kentucky College of Medicine and Innova Institute for Medical Education. The University of Kentucky College of Medicine is accredited by the ACCME to provide continuing medical education for physicians.

The University of Kentucky College of Medicine designates this educational activity for a maximum of six (6) Category 1 credits toward the AMA Physician's Recognition Award. Each physician should claim only those hours of credit he or she actually spent in the educational activity.

The University of Kentucky College of Medicine presents this activity for educational purposes only. Readers are expected to use their own expertise and judgment while engaged in the practice of medicine. All information is reviewed by professionals who are recognized as experts in their field.

Pharmacist Accreditation

The University of Kentucky College of Pharmacy is approved by the American Council on Pharmaceutical Education as a provider of continuing pharmaceutical education.

This program has been assigned ACPE No. 022-999-04-006-H04 and will award six (6) contact hours (0.6 CEUs) of continuing pharmacy education credit in states that recognize ACPE providers. Statements of credit will indicate hours and CEUs based on participation. The college complies with the Criteria for Quality for continuing education programming.

The University of Kentucky College of Pharmacy presents this activity for educational purposes only. Readers are expected to utilize their own expertise and judgment while engaged in the practice of pharmacy. All information is reviewed by professionals who are recognized as experts in their field.

To receive credit for this continuing education activity, participants must complete, sign, and mail the course evaluation form to:

Attn: Distance Education
Continuing Education Office
Colleges of Pharmacy and Medicine
University of Kentucky
One Quality Street, 6th Floor
Lexington, KY 40507-1428

Program Release Date: February 1, 2004
Program Expiration Date: January 31, 2005

Disclosure Statement

The University of Kentucky Colleges of Pharmacy and Medicine Continuing Education Office endorses the standards of the Accreditation Council for Continuing Medical Education and the guidelines of the Association of American Medical Colleges, in that contributors to continuing medical education activities disclose significant relationships with commercial companies whose products or services are discussed in educational presentations.

Significant relationships include receiving from a commercial company research grants, consultant fees, honoraria, travel or other benefits, or any self-managed equity interest in a company.

Disclosure of a relationship is not intended to suggest or condone any bias in any presentation, but is made to provide participants with information that might be of potential importance in their evaluation of a presentation.

Significant relationships exist with the following companies/organizations whose products or services may be discussed:

Donald H. Batts, MD, FACP

Dr Batts is a consultant for Pfizer Inc, Cubist Pharmaceuticals, and Takeda Pharmaceuticals; he serves on the speakers' bureaus for Pfizer, Cubist, Ortho Biotech, and Bayer.

Marin H. Kollef, MD

Dr Kollef serves on the speakers' bureaus for Merck & Co., Inc., and Pfizer Inc. He has received grants and research support from Merck and Bayer.

Benjamin A. Lipsky, MD, FACP, FIDSA

Dr Lipsky has received grants and research support from Pfizer Inc, Merck & Co., Inc., Cubist Pharmaceuticals, and Vicuron Pharmaceuticals. He is a consultant for Pfizer, Merck, Cubist, Vicuron, and KCI, and he serves on the speakers' bureaus for Pfizer and Merck.

David P. Nicolau, PharmD, FCCP

Dr Nicolau has received grants and research support from Aventis Inc, AstraZeneca, and Cubist Pharmaceuticals and serves as a consultant for Pfizer Inc and Wyeth.

John A. Weigelt, MD, DVM

Dr Weigelt has received grants and research support from Pfizer Inc, Wyeth, and Bristol-Myers Squibb Company. He serves as a consultant for Pfizer and BMS and serves on the speakers' bureaus for Pfizer, Wyeth, and Merck & Co., Inc.

CREATION OF A NOVEL CLASS:

TABLE OF CONTENTS

THE OXAZOLIDINONE ANTIBIOTICS

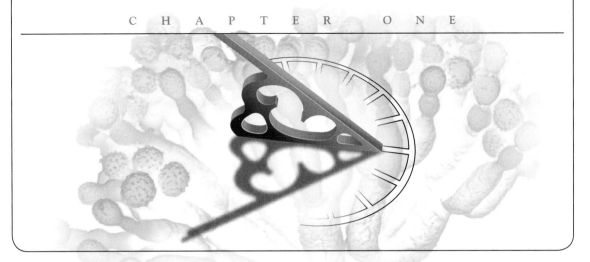

CREATION OF A NOVEL CLASS:

THE RISE OF RESISTANCE
AND THE NEED FOR NOVEL ANTIBACTERIAL AGENTS

EDITOR

Donald H. Batts, MD, FACP

LEARNING OBJECTIVES

After completion of this chapter, readers should be able to:

1. Understand the importance of the discovery of antibiotics in the course of human history.

2. Discuss the threat posed by the rise of bacterial resistance.

3. Identify key causes of bacterial resistance.

4. Implement strategies for reducing the rise of resistance in bacterial pathogens.

THE OXAZOLIDINONE ANTIBIOTICS

The antibiotic miracle achieved with the discovery of penicillin in the 20th century is eroding as a result of the rise of antimicrobial resistance among many common pathogens. Until recently, no new class of antibiotic had been introduced for several decades, and new agents were merely analogs within existing classes. These were modified to improve either pharmacokinetics or pharmacodynamics or, more importantly, to stay ahead of bacterial mutations and the subsequent development of new resistance mechanisms. With the introduction of linezolid and the oxazolidinone class of antibiotics, clinicians gained a new therapeutic weapon in the arsenal against bacterial infections caused by gram-positive pathogens. Its unique mechanism of action offers treatment for pathogens resistant to other antibiotic classes.

became available, unmonitored use by patients at home could result in inadequate therapy. His words proved to be prophetic.

The Golden Age of Antibiotics

Before the development of antibiotics, microbial infection exacted a huge toll on human life.[3] In 1900, the average life span in the United States was 47 years, and 30.4% of all deaths occurred in children under the age of 5 years.[1,4] At that time, the 3 leading causes of death were pneumonia, tuberculosis, and diarrhea/enteritis. The crude death rate for infectious diseases alone was 800 per 100,000 individuals (Figure 1).[1]

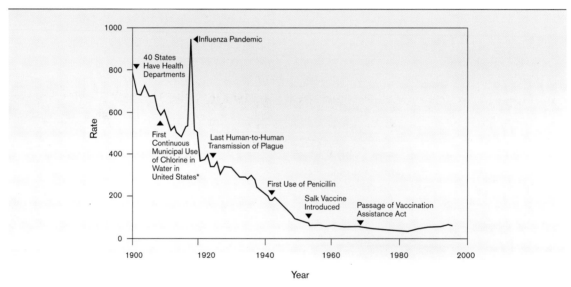

Figure 1. Crude death rate (per 100,000 population per year) for infectious diseases, United States, 1900-1996.
*American Water Works Association. Water chlorination principles and practices. In: *AWWA Manual M20*. Denver, Colo: American Water Works Association; 1973. Adapted from Armstrong GL, Conn LA, Pinner RW. Trends in infectious disease mortality in the United States during the 20th century. *JAMA.* 1999;48:61-66. Reprinted from the Centers for Disease Control and Prevention. Achievements in public health, 1900-1999: control of infectious diseases. *MMWR Morb Mortal Wkly Rep.* 48:621-629.

The discovery of antibiotics in the first half of the 20th century ranks as one of the single greatest achievements in human history. Antibiotics were first used in significant quantities during World War II,[1] yet evidence of antibiotic resistance emerged almost simultaneously with Alexander Fleming's discovery of penicillin in the late 1920s.[2] As early as 1945, Fleming warned that resistance might develop from inadequate treatment with these agents or misuse of the drugs. He warned that when oral penicillin

In comparison, in 1999 the life expectancy at birth was 76.7 years, the death rate in children younger than 5 years was 1.4%, and the total crude death rate was 877 per 100,000 individuals.[1,5] Nearly a third (265.9/100,000) of those deaths in 1999 were attributable to heart disease, another 201.6 to cancer, and 61.4 to cerebrovascular disease.[5] Influenza and pneumonia combined contributed only 23.4 deaths per 100,000 individuals. Septicemia, the only other infectious disease to be listed among the top

15 causes of death in 1999, contributed 11.3 deaths per 100,000 individuals. Septicemia plus influenza and pneumonia combined constituted just 4% of the total death rate. The infant mortality rate also declined significantly with the advent of antibiotics, decreasing 93% between 1915 and 1997.[1] The greatest reductions occurred in the 1940s, concurrent with the introduction of antibiotic therapy, and then again in the 1970s, when major technological advances were made in neonatal care. Accordingly, in just a century, astounding progress had been made in reducing the mortality associated with bacterial disease.[1]

An examination of primary care practices on the eve of the antibiotic revolution reveals much the same pattern. Minor surgical procedures such as tonsillectomy, adenoidectomy, incision and drainage for mastoiditis, and myringotomy for otitis media formed a major part of what was then called general practice.[6] In contrast, physical examinations and treatment for hypertension, minor trauma, and acute pharyngitis are the 4 most common elements in a comparable practice today.

We now live in an era in which the principal causes of death are diseases of old age or lifestyle, such as heart disease, cancer, stroke, or chronic obstructive pulmonary disease.[1,7] We prick a finger on a rose thorn, gash a knuckle while working on the car, or develop bronchitis and rarely worry about it, confident that an antibiotic prescription will take care of any problems that arise. However, this is a luxury in the course of human history, one that is increasingly threatened by the rise of microbial resistance.[1] This resistance threatens to render ineffective our current treatment options for serious common ailments such as pneumonia, skin and skin structure infections, septicemia, and upper respiratory tract infections. It threatens to return us to an era when we were largely at the mercy of microbes.

Breakpoints

Before exploring the issue of resistance, a basic understanding of breakpoints is necessary. Bacterial resistance and susceptibility are defined in terms of minimal inhibitory concentration (MIC) breakpoints. An MIC_{50} is the concentration that must be achieved to inhibit growth of 50% of the organisms tested, while an MIC_{90} is the concentration required to inhibit growth of 90% of the organisms tested.[7] Pathogenic strains are defined as susceptible,

intermediate (ie, exhibiting intermediate resistance), or resistant.

Breakpoints in the United States are defined by the National Committee for Clinical Laboratory Standards (NCCLS) and the Food and Drug Administration. Internationally, there are several other standards, including the British Society for Antimicrobial Chemotherapy (BSAC), and the Comite de l'Antibiogramme de la Société Française Microbiologie (CA-SFM).[8] Although considerable agreement exists among international standards,[9] differences do exist. For instance, the NCCLS defines isolates of *Staphylococcus aureus* with MICs of 32 µg/mL or greater as vancomycin-resistant *Staphylococcus aureus* (VRSA) and those with MICs of 4 µg/mL or less as susceptible, but the BSAC considers any strain with an MIC of 8 µg/mL or greater to be VRSA.[8] The following table presents MICs for *Streptococcus pneumoniae* to 11 antibiotics.

Table. MICs for *Streptococcus pneumoniae* Isolates to 11 Antibiotics

Antibiotic	MIC_{50} (µg/mL)	MIC_{90} (µg/mL)
Penicillin	0.03	2
Ceftriaxone	0.015	1
Cefepime	0.06	1
Meropenem	0.015	0.5
Erythromycin	0.125	8
Clindamycin	0.125	0.5
Ciprofloxacin	2	4
Levofloxacin	1	2
Chloramphenicol	4	4
Linezolid	0.5	1
Quinupristin-dalfopristin	0.5	0.5

MIC_{50} = minimum concentration needed to inhibit 50% of organisms; MIC_{90} = minimum concentration needed to inhibit 90% of organisms. Adapted from Quale J, Landman D, Ravishankar J, Flores C, Bratu S. *Streptococcus pneumoniae*, Brooklyn, New York: fluoroquinolone resistance at our doorstep. *Emerg Infect Dis* [serial online]. 2002 Jul [cited 2003 October 30];8. Available at: www.cdc.gov/ncidod/eid/vol8no6/pdf/01-0275.pdf.

The Rise of Resistance

Although evidence of resistance surfaced almost concurrently with the discovery of antibiotics, the potential threat was not apparent until much later. Despite the appearance of penicillin-resistant strains of staphylococci in hospitals by the late 1940s, resistance at first was largely confined to city hospitals.[2] Penicillin-resistant strains began to emerge in the community in the 1960s and 1970s, but the discovery of new antibiotic classes appeared to keep the problem under control. But in the late 1980s and early 1990s, with the pace of drug discovery slowing and multidrug-resistant pathogens increasing dramatically worldwide, the danger posed by microbes such as staphylococci and streptococci became obvious.[10] It was clear to the international medical community that a serious problem was emerging. The exception to this is *Streptococcus pyogenes*, which even in a recently published study from a major US surveillance program has yet to demonstrate any penicillin resistance, though 5.5% of isolates were resistant to erythromycin.[11]

As Fleming predicted at the start of the antibiotic age, abuse has exacerbated the problem of resistance.[2] Unfortunately, inappropriate use of antibiotics is fairly common. Antibiotics are the second largest category of drugs prescribed by primary care physicians after drugs for the central nervous system.[12] Estimates have placed the inappropriate prescribing of antibiotics, particularly for colds, bronchitis, and likely viral upper respiratory tract infections, at more than 50% (95% confidence interval [CI], 30%-71%; 44%-60%; and 59%-73%, respectively).[13] In most cases, viral infections are self-limiting and do not require antibiotic treatment or prophylaxis.[14] Excessive use of these agents for nonbacterial infections places unnecessary selective pressure on bacterial pathogens.[15] Drug use–mediated selective pressure appears to be the most important factor in the emergence of resistance.[16]

Use of agents that have not demonstrated efficacy for the most likely pathogen involved in an infection, or use of agents that do not achieve adequate concentrations at the site of infection, may also increase the likelihood of antimicrobial resistance.[17] For example, aminoglycoside antibiotics do not work at low pH levels or in anaerobic environments, and they are not transported into cells. As a result, these agents are inappropriate choices for undrained abscesses.[14] Vancomycin is a glycopeptide that is active against gram-positive, but not gram-negative, infections. As such, it would not be an appropriate choice to treat infections where *Escherichia coli* is the likely causative pathogen.[18]

Treatment with antimicrobial agents at subtherapeutic doses is another serious problem, increasing the probability of clinical failure and emergent resistance.[19] Microbes that survive are more likely to have some level of innate resistance, which may then be amplified by repeated inadequate therapy.[20,21] Subtherapeutic doses occur for a number of reasons. In some cases, fear of drug toxicity, such as the ototoxicity found with vancomycin, may encourage the clinician to use lower doses.[22] Patient compliance may also play a role, in that failure to finish an antibiotic course or to adhere to a regimen can result in subtherapeutic doses.[23] Patients may also hoard antibiotics and then engage in unsupervised use for what they feel is an appropriate indication. Noncompliance is a serious issue with all medications.[24] Estimates are that most patients take between 33% and 94% of their prescribed course of drugs. Because the rise of resistance among pathogenic organisms has the potential to spread throughout the community, noncompliance with antibiotic therapy has implications well beyond the individual patient.

Cross-Resistance

Many pathogens now exhibit multidrug resistance. This resistance may be the result of bacterial exposure to multiple agents, or it may occur without prior exposure to agents that are chemically related or have similar mechanisms of action to agents that have been in use.[25,26] An example of the latter scenario occurred in Taiwan, where resistance to quinupristin-dalfopristin was noted before the introduction of that compound, presumably because of an agent (virginiamycin) with a similar chemical structure that was used in animal feed.[27] The situation in Taiwan is discussed in greater detail later in this chapter.

Cross-resistance can arise within a drug class or across classes.[28] For example, mutations of the topoisomerase IV and DNA gyrase within *S pneumoniae* threaten to render the entire fluoroquinolone class of drugs ineffective in treating infections with that pathogen. Cross-class resistance occurs by 1 of 2 mechanisms—overlapping targets or drug efflux.[29] Bacterial efflux pumps afford relative resistance and account for cross-resistance between many antibiotic classes, including β-lactams, aminoglycosides, and tetracyclines.[30] Cross-resistance between the macrolides, lincosamides, and streptogramins is the result of overlapping ribosomal targets, and the level of resistance conferred is high.[29,31,32] The *erm* gene, which results in target modification, confers resistance to most macrolides, lincosamides, and streptogramin B compounds and is known as MLS_B resistance.[31,33-35] However, cross-resistance cannot be assumed for these 3 drug classes, as the M phenotype often found in American strains of pneumococci does not contain an *erm* methylase and confers resistance only to erythromycin.[31,32] In these strains the presence of a *mef* gene appears to enable the bacteria to efflux the erythromycin.[32]

While antibiotic therapy in humans may create selective pressure and induce resistance and cross-resistance, the use of antiseptic agents in a large number of household products, including soaps, dishwashing liquids, toothpastes, and lotions, also may contribute to the problem of resistance.[36-38] In the early 1990s, only a few dozen of these antiseptic products were available, but by 2001 the number had risen to more than 700.[36] Triclosan, a common antiseptic, has been added to everything from cleaning products to bed linens and towels.[36,39] Some strains of *Pseudomonas aeruginosa* have become triclosan resistant, and evidence suggests that widespread use of this agent may promote the selection of multidrug-resistant bacteria.[39] This cross-resistance appears to be mediated by multidrug efflux pumps.[39] Interestingly, there is no evidence that use of these antiseptic products provides any benefit to healthy individuals.[36]

The Role of Veterinary Use of Antibiotics

The pervasive use of antibiotics in aquaculture and veterinary medicine also has contributed significantly to antimicrobial cross-resistance.[40] The intensive use of these agents in farming to increase animal growth and improve health has placed organisms such as *Salmonella enterica* under selective pressure, and multidrug-resistant strains have been detected. In the United States, the use of the fluoroquinolones sarafloxacin and enrofloxacin for the control of *E coli* in poultry in the mid-1990s raised concerns about the risk of transfer of resistance

genes to pathogens affecting humans, particularly in light of the fact that cross-resistance affects all agents in this class.[41]

A 1996 veterinary monitoring program revealed considerable resistance among *Salmonella* isolates to tetracycline in cattle (24%), chickens (34%), swine (50%), and turkeys (47%).[41] Ampicillin-resistant *Salmonella* isolates ranged from 7% in turkeys to 14% in cattle and chickens, while sulfa resistance ranged from 14% in chickens to 68% in turkeys. Although fluoroquinolone resistance was not found, nor had it been demonstrated at that time that such resistance could be transferable, the National Antimicrobial Resistance Monitoring System (NARMS) found that 14% of *Campylobacter* isolates collected from individuals with infections during the years 1997 to 2000 were resistant to ciprofloxacin.[42]

The fluoroquinolones and ceftriaxone are used to treat invasive *Salmonella* infection, but resistance to these agents in *Salmonella* isolates from humans has been rare in the United States.[43] However, in 2000, an isolate of *S enterica* serotype Typhimurium cultured from an infected 12-year-old child proved resistant to ceftriaxone and 12 other antimicrobial agents. This was particularly disturbing; the other agents used to treat this disease, the fluoroquinolones, are not approved for use in children. Molecular analysis showed that the isolate in question was identical to one found in cattle. Global distribution of multidrug-resistant *Salmonella* clones has been observed.[44] A study by White and colleagues[45] found that 20% of ground meat samples in the Washington, DC area were contaminated with *Salmonella* serotypes. Ceftriaxone-resistant *Salmonella* isolates were found, as was multidrug-resistant *S enterica*.

It has been suggested that vancomycin resistance among enterococci may have been provoked by the use of avoparcin in farm animals in Europe,[46,47] a compound that has since been withdrawn from the market.[48] Use of the streptogramin virginiamycin has raised concerns about possible development of cross-resistance among *Enterococcus faecalis* and *Enterococcus faecium* to quinupristin-dalfopristin,[49] as this combination antibiotic has been approved for use in people infected with vancomycin-resistant *E faecium*.[48] Although a study by McDonald et al[48] found evidence of quinupristin-dalfopristin–resistant *E faecium* in chickens purchased in supermarkets in 4 states, little resistance was found among enterococci isolated from humans through mid-1999.

Rise of Resistance in the Developing World

Socioeconomic difficulties and cultural attitudes contribute to the problem of antibiotic resistance in the developing world.[15] A lack of well-trained health care personnel in many of these countries results in antibiotics being prescribed by health workers who may not be aware of the harmful effects of antibiotic misuse. In many developing countries, antibiotics can be purchased easily without a prescription. Cultural attitudes also may foster antibiotic abuse, as it is a commonly held belief in many countries that antibiotics can cure all types of illnesses. Economic factors contribute to the abuse as well. For instance, small aliquots of antibiotic agents often are sold at roadside stands, patients often fail to return to the doctor for follow-up visits because of the expense, and patients often are not able to purchase the complete regimen prescribed. Consequently, subtherapeutic doses may be taken, with resultant clinical failure and selection for resistant strains.

This contributes to global dissemination of resistant microbes. Crowding and poor sanitation may contribute to the spread of resistant pathogens within developing countries, while emigration and international travel spread resistance beyond the borders of these countries and around the world.[15] Lack of resources, armed conflicts, and political corruption hamper attempts to combat inappropriate antibiotic use.

International Surveillance Programs

Worldwide surveillance of antimicrobial resistance has been a priority of the international medical community for a number of years, and several programs have been initiated to monitor the development of resistance in several clinically important human pathogens. The Alexander Project, which was established in 1992, is an ongoing multicenter surveillance study of antimicrobial resistance in the major pathogens involved in community-acquired lower respiratory tract infection.[50]

From 1992 to 1995, monitoring was conducted at 5 centers in the United States and 10 centers in Europe.[50] In 1996 and 1997, recognition of the global nature of resistance prompted expansion of surveillance to include centers in Central and South America, the Middle East, South Africa, Hong Kong, and European countries not previously covered.[51] Results from the 1996-1997 study indicated that resistance varied considerably from country to country—and even within countries; an overall trend toward increasing resistance in both S pneumoniae and Haemophilus influenzae was noted. Surprisingly high levels of penicillin-resistant S pneumoniae in Hong Kong (≥50%) highlighted the need to monitor pathogens in multiple centers.

The SENTRY Antimicrobial Surveillance Program was initiated in 1997 to monitor resistance patterns among the major pathogens in both nosocomial and community-acquired infections through an international network of sentinel hospitals in the United States, Canada, Europe, Latin America, and the Asia-Pacific region.[16] Five major types of infection are monitored, including (1) bloodstream infections, (2) community-acquired respiratory tract infections, (3) pneumonia in hospitalized patients, (4) skin and soft tissue or wound infections, and (5) urinary tract infections. As with the Alexander Project, significant regional differences have been found in resistance patterns for the major respiratory tract pathogens S pneumoniae, H influenzae, and Moraxella catarrhalis. Particularly high rates of penicillin-resistant (28.9%) and clindamycin-resistant (20.0%) S pneumoniae were found in the Asia-Pacific region, whereas the highest rates of β-lactamase–producing H influenzae were found in the United States (33%) and Canada (29%).

Methicillin resistance in S aureus is often used as a benchmark for gauging the tide of virulent bacterial resistance. Oxacillin resistance in this pathogen is equivalent to methicillin resistance, and an oxacillin MIC of greater than or equal to 4 μg/mL defines methicillin-resistant Staphylococcus aureus (MRSA). In another review of SENTRY data, oxacillin resistance was examined in samples of S aureus obtained from hospitalized patients in the Asia-Pacific area and South Africa.[52] Isolates were collected from all major infection sites outlined in the SENTRY study protocol: respiratory tract, blood, skin and soft tissue, and urine. The data suggested that, in this region of the world, S aureus was the most common cause of pneumonia and infection of the bloodstream and skin and soft tissue. The percentage of oxacillin-resistant strains ranged from 5% of isolates in the Philippines to nearly 70% in Japan and Hong Kong. Reflecting the often highly regional character of resistance, only 28% of isolates from China were oxacillin resistant. Multidrug-resistant strains were common.

Prevalence of Resistant Strains

S pneumoniae is one of the most virulent human pathogens and a common cause of pneumonia.[53] Before 1980, more than 99% of S pneumoniae isolates in the United States were susceptible to penicillin.[13] However, by 2000, a study by Doern et al[54] demonstrated that penicillin-resistant strains of S pneumoniae in the United States ranged from 5.2% to 56.1%. Alarming levels of resistance were found to other antibiotics as well. Resistance ranged from 3.0% to 39.0% for ceftriaxone; 6.1% to 53.7% for erythromycin; 7.3% to 50.0% for tetracycline; 13.5% to 53.7% for trimethoprim-sulfamethoxazole (TMP-SMX); and 1.9% to 27.3% for chloramphenicol. The overall national rate of penicillin resistance at that time was 34.2%, with 21.5% of isolates demonstrating high-level resistance (MIC≥2 μg/mL). Nearly a quarter (22.4%) of the isolates were resistant to at least 3 different classes of antibiotics, and 28.6% of strains were resistant to 5 different classes.

Resistance to the fluoroquinolones among S pneumoniae isolates generally was low—1.2% to 1.6%; however, 21 ciprofloxacin-resistant strains were isolated, 2 with MICs above 64 μg/mL.[54] Although fluoroquinolone resistance generally has remained stable in the United States, higher rates have been reported elsewhere in the world, a phenomenon that warrants close monitoring.[55]

Overall macrolide resistance rose from 10.3% in 1995 to 26.2% in 2000.[54] This may be the result of increasing use of these agents; a similar trend has been noted for azithromycin and clarithromycin, as well as for the fluoroquinolones.[56] This is cause for concern, as these agents frequently are prescribed for patients who are hospitalized with pneumonia. Fortunately, resistance was not found for vancomycin, quinupristin-dalfopristin, or newer agents such as the ketolides or linezolid.[54]

The study also found geographic variations in resistance, with the southeastern United States experiencing the highest levels.[54] Middle ear fluid and sinus isolates recovered from children aged 5 years or younger demonstrated the highest levels of resistance, but inpatient and outpatient rates were comparable.

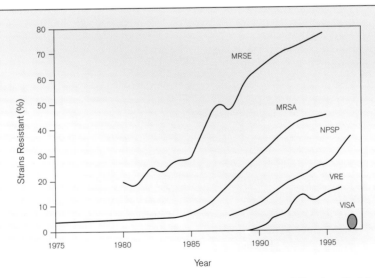

Figure 2. Trends in antimicrobial resistance among gram-positive organisms in the United States. MRSE = methicillin-resistant *Staphylococcus epidermidis*; MRSA = methicillin-resistant *Staphylococcus aureus*; NPSP = non-penicillin–susceptible pneumococci; VRE = vancomycin-resistant enterococci; VISA = vancomycin-intermediate-resistant *Staphylococcus aureus*. Originally published in Paladino JA. Economic justification of antimicrobial management programs: implications of antimicrobial resistance. *Am J Health Syst Pharm.* 2000;57(20s):10-12. © 2000, American Society of Health-System Pharmacists, Inc. All rights reserved. Reprinted with permission. (R0351).

Investigators noted an alarming increase in high-level penicillin resistance over a period of only a few years.[54] Approximately 63% of penicillin-nonsusceptible strains demonstrated high-level resistance. These highly resistant strains were present in all 3 major specimen categories: upper respiratory tract (68.9%), lower respiratory tract (59.9%), and invasive isolates (59.8%). This rapid spread of multidrug and high-level resistance appears to have been accomplished through proliferation of a few major pneumococcal clones.

Conversely, Canadian data reveal that pneumococcal resistance to penicillin and TMP-SMX remained fairly stable between 1994 and 2000, with 12% to 13% of isolates resistant to penicillin (P=.07) and approximately 11% resistant to TMP-SMX (P=.07).[57] However, macrolide resistance had increased from 2.8% in 1995 to 11.6% (P=.001) in 2000.

Interestingly, the ketolides, which are semisynthetic 14-membered ring macrolides,[57,58] maintained efficacy against S pneumoniae despite increases in macrolide resistance.[59,60] As expected, resistance among pneumococci was not found for linezolid.[57] The authors conclude that these newer antimicrobial agents appeared to have potential for the treatment of multidrug-resistant infections.

Other virulent pathogens have exhibited resistance as well. Methicillin-resistant S aureus was observed in the 1970s but at very low levels until 1985, when its incidence began to increase dramatically. By 1997, MRSA constituted nearly 50% of S aureus strains.[61] Methicillin-resistant Staphylococcus epidermidis (MRSE) first appeared in 1980 in approximately 20% of isolates, but it has since increased to nearly 80% of strains. Although vancomycin had been in use for decades, vancomycin-resistant enterococci (VRE) had been found only in hospitals before the early 1990s. But by 1997, VRE constituted nearly 20% of enterococcal isolates. Vancomycin-intermediate-resistant Staphylococcus aureus (VISA) appeared in 1997 (Figure 2).

Within the last 2 years, high-level resistance to vancomycin has been identified among isolates of S aureus in the United States.[62-64] Given the virulent nature of this pathogen, this development is particularly alarming. Genetic analysis suggests that a transfer of the vanA gene complex occurred from a vancomycin-resistant strain of E faecalis to S aureus, underscoring the importance of interspecies transfer as a source for rapidly emerging resistance.[63]

As demonstrated by the results of both the Alexander Project and SENTRY, local resistance patterns can differ significantly from one country to another and within countries as well, depending on prescribing patterns. South African enterococcal resistance patterns to 15 antimicrobial agents were investigated by Struwig et al.[65] Multidrug resistance was common. Approximately 70% of E faecium isolates were resistant to ampicillin and an aminoglycoside, but only 1.4% of E faecalis isolates displayed this pattern. High levels of resistance were found for gentamicin and kanamycin-amikacin; 39.9% of E faecalis isolates were resistant to these agents, as were 46.8% of E faecium isolates. Nearly equal numbers of isolates of these 2 pathogens were resistant to ciprofloxacin and an aminoglycoside (approximately 14%), while 25.5% of E faecium and 9.4% of E faecalis isolates were resistant to kanamycin-amikacin but susceptible to gentamicin.

In Taiwan between 1996 and 1999, gram-positive bacteria were assessed for resistance to 10 compounds, including quinupristin-dalfopristin, oxacillin, vancomycin, teicoplanin, gentamicin, ciprofloxacin, trovafloxacin, moxifloxacin, rifampin, and linezolid.[27] Although quinupristin-dalfopristin had yet to be introduced into clinical practice, intermediate resistance to this agent was noted in 30% of MRSA strains. Quinupristin-dalfopristin resistance was also found in 76% of vancomycin-susceptible enterococci. This surprisingly high level of resistance to a compound that had yet to be introduced was attributed to long-time use of virginiamycin in animal feed. Additionally, 97% of MRSA strains were resistant to ciprofloxacin. Linezolid demonstrated the greatest efficacy against all isolates tested, including glycopeptide-resistant and quinupristin-dalfopristin–resistant isolates.

The occasionally localized nature of resistance patterns was demonstrated in a more recently published study of fluoroquinolone resistance in S pneumoniae in Brooklyn, NY.[66] In western areas of Brooklyn, a borough of New York City, higher levels of penicillin and fluoroquinolone resistance were noted than in other areas of the city (P=.046). Furthermore, the genes that impart resistance can demonstrate distinctly local patterns. In the Brooklyn study, investigators found that the Spanish/USA 23F clone predominated in the western half of the borough, while the

Spanish/French 9/14 clone predominated in the eastern half. Of clinical importance, these clones also have different cross-resistance patterns.[7-9,14,67,68]

The True Costs of Resistance

Although the greatest cost of bacterial resistance is clinical failure, resistance also has a considerable economic impact. Direct costs include medical expenditures associated with the additional care necessitated by a resistant infection. These may include use of more expensive antibiotics, longer hospital stays, and expenses associated with patient isolation procedures. A 1999 study of resistant *S aureus* infections in New York City hospitals revealed that MRSA infections cost an additional $2500 over the average cost of $31,500 for a methicillin-susceptible *Staph-*

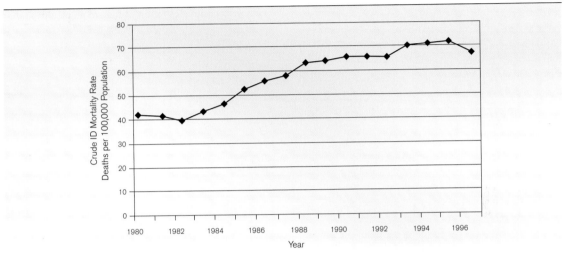

Figure 3. Infectious disease mortality in the United States, 1980 through 1996. ID = infectious diseases. Source: Centers for Disease Control and Prevention. *Preventing Emerging Infectious Diseases: A Strategy for the 21st Century* [slide presentation]. 1998. Available at: http://www.cdc.gov/ncidod/emergplan/slideset/3.htm. Accessed September 30, 2003.

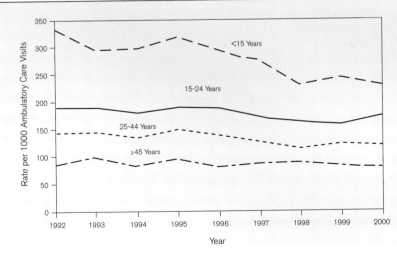

Figure 4. Trends in annual antimicrobial prescribing rates by age, United States, 1992 through 2000. Note: Trend for visits by patients aged <15 years, *P*<.001; for visits by patients aged 15-24 years, *P*=.007; for visits by patients aged 25-44 years, *P*=.001. Reprinted from McCaig LF, Besser RE, Hughes JM. Antimicrobial drug prescriptions in ambulatory care settings, United States, 1992-2000. *Emerg Infect Dis* [serial online]. 2003 Apr [cited 2003 October 30];9. Available from: www.cdc.gov/ncidod/eid/vol9no4/pdfs/02-0268.pdf.

ylococcus aureus (MSSA) infection. Nosocomial MRSA infections cost an additional $3700 over the estimated $27,700 cost of a nosocomial MSSA infection.[69] Additionally, the death rate was 2.5 times higher in MRSA infections (21%) than in MSSA infections (8%). Other studies have found even higher costs. In a study conducted in France, the mean total costs of treating MRSA infections exceeded those of controls by $9275.[70]

A cost that is less easily quantified is the tremendous expense involved in developing new drugs to combat infections that have become resistant to currently available compounds. In 2001, Joseph DiMasi of the Tufts Center for the Study of Drug Development released a study of drug development costs that pegged the average cost of developing a new prescription drug at $802 million.[71] This is nearly 4 times the average cost estimated in 1987 ($231 million). Had inflation been the only factor involved in increasing costs, that figure would be $318 million. However, the rising cost of clinical trials and the difficulty of recruiting study subjects, as well as the increased focus on developing drugs to treat chronic and degenerative diseases, added considerably to the price tag. These costs also include the significant expense of project failures. As the relatively obvious bacterial targets are exploited, finding new targets for antibiotic action may increase these costs.

Some consumer groups dispute these figures as exaggerated and estimate that costs are considerably lower, running approximately $200 million for each new compound.[72,73] Given the risky nature of the drug development process, it is difficult to detail all the costs involved in bringing new agents to market, and the truth no doubt lies somewhere between these figures.

Summary

It has become clear that bacterial resistance has some impact on clinical outcomes. A review of data from the National Center for Health Statistics reveals that mortality associated with infectious diseases in the United States has risen from 41 deaths per 100,000 individuals in 1980 to 65 per 100,000 in 1992 (Figure 3).[74] Although much of this is attributable to the emergence of human immunodeficiency virus as a major pathogen, mortality due to respiratory tract infections increased 20%, from 25 to 30 deaths per 100,000, while deaths due to septicemia rose 83%, from 4.2 to 7.7 per 100,000.

Nevertheless, there are encouraging signs. A study by McCaig et al[56] revealed a decrease in antimicrobial prescribing rates in ambulatory care settings from 1992 through 2000 (Figure 4). Rates decreased from 151 million (95% CI, 132-169) to 126 million (95% CI, 112-141). This reversed a trend of increasing levels of antibiotic prescriptions that had been noted in National Ambulatory Medical Care Survey (NAMCS) data from 1980 through 1992. The reduction was most evident for children younger than 15 years (P=.001). In this age group, prescription rates decreased by 34% in physicians' offices and by 13% in emergency departments. The authors suggest that attempts to educate clinicians and the public about the dangers of antibiotic overuse may have had the desired effect. Although prescriptions in most antibiotic categories declined during this period, an increase was noted in the use of newer broad-spectrum agents, such as azithromycin, clarithromycin, quinolones, and amoxicillin-clavulanate.

One hopes that more prudent use of antibiotics may ultimately result in falling levels of antimicrobial resistance among bacterial pathogens. The importance of preserving the effectiveness of our current antibiotic arsenal cannot be overstated. However, it appears that, for the foreseeable future, it remains necessary to continue to research and develop new agents and classes of antibiotics to prevent clinical failures and remain above the rising tide of resistance. At this time, some of the newer fluoroquinolones, the ketolides, and the oxazolidinones seem to offer our best hope.

References

1. Centers for Disease Control and Prevention. Achievements in public health, 1900-1999: control of infectious diseases. *MMWR Morb Mortal Wkly Rep.* 1999;48:621-629.

2. Levy SB. *The Antibiotic Paradox.* 1st ed. New York, NY: Plenum Press; 1992:1, 7.

3. Sartin JS, Perry HO. From mercury to malaria to penicillin: the history of the treatment of syphilis at the Mayo Clinic—1916-1955. *J Am Acad Dermatol.* 1995;32:255-261.

4. Centers for Disease Control and Prevention, Office of Women's Health. Women's health—prevention works for women. Aging. Available at: http://www.cdc.gov/od/spotlight/nwhw/pubs/aging.htm. Accessed May 6, 2003.

5. Hoyert DL, Arias E, Smith B, Murphy SL, Kochanek KD. Deaths: final data for 1999. *Natl Vital Stat Rep.* 2001;49:1-113.

6. Haddy RI, Hill JM, Costarella BR, et al. A comparison of rural family practice in the 1930s and today. *J Fam Pract.* 1993;36:65-69.

7. Jacobs MR. Emergence of antibiotic resistance in upper and lower respiratory tract infections. *Am J Manag Care.* 1999;5(suppl 11): S651-S661.

8. Tenover FC, Biddle JW, Lancaster MV. Increasing resistance to vancomycin and other glycopeptides in *Staphylococcus aureus. Emerg Infect Dis.* 2001;7:327-332.

9. Hallgren A, Abednazari H, Ekdahl C, et al. Antimicrobial susceptibility patterns of enterococci in intensive care units in Sweden evaluated by different MIC breakpoint systems. *J Antimicrob Chemother.* 2001;48:53-62.

10. Doern GV. Antimicrobial resistance with *Streptococcus pneumoniae*: Much ado about nothing? *Semin Respir Infect.* 2001;16:177-185.

11. Doern GV, Brown SD. Antimicrobial susceptibility among community-acquired respiratory tract pathogens in the USA: data from PROTEKT US 2000-01. *J Infect.* 2004;48:56-65.

12. McCaig LF, Hughes JM. Trends in antimicrobial drug prescribing among office-based physicians in the United States. *JAMA.* 1995;273:214-219.

13. Gonzales R, Steiner JF, Sande MA. Antibiotic prescribing for adults with colds, upper respiratory tract infections, and bronchitis by ambulatory care physicians. *JAMA.* 1997;278:901-904.

14. Chambers HF, Sande MA. Antimicrobial agents: general considerations. In: Hardiman JG, Limbird LE, Molinoff PB, Ruddon RW, Goodman Gilman A, eds. *Goodman & Gilman's The Pharmacological Basis of Therapeutics.* 9th ed. New York, NY: McGraw-Hill Health Professions Division; 1996:1029-1056.

15. Okeke IN, Lamikanra A, Edelman R. Socioeconomic and behavioral factors leading to acquired bacterial resistance to antibiotics in developing countries. *Emerg Infect Dis.* 1999;5:18-27.

16. Hoban DJ, Doern GV, Fluit AC, Roussel-Delvallez, RN. J. Worldwide prevalence of antimicrobial resistance in *Streptococcus pneumoniae, Haemophilus influenzae,* and *Moraxella catarrhalis* in the SENTRY Antimicrobial Surveillance Program, 1997-1999. *Clin Infect Dis.* 2001;32(suppl 2):S81-S93.

17. Ho PL, Yung RW, Tsang DN, et al. Increasing resistance of *Streptococcus pneumoniae* to fluoroquinolones: results of a Hong Kong multicentre study in 2000. *J Antimicrob Chemother.* 2001;48:659-665.

18. Chambers HF. Beta-lactam antibiotics & other inhibitors of cell wall synthesis. In: Katzung BG, ed. *Basic & Clinical Pharmacology.* 8th ed. New York, NY: Lange Medical Books/McGraw-Hill Medical Publishing Division; 2001:754-773.

19. Lesar TS, Rotschafer JC, Strand LM, Solem LD, Zaske DE. Gentamicin dosing errors with four commonly used nomograms. *JAMA.* 1982;248:1190-1193.

20. Kollef MH. Inadequate antimicrobial treatment: an important determinant of outcome for hospitalized patients. *Clin Infect Dis.* 2000;31(suppl 4):S131-S138.

21. Thomas JK, Forrest A, Bhavnani SM, et al. Pharmacodynamic evaluation of factors associated with the development of bacterial resistance in acutely ill patients during therapy. *Antimicrob Agents Chemother.* 1998;42:521-527.

22. Kapusnik-Uner JE, Sande MA, Chambers HF. Antimicrobial agents: tetracyclines, chloramphenicol, erythromycin, and miscellaneous antibacterial agents. In: Hardiman JG, Limbird LE, Molinoff PB, Ruddon RW, Goodman Gilman A, eds. *Goodman & Gilman's The Pharmacological Basis of Therapeutics.* 9th ed. New York, NY: McGraw-Hill Health Professions Division; 1996:1123-1153.

23. Carey B, Cryan B. Antibiotic misuse in the community—a contributor to resistance? *Ir Med J.* 2003;96:43-44, 46.

24. Morris LS, Schulz RM. Patient compliance—an overview. *J Clin Pharm Ther.* 1992;17:283-295.

25. Soltani M, Beighton D, Philpott-Howard J, Woodford N. Mechanisms of resistance to quinupristin-dalfopristin among isolates of *Enterococcus faecium* from animals, raw meat, and hospital patients in Western Europe. *Antimicrob Agents Chemother.* 2000;44:433-436.

26. Werner G, Klare I, Witte W. Association between quinupristin/dalfopristin resistance in glycopeptide-resistant *Enterococcus faecium* and the use of additives in animal feed. *Eur J Clin Microbiol Infect Dis.* 1998;17:401-402.

27. Luh KT, Hsueh PR, Teng LJ, et al. Quinupristin-dalfopristin resistance among gram-positive bacteria in Taiwan. *Antimicrob Agents Chemother.* 2000;44:3374-3380.

28. Doern GV. Antimicrobial use and the emergence of antimicrobial resistance with *Streptococcus pneumoniae* in the United States. *Clin Infect Dis.* 2001;33(suppl 3):S187-S192.

29. Courvalin P. The antibiotic food-chain gang. *Emerg Infect Dis.* 2001;7:489-490.

30. Paulsen IT, Brown MH, Skurray RA. Proton-dependent multidrug efflux systems. *Microbiol Rev.* 1996;60:575-608.

31. Sutcliffe J, Tait-Kamradt A, Wondrack L. *Streptococcus pneumoniae* and *Streptococcus pyogenes* resistant to macrolides but sensitive to clindamycin: a common resistance pattern mediated by an efflux system. *Antimicrob Agents Chemother.* 1996;40:1817-1824.

32. Tait-Kamradt A, Clancy J, Cronan M, et al. *mefE* is necessary for the erythromycin-resistant M phenotype in *Streptococcus pneumonia. Antimicrob Agents Chemother.* 1997;41:2251-2255.

33. Fernandez-Munoz R, Monro RE, Torres-Pineod R, Vasquez D. Substrate- and antibiotic-binding sites at the peptidyl-transferase centre of *Escherichia* ribosomes. Studies on the chloramphenicol, lincomycin and erythromycin sites. *Eur J Biochem.* 1971;23:185-193.

34. Lai CJ, Weisblum B. Altered methylation of ribosomal RNA in an erythromycin-resistant strain of *Staphylococcus aureus. Proc Natl Acad Sci USA.* 1971;68:856-860.

35. Leclerq R, Courvalin P. Mechanisms of resistance to macrolides and functionally related antibiotics. In: Bryskier AJ, Butzler JP, Neu HC, Tulkens PM, eds. *Macrolides, Chemistry, Pharmacology and Clinical Uses.* Paris, France: Arnette, Blackwell; 1993.

36. Levy SB. Antibacterial household products: cause for concern. *Emerg Infect Dis.* 2001;7(3 suppl):512-515.

37. Heath RJ, Rubin JR, Holland DR, Zhang E, Snow ME, Rock CO. Mechanism of triclosan inhibition of bacterial fatty acid synthesis. *J Biol Chem.* 1999;274:11110-11114.

38. McMurry LM, McDermott PF, Levy SB. Genetic evidence that InhA of *Mycobacterium smegmatis* is a target for triclosan. *Antimicrob Agents Chemother.* 1999;43:711-713.

39. Chuanchuen R, Beinlich K, Hoang TT, Becher A, Karkhoff-Schweizer

RR, Schweizer HP. Cross-resistance between triclosan and antibiotics in *Pseudomonas aeruginosa* is mediated by multidrug efflux pumps: exposure of a susceptible mutant strain to triclosan selects nfxB mutants overexpressing MexCD-OprJ. *Antimicrob Agents Chemother.* 2001;45:428-432.

40. Nastasi A, Mammina C. Presence of class I integrons in multidrug-resistant, low-prevalence *Salmonella* serotypes, Italy. *Emerg Infect Dis.* 2001;7:455-458.

41. Tollefson L, Angulo FJ, Fedorka-Cray PJ. National surveillance for antibiotic resistance in zoonotic enteric pathogens. *Vet Clin North Am Food Anim Pract.* 1998;14:141-150.

42. McClellan J, Rossiter S, Joyce K, Stamey K, Anderson A, and the NARMS Working Group. Prevalence and consequences of fluoroquinolone-resistant *Campylobacter* infections: NARMS 1997-2000. Paper presented at: International Conference on Emerging Infectious Diseases. March 24-27, 2002; Atlanta, Ga. Available at: http://www.cdc.gov/namrs/pub/presentations/iced/mclellan_j.htm. Accessed May 6, 2003.

43. Fey PD, Safranek TJ, Rupp ME, et al. Ceftriaxone-resistant salmonella infection acquired by a child from cattle. *N Engl J Med.* 2000;342:1242-1249.

44. Davis MA, Hancock DD, Besser TE, et al. Changes in antimicrobial resistance among *Salmonella enterica* serovar Typhimurium isolates from humans and cattle in the Northwestern United States, 1982-1997. *Emerg Infect Dis.* 1999;5:802-806.

45. White DG, Zhao S, Sudler R, et al. The isolation of antibiotic-resistant *Salmonella* from retail ground meats. *N Engl J Med.* 2001;345:1147-1154.

46. Klare I, Heier H, Claus H, Reissbrodt R, Witte W. *vanA*-mediated high-level glycopeptide resistance in *Enterococcus faecium* from animal husbandry. *FEMS Microbiol Lett.* 1995;125:165-171.

47. Aarestrup FM. Occurrence of glycopeptide-resistance among *Enterococcus faecium* isolates from conventional and ecological poultry farms. *Microb Drug Resist.* 1995;1:255-257.

48. McDonald LC, Rossiter S, Mackinson C, et al. Quinupristin-dalfopristin-resistant *Enterococcus faecium* on chicken and in human stool specimens. *N Engl J Med.* 2001;345:1155-1160.

49. Welton LA, Thal LA, Perri MB, et al. Antimicrobial resistance in enterococci isolated from turkey flocks fed virginiamycin. *Antimicrob Agents Chemother.* 1998;42:705-708.

50. Felmingham D, Gruneberg RN. A multicentre collaborative study of the antimicrobial susceptibility of community-acquired, lower respiratory tract pathogens 1992-1993: the Alexander Project. *J Antimicrob Chemother.* 1996;38(suppl A):1-57.

51. Felmingham D, Gruneberg RN, and the Alexander Project Group. The Alexander Project 1996-1997: latest susceptibility data from this international study of bacterial pathogens from community-acquired lower respiratory tract infections. *J Antimicrob Chemother.* 2000;45:191-203.

52. Bell JM, Turnidge JD, and SENTRY APAC Participants. High prevalence of oxacillin-resistant *Staphylococcus aureus* isolates from hospitalized patients in Asia-Pacific and South Africa: results from SENTRY Antimicrobial Surveillance Program, 1998-1999. *Antimicrob Agents Chemother.* 2002;46:879-881.

53. Bloch KC. Infectious diseases. In: McPhee SJ, Lingappa VR, Ganong WF, eds. *Pathophysiology of Disease: An Introduction to Clinical Medicine.* 4th ed. New York, NY: Lange Medical Books/McGraw-Hill Professional; 2003:58-90.

54. Doern GV, Heilmann KP, Huynh HK, Rhomberg PR, Coffman SL, Brueggemann AB. Antimicrobial resistance among clinical isolates of *Streptococcus pneumoniae* in the United States during 1999-2000, including a comparison of resistance rates since 1994-1995. *Antimicrob Agents Chemother.* 2001;45:1721-1729.

55. Brueggemann AB, Coffman SL, Rhomberg P, et al. Fluoroquinolone resistance in *Streptococcus pneumoniae* in United States since 1994-1995. *Antimicrob Agents Chemother.* 2002;46:680-688.

56. McCaig LF, Besser RE, Hughes JM. Antimicrobial drug prescription in ambulatory care settings, United States, 1992-2000. *Emerg Infect Dis.* 2003;9:432-437.

57. Low DE, de Azavedo J, Weiss K, et al. Antimicrobial resistance among clinical isolates of *Streptococcus pneumoniae* in Canada during 2000. *Antimicrob Agents Chemother.* 2002;46:1295-1301.

58. Chambers HF. Chloramphenicol, tetracyclines, macrolides, clindamycin, & streptogramins. In: Katzung BG, ed. *Basic & Clinical Pharmacology.* 8th ed. New York, NY: Lange Medical Books/McGraw-Hill Medical Publishing Division; 2001:774-783.

59. Capobianco JO, Cao Z, Shortridge VD, Ma Z, Flamm RK, Zhong P. Studies of the novel ketolide ABT-773: transport, binding to ribosomes, and inhibition of protein synthesis in *Streptococcus pneumoniae.* *Antimicrob Agents Chemother.* 2000;44:1562-1567.

60. Morosini MI, Canton R, Loza E, et al. In vitro activities of telithromycin against Spanish *Streptococcus pneumoniae* isolates with characterized macrolide resistance mechanisms. *Antimicrob Agents Chemother.* 2001;45:2427-2431.

61. Paladino JA. Economic justification of antimicrobial management programs: implications of antimicrobial resistance. *Am J Health Syst Pharm.* 2000;57(suppl 2):S10-S12.

62. Severin A, Tabei K, Tenover F, Chung M, Clarke N, Tomasz A. High level oxacillin and vancomycin resistance and altered cell wall composition in *Staphylococcus aureus* carrying the staphylococcal *mecA* and the enterococcal *vanA* gene complex. *J Biol Chem.* 2003; In press.

63. Centers for Disease Control and Prevention. *Staphylococcus aureus* resistant to vancomycin—United States, 2002. *MMWR Morb Mortal Wkly Rep.* 2002;51:565-567.

64. Centers for Disease Control and Prevention. Public health dispatch: vancomycin-resistant *Staphylococcus aureus*—Pennsylvania, 2002. *MMWR Morb Mortal Wkly Rep.* 2002;51:902.

65. Struwig MC, Botha PL, Chalkley LJ. In vitro activities of 15 antimicrobial agents against clinical isolates of South African enterococci. *Antimicrob Agents Chemother.* 1998;42:2752-2755.

66. Quale J, Landman D, Ravishankar J, Flores C, Bratu S. *Streptococcus pneumoniae*, Brooklyn, New York: fluoroquinolone resistance at our doorstep. *Emerg Infect Dis.* 2002;8:594-597.

67. National Committee for Clinical Laboratory Standards. Performance standards for antimicrobial susceptibility testing; twelfth informational supplement. Wayne, Pa: National Committee for Clinical Laboratory Standards. Document M100-S12. 2002;22:1-118.

68. Kaplan SL, Mason EO Jr. Management of infections due to antibiotic-resistant *Streptococcus pneumoniae*. *Clin Microbiol Rev.* 1998;11:628-644.

69. Rubin RJ, Harrington CA, Poon A, Dietrich K, Greene JA, Moiduddin A. The economic impact of *Staphylococcus aureus* infection in New York City hospitals. *Emerg Infect Dis.* 1999;5:9-17.

70. Chaix C, Durand-Zaleski I, Alberti C, Brun-Buisson C. Control of endemic methicillin-resistant *Staphylococcus aureus*. A cost-benefit analysis in an intensive care unit. *JAMA.* 1999;282:1745-1751.

71. Tufts Center for the Study of Drug Development pegs cost of a new prescription medicine at $802 million [news release]. Philadelphia, Pa: Tufts University; November 30, 2001. Available at: http://csdd.tufts.edu/newsevents/recentnews.asp?newsid=6. Accessed June 23, 2003.

72. Connolly C. Price tag for a new drug: $802 million. Findings of Tufts University study are disputed by several watchdog groups. *Washington Post.* Saturday, December 1, 2001;Sect A: A10.

73. Tufts drug study sample is skewed: true figure of R&D costs likely is 75 percent lower [press release]. Washington, DC: Public Citizen; December 4, 2001. Available at: http://www.citizen.org/pressroom/release.cfm?ID=954. Accessed June 23,2003.

74. Pinner RW, Teutsch SM, Simonsen L, et al. Trends in infectious diseases mortality in the United States. *JAMA.* 1996;275:189-193.

CHAPTER ONE CME QUESTIONS

1. When did the first evidence of antibiotic resistance surface?
   a. Almost simultaneously with Alexander Fleming's discovery of penicillin in the late 1920s
   b. In the early 1940s
   c. In the 1950s
   d. In the 1960s

2. Before the use of antibiotics to treat bacterial disease, what was the crude death rate per 100,000 population from infectious diseases?
   a. 150
   b. 500
   c. 800
   d. 900

3. Inappropriate prescribing of antibiotics for colds, bronchitis, and upper respiratory tract infections with a likely viral origin is implicated in the rise of antibiotic resistance and has been estimated to constitute more than what percentage of prescriptions for those illnesses?
   a. 25%
   b. 33%
   c. 50%
   d. 75%

4. By 1999-2000, what was the approximate range of resistance to penicillin among strains of *Streptococcus pneumoniae* in the United States?
   a. 2% to 15%
   b. 5% to 56%
   c. 10% to 67%
   d. 25% to 75%

5. Which of the following factors has been implicated in the rise of bacterial resistance to antibiotics?
   a. Use of subtherapeutic doses of medication
   b. Inappropriate use of antibiotics for nonbacterial disease
   c. Use of an inappropriate antibiotic to treat a particular pathogen
   d. Patient failure to comply with the dosing regimen and to finish all antibiotic medication
   e. All of the above

CREATION OF A NOVEL CLASS:

A HISTORY OF ANTIBIOTICS

EDITOR

Donald H. Batts, MD, FACP

LEARNING OBJECTIVES

After completion of this chapter, readers should be able to:

1. Discuss the early development of antibiotics.

2. Differentiate major antibiotic classes.

3. Identify antibiotic mechanisms of action.

4. Describe bacterial mechanisms of resistance.

THE OXAZOLIDINONE ANTIBIOTICS

For thousands of years, human beings fought bacterial infections with herbal remedies and chemical compounds. In the late 15th century, Europeans began to treat syphilis (*Treponema pallidum* infection) with mercury, a practice that continued well into the 20th century.[1,2] Nearly 2500 years ago, the Chinese first used a concoction of moldy soybean curd to cure skin infections (*Staphylococcus aureus*).[3] More recently, researchers have found that tempe, a fungal fermented soybean product, may inhibit adhesion of *Escherichia coli* to the brush-border membrane of the small intestine in piglets.[4] Other naturally occurring antibiotics in plants, such as the allium found in onions and garlic, have been used for centuries in folk medicine to treat infections.[5,6]

In some cases, the discovery of antibiotic qualities in plants has considerably changed the course of history. Centuries before the arrival of the Europeans, South American Indians used the bark of the cinchona tree to treat malaria (caused by *Plasmodium* species).[7-9] However, by 1630, Europeans were also using the quinine derived from cinchona bark to treat malaria.[7,8] Expanded use of this therapy in the 19th century allowed European conquest of territory in areas formerly considered inaccessible because of high rates of endemic malaria.[7] The medicinal benefits of cinchona bark continued to be explored and led to the development of the synthetic derivatives chloroquine, amodiaquine, primaquine, and mefloquine.[8,10] Further research into the compound chloroquine ultimately resulted in the creation of the quinolone antibiotics.[10]

However, not until the mid-19th century, with the work of Louis Pasteur on a variety of vaccines and pathogens, including anthrax (*Bacillus anthracis*), and that of Robert Koch on the anthrax life cycle, was modern microbiology founded.[11,12] In 1877, Pasteur and Joubert noted that anthrax bacilli, which grew rapidly in sterile urine, would soon die if other airborne bacteria were introduced into the urine at the same time.[13] Thus, the concept that bacterial byproducts might prove toxic to other microbes was formulated.

Early Research Begins to Bear Fruit

With the advent of the 20th century, progress was made in the development of treatments for these recently discovered pathogens. In 1908, Paul Gelmo, an Austrian chemist, synthesized *para*-aminobenzenesulfonamide, a compound that would eventually lead to the development of the sulfonamides or sulfa drugs.[14] However, the first successful antimicrobial compound was an arsphenamine with the trade name of Salvarsan, developed by the German medical researcher Paul Ehrlich in 1910 for the treatment of syphilis.[15] Alexander Fleming's discovery in 1928 that a mold named *Penicillium notatum* would inhibit *S aureus* was one of the defining moments in pharmacological history.[16,17] Unfortunately, 12 years or more elapsed before this discovery was put into practical application.[16-21]

Meanwhile, the early work of Gelmo was rediscovered by a German physician named Gerhard Domagk. In 1927, the very large German chemical company I.G. Farbenindustrie hired Domagk to screen various dyes for pharmaceutical activity.[22-24] Domagk reasoned that the azo dyes might have antimicrobial activity because their double nitrogen bond, which gives them a strong affinity for the proteins in fabrics and leather and makes them excellent dyes, might allow them to also attach to bacterial proteins. Domagk tested a new orange-red dye, sulfamidochrysoidine, on laboratory rats and rabbits that had been infected with streptococci and found that the new compound was highly effective against the bacteria and was not toxic. Researchers soon discovered that Prontosil, as this agent was called, was not the active compound.[22] Instead, it served as a prodrug for its active metabolite, sulfanilamide (*p*-aminobenzenesulfonamide), which inhibited bacterial reproduction and allowed the body's immune system to mount an effective defense.

Other related compounds or sulfa drugs were discovered in the late 1930s and early 1940s, although only a few were medically important.[22] Among those were sulfapyridine, used to treat Winston Churchill during World War II; sulfathiazole; sulfadiazine; and sulfaguanidine. However, researchers discovered that these very useful compounds had serious adverse effects and that many clinically important bacteria developed resistance to them.[18,22,24,27]

Fortunately, other avenues of antibiotic research were being pursued at that time. A group of scientists in Britain were expanding on the early work of Alexander Fleming. Although Fleming had recognized the importance of his discovery that *Penicillium* mold would inhibit bacterial growth, he had been unable to extract the active substance, which he had named penicillin.[16] In the 1930s, under the direction of Howard Florey, the British group, which included Ernst Chain and Edward Abraham, worked to extract and purify the penicillin.[16,17] By May of 1940, the group was ready to test the purified penicillin extract. Eight mice were injected with a lethal dose of streptococcal bacteria. Four were given the purified penicillin, and 4 were not. Those given penicillin recovered from their infection and lived; the other mice died.[17,24,28] In 1941, the first patient, a man who had contracted a massive bacterial infection from a rose thorn, was treated with the new drug. Although the man began an initial recovery, not enough penicillin was available to provide adequate treatment. Despite heroic efforts to extract additional penicillin from the patient's urine, he soon relapsed and died.[28] However, by 1943, mass production of the drug had begun in the United States, and penicillin was making an invaluable contribution to medical science.[24,28]

After World War II, antibiotic discoveries began to accelerate. Many researchers were stimulated by the work of Fleming, Florey, Chain, and Abraham and began to look at other microorganisms as potential antimicrobial agents. Between 1939 and 1943, Selman Waksman, who had emigrated from Russia to the United States in 1910, began systematically examining soil fungi, particularly actinomycetes, in an effort to identify potential therapeutic agents.[29] Over a 10-year period, Waksman and colleagues discovered 3 antibiotic agents with important clinical implications: actinomycin in 1940, streptomycin in 1944, and neomycin in 1949.[23,29-31]

In Cagliari, Italy, Giuseppe Brotzu, a professor at the University of Cagliari and director of the school's Institute of Hygiene, was intrigued by a phenomenon he noted near a local sewage outlet. The unfiltered sewage poured directly into the sea, clouded the water for several hundred feet, and then abruptly disappeared. Water farther out was clear and apparently devoid of the pathogens he was able to isolate from the polluted water. In July 1945, Brotzu isolated a fungus, *Cephalosporium acremonium*, that had potent antibiotic activity against a variety of pathogens, including staphylococci, streptococci, *B anthracis*, *Salmonella typhi*, and *Vibrio cholerae*.[24,32,33] However, a lack of facilities and financial support prevented him from developing his discovery, and, after the publication of the results of his findings, he sent a sample of *C acremonium* to the Laboratory of Pathology at Oxford University.[32,34] There, Edward Abraham, who had worked with Florey and Chain on penicillin, took Brotzu's discovery further,

ultimately purifying cephalosporin C from the sample and determining its chemical structure.[16,32,34] The cephalosporins, as this newest class of antibiotics was termed, were capable of destroying penicillin-resistant bacteria.[32,34,35]

The discovery of chloramphenicol in 1947 and the tetracyclines in 1948 led to the first effective treatment for Rocky Mountain spotted fever (*Rickettsia rickettsii*).[36] Before the availability of these antibiotics, approximately 30% of infected individuals died, and even today the disease remains a serious illness, with a 3% to 5% mortality rate. Chloramphenicol is produced by *Streptomyces venezuelae*, an organism that was first isolated from soil samples in Venezuela, whereas the tetracyclines were developed from antibiotic-producing microorganisms found in soil samples collected from around the world.[37] The tetracyclines were soon found to have efficacy against both aerobic and anaerobic gram-positive and gram-negative bacteria in addition to their effectiveness against the rickettsiae. Chloramphenicol has a wide spectrum of activity as well, but it quickly became apparent that its toxic effects limited its use to the most serious infections. Because it can cause fatal blood dyscrasias, chloramphenicol is reserved for illnesses such as meningitis, typhus, and typhoid fever in addition to Rocky Mountain spotted fever.

Soil samples again proved their value when *Streptomyces erythraeus* was isolated by McGuire and colleagues in 1952 from a sample of soil taken from the city of Iloilo on the Island of Paray in the Philippines.[37-39] Erythromycin became the first, and for 40 years was the only macrolide antibiotic.[37] Clarithromycin and azithromycin are semisynthetic derivatives of erythromycin that were developed in the closing years of the 20th century. Erythromycin was particularly valuable because it could be used in patients with penicillin allergies[39]; however, gastrointestinal intolerance limited its use.[37] Vancomycin, a glycopeptide developed in 1956, was obtained from *Streptomyces orientalis*, an actinomycete found in soil samples from Indonesia and India.[37,40-42] Both vancomycin and another glycopeptide, teicoplanin, demonstrated a high degree of efficacy against pathogens resistant to other antimicrobials, and only recently has resistance to these compounds been found.[40] However, the increase in resistance to such powerful agents was alarming indeed and underscored the need for an ever-increasing arsenal of antibiotics.[43,44]

Table 1. Timeline for Select Antibiotic Classes[10,23,25,40,41]

Class	Year	Discoverer	Source
β-Lactams			
Penicillins	1928	Fleming, Florey, Chain	*Penicillium* species
Cephalosporins	1945	Brotzu, Abraham	*Cephalosporium acremonium*
Sulfonamides	1908	Gelmo	*para*-Aminobenzenesulfonamide
	1932	Domagk	Sulfamidochrysoidine (dye)
Aminoglycosides	1940	Waksman	*Actinomyces* species
Macrolides	1952	McGuire	*Streptomyces erythraeus*
Glycopeptides	1956	Eli Lilly[23,25,40,41]	*Streptomyces orientalis*
Quinolones	1962[10]	Lesher, Froelich, Gruett	Chloroquine
Fluoroquinolones	1980	Irikura[25]	
Oxazolidinones	Late 1970s	DuPont, Upjohn	

Although quinolone compounds such as nalidixic acid had been available for years, their use was limited to the treatment of urinary infections.[10] However, with the introduction in the 1980s of the fluorinated 4-quinolones, such as ciprofloxacin and ofloxacin, a highly valuable synthetic class of antimicrobials became available.[24,45] These compounds had a broad spectrum of activity against pathogens that had become resistant to many other antibiotics and were a welcome addition to an embattled armamentarium. However, their use in pediatric populations and pregnant women was restricted by adverse effects.[24,45]

The oxazolidinones, a group of synthetic antibiotics with activity against gram-positive organisms, were first discovered in the 1970s.[46] However, nearly 30 years elapsed before the first agent in this class, linezolid, was approved for the treatment of pneumonia and skin and skin structure infections. Three subclasses of oxazolidinones were developed.[43] These included piperazine, indoline, and tropone, with the greatest potential being found in the first subclass. The 2 candidates that emerged from the piperazine subclass were eperezolid and linezolid. Linezolid appeared to have the superior pharmacokinetic profile and was thus chosen for continued human clinical evaluation. The creation of linezolid is outlined in greater detail in the following chapter. Table 1 presents a timeline for the history of a number of classes of antibiotics.

The Antibiotic Classes

Most antibiotic agents have been developed from naturally occurring compounds, usually fungi (eg, penicillins, cephalosporins), actinomycetes (eg, aminoglycosides, glycopeptides, macrolides), or other bacteria (eg, polypeptides). Synthetic antibiotics include the sulfonamides, derived from dyes; the quinolones, derived from byproducts of chloroquine synthesis; and the oxazolidinones. Many of the later agents developed in a particular antibiotic class are variations of earlier compounds.[44] With the exception of the oxazolidinones and cationic peptides, both of which act on unconventional bacterial targets, the currently available antibiotic classes are directed at only 15 different bacterial targets.

The major antibiotic classes include the β-lactams (ie, penicillins, cephalosporins, carbapenems, monobactams), aminoglycosides (ie, streptomycin, gentamicin), macrolides (ie, erythromycin, clarithromycin, azithromycin), glycopeptides (ie, vancomycin, teicoplanin, daptomycin), polypeptides (ie, polymyxin, bacitracin), sulfonamides, quinolones, lincomycins (ie, clindamycin), tetracyclines (ie, tetracycline, doxycycline), rifamycins (ie, rifampicin), oxazolidinones, ketolides, and the combination agents trimethoprim-sulfamethoxazole and quinupristin-dalfopristin.

Antibiotics work either through bacteriostatic mechanisms—they inhibit bacterial growth and allow the host's own immune system to rid the body of infection—or through bactericidal mechanisms—they kill bacteria directly.[47] Some antibiotics are bacteriostatic with some pathogens yet bactericidal with others. Selective toxicity is the basis of antimicrobial therapy. Chemical compounds are chosen for their effects on particular bacterial targets because those targets are unique to the bacteria; thus, the agent's primary mode of action is unlikely to affect human cells. Inhibitors of cell wall synthesis, such as the β-lactam antibiotics, do not interfere with human or animal cells because those cells lack cell walls. β-Lactam antibiotics inhibit the last step in peptidoglycan synthesis and disrupt cell wall formation; however, they require that bacteria be in a growth phase to be effective. Cell membrane inhibitors such as polymyxin interfere with the structure or function of the bacterial cell membrane and lead to leakage of the intracellular contents.[13,47] Although differences exist between bacterial and eukaryotic cell membranes, until recently these compounds were not used systemically because of concerns about toxicity.[47] However, with the emergence of multidrug-resistant gram-negative infections, particularly those caused by *Pseudomonas aeruginosa* and *Acinetobacter*, polymyxin B has been used to effectively treat these infections with a lower rate of nephrotoxicity than previously reported.[48]

Some protein synthesis inhibitors operate by interfering with the function of the 30S or 50S ribosomal subunits to cause a reversible inhibition of protein synthesis. These agents are bacteriostatic and include chloramphenicol, the tetracyclines, erythromycin, and clindamycin.[13] Others, including the aminoglycosides, bind to the 30S ribosomal subunit to alter protein synthesis, which leads to cell death. Agents that affect nucleic acid metabolism, through the inhibition of either DNA-dependent RNA polymerase or DNA gyrase, include the rifamycins (the former mechanism) and the quinolones (the latter mechanism). The final antibiotic mechanism is the interference with specific metabolic steps essential to microbial organisms. Known as antimetabolites, this group includes trimethoprim and the sulfonamides.

Pathogenic Targets

Antibiotics are classified as *broad spectrum*, meaning they kill or inhibit a wide range of gram-positive and gram-negative bacteria; *narrow spectrum*, meaning their efficacy is generally limited to gram-negative or gram-positive bacteria; and *limited spectrum*, indicating the agent in question is effective primarily against a single pathogen.[47] Although broad-spectrum antibiotics may appear to be the best choice at first glance, given the frequent difficulty determining the causative pathogen in many infections, overuse of broad-spectrum agents can induce greater resistance in affected bacteria. Moreover, superinfection, which occurs when the body's normal flora is altered by the use of antibiotics, allows opportunistic pathogens a chance to invade and cause an infection and is more likely to arise with the use of broader-spectrum agents.[13] Thus, generally speaking, when an infection is strongly suspected as being caused by a particular pathogen, the best plan is to select an antibiotic with (1) efficacy against the suggested microbe and (2) the narrowest spectrum possible. Table 2 presents a number of antibiotics and their mechanisms of action.

Resistance Mechanisms

Even during the golden era of antibiotics, there were indications that resistance might develop. Alexander Fleming cautioned in an interview with *The New York Times* in 1945 that misuse of penicillin could lead to selection for resistance among bacteria.[49] As early as 1946, one hospital reported that 14% of *Staphylococcus* isolates were resistant to penicillin, and by 1950 in that same hospital, the rate of resistant strains increased to 59%.

Mechanisms of bacterial resistance are almost as diverse as the bacteria themselves; however, they can be grouped into 4 general types.[50,51] By altering the proteins in the antibiotic target site or creating a competitive second target site, bacteria inhibit the ability of antibiotics to attach and thus disrupt bacterial function.[50,52] Such a mechanism is evident in penicillin-resistant *Streptococcus pneumoniae*, which alters the penicillin-binding proteins. Other bacteria, such as β-lactamase–producing *Haemophilus influenzae*, make enzymes that inactivate or destroy the antibiotic before it reaches the target site. Other bacteria decrease the permeability of their cell membranes to antibiotic penetration or develop an active transport system, such as an efflux pump. This latter mechanism is found in some bacteria resistant to macrolides. Either of these 2 last mechanisms results in inadequate intracellular accumulations of the antibiotic.[50] Pathogens sometimes exhibit more than one mechanism of resistance.[50,52,53]

Resistance can be absolute or relative. For instance, in the case of macrolide antibiotics, the efflux pump confers relative resistance, and minimal inhibitory concentrations of 1 µg/mL to 32 µg/mL suggest an efflux pump because higher concentrations of the agent can overcome resistance.[53] Ribosomal methylation, another form of macrolide resistance, is absolute, and minimal inhibitory concentrations of greater than 64 µg/mL suggest this latter mechanism.

Resistance may be inherent, occurring naturally as an intrinsic property of the bacteria, or it may arise as the result of a mutation.[50,51,54] Additionally, resistance can be acquired from other pathogens through transformation, conjugation, or transduction.[27,47,51] In the case of an organism such as *P aeruginosa*, resistance may have been acquired long before the advent of the antibiotic era, as this microbe's natural habitat includes the soil, where it would have been exposed to many of the actinomycetes, molds, and bacilli commonly used to create antimicrobials.[47,55] The pressure exerted on a bacterial population by antimicrobial therapy can result in the rapid rise of resistance, selecting for those

Table 2. Antibiotic Mechanisms of Action, Killing Method, and Spectrum of Activity[3,10,40,47,48]

Mechanism of Action	Classes/Agents	Killing Method	Spectrum
Inhibition of cell wall synthesis	Penicillins	T-d, bactericidal*	G+ bacteria
	Cephalosporins	T-d, bactericidal*	G+ bacteria
	Semisynthetic penicillins	T-d, bactericidal*	G+/G- bacteria
	Glycopeptides	T-d, bactericidal*	G+ bacteria, especially *Staphylococcus* species
	Bacitracin	T-d, bactericidal	G+ bacteria
Disruption of cell membrane	Polymyxin B, E	C-d, bactericidal	G- bacteria
	Polyenes	C-d, bactericidal	Fungi
Protein synthesis inhibition	Aminoglycosides	C-d, bactericidal	G+/G- bacteria
	Tetracyclines	T-d, bacteriostatic	G+/G- bacteria, *Rickettsia* species
	Macrolides	T-d, bacteriostatic	G+/G-, excluding *Enterococcus, Neisseria, Legionella, Mycoplasma* species
	Lincosamides	T-d, bacteriostatic	G+/G- bacteria, especially anaerobic *Bacteroides* species
	Chloramphenicol	T-d, bacteriostatic	G+/G- bacteria
	Oxazolidinones	T-d, bacteriostatic	G+ bacteria, especially *Staphylococcus, Streptococcus* species
Nucleic acid metabolism interruption (antimetabolites)	Fluoroquinolones	C-d, bactericidal	G+/G- bacteria
	Sulfonamides	T-d, bacteriostatic	G+/G- bacteria
	Metronidazole	C-d, bactericidal	Anaerobic bacteria and protozoa, especially *Trichomonas* species

T-d = time-dependent killing; C-d = concentration-dependent killing; G+ = gram-positive organism; G- = gram-negative organism.
*Bactericidal only during active growth and cell wall synthesis.

features that occur either through mutation or acquisition and conferring the greatest chance for survival. Enterococci often exhibit an inherent resistance to cephalosporins, semisynthetic penicillinase-resistant penicillins, low levels of aminoglycosides, and clindamycin.[51,56] They have also acquired resistance to tetracyclines; erythromycin; chloramphenicol; trimethoprim; vancomycin; and high levels of clindamycin, aminoglycosides, and penicillins. Interestingly, a β-lactamase identical to that produced by *S aureus* and first identified in the mid-1940s was found in *Enterococcus faecalis* by 1981.[56]

Advances in genetics have enabled researchers to identify many of the genes responsible for resistance in various species of bacteria. The β-lactamase responsible for β-lactam resistance in enterococci has been demonstrated to be encoded on transferable plasmids in several *E faecalis* strains and is identical to that present on several staphylococcal plasmids.[56] More recently, genetic mutations that encode for quinolone resistance have been identified in *E coli*, and transmissible resistance to quinolones has also been discovered on a plasmid, despite the idea that plasmid-mediated transference of quinolone resistance was long considered highly unlikely.[57]

Although β-lactam resistance has been a problem for many years,[58] bacterial resistance to quinolones and fluoroquinolones is a more recent and disturbing phenomenon. High levels of resistance—44.5% to norfloxacin and 40.5% to ciprofloxacin—have been found among *Campylobacter* isolates in Crete among patients with acute diarrhea.[59] The same study found that 31.5% of *Salmonella enterica*, 58.3% of *Shigella* species, and 31.5% of enteropathogenic *E coli* are resistant to ampicillin, whereas 4.4% of *S enterica*, 30.5% of *Shigella* species, and 18.5% of *E coli* are resistant to trimethoprim-sulfamethoxazole.[59] Data suggest that levofloxacin may promote fluoroquinolone resistance in *S pneumoniae*, an alarming finding considering how often this agent is used for lower respiratory tract infections.[60,61] Given the extensive cross-resistance noted among the fluoroquinolones, ciprofloxacin is likely to provoke similar levels of resistance.[62]

Equally alarming is the resistance found in some pathogens to vancomycin, which until recently was the last defense against resistant strains and was often used in the treatment of nosocomial infections.[63] The emergence of vancomycin-resistant enterococci in hospital settings is of great concern. Fears are that vancomycin-resistant enterococci may serve as a reservoir for vancomycin-resistant genes that may eventually find their way into more virulent bacterial populations, such as the staphylococci.[64] Genetic research has indicated that resistance, which has been found in both gram-positive and gram-negative bacteria, may have developed out of adaptive mechanisms found in glycopeptide-producing bacteria.[63] Glycopeptides such as vancomycin normally disrupt cell wall formation by preventing peptidoglycan cross-linking. Ligases from *Streptomyces toyocaensis* and *Amycolatopsis orientalis*, both of which produce glycopeptides, protect the bacteria by reprogramming cell wall termini and reducing the affinity for the antibiotic compound 1000-fold during its biosynthesis.[63,64] Interestingly, *vanA* and *vanB*, 2 depsipeptide ligases found in vancomycin-resistant enterococci, have shown a high degree of homology to those found in *S toyocaensis* and *A orientalis*, suggesting that these adaptations may have originated from the glycopeptide-producing organisms.[64]

Summary

The discovery of antibiotics in the first half of the 20th century and the subsequent introduction of numerous antimicrobial agents into medical practice in the second half of the 20th century stand as one of the greatest accomplishments in human history. The number of lives saved through the use of these drugs is incalculable. However, the resilience of pathogenic organisms has proved to be more than a match for medical science, and this great achievement is now threatened by the rise of bacterial resistance. Preventing a return to the preantibiotic era, when a pinprick could prove fatal, requires a concerted effort (1) on the part of the pharmaceutical industry to identify novel bacterial targets and develop new, effective antimicrobial agents and (2) on the part of the medical community to promote and practice judicious use of available antibiotics to preserve their effectiveness.

References

1. Weissmann K. Neurosyphilis, or chronic heavy metal poisoning: Karen Blixen's lifelong disease. *Sex Transm Dis.* 1995;22:137-144.
2. Sartin JS, Perry HO. From mercury to malaria to penicillin: the history of the treatment of syphilis at the Mayo Clinic—1916-1955. *J Am Acad Dermatol.* 1995;32(2 pt 1):255-261.
3. Whittem R, Gaon D. Principles of antimicrobial therapy. *Vet Clin North Am Small Anim Pract.* 1998;28:197-213.

4. Kiers JL, Nout MJ, Rombouts FM, Nabuurs MJ, van der Meulen J. Inhibition of adhesion of enterotoxigenic *Escherichia coli* K88 by soya bean tempe. *Lett Appl Microbiol.* 2002;35:311-315.

5. Sivam GP. Protection against *Helicobacter pylori* and other bacterial infections by garlic. *J Nutr.* 2001;13:1106S-1108S.

6. Griffiths G, Trueman L, Crowther T, Thomas B, Smith B. Onions—a global benefit to health. *Phytother Res.* 2002;16:603-615.

7. Lee MR. Plants against malaria. Part 1: cinchona or the Peruvian bark. *J R Coll Physicians Edinb.* 2002;32:189-196.

8. Tagboto S, Townson S. Antiparasitic properties of medicinal plants and other naturally occurring products. *Adv Parasitol.* 2001;50: 199-295.

9. Willcox L, Cosentino MJ, Pink R, Bodeker G, Wayling S. Natural products for the treatment of tropical diseases. *Trends Parasitol.* 2001;17:58-60.

10. Emmerson AM, Jones AM. The quinolones: decades of development and use. *J Antimicrob Chemother.* 2003;51(suppl 1):13-20.

11. Baxter AG. Louis Pasteur's beer of revenge. *Nat Rev Immunol.* 2001;1:229-232.

12. Fry DE. In vino veritas. *Surg Infect (Larchmt).* 2001;2:185-191.

13. Chambers HF, Sande MA. Antimicrobial agents. General considerations. In: Hardman JG, Limbird LE, Molinoff PB, Ruddon RW, Goodman Gilman A, eds. *Goodman & Gilman's The Pharmacological Basis of Therapeutics.* 9th ed. New York, NY: McGraw-Hill Health Professions Division; 1996:1029-1056.

14. The Columbia Encyclopedia, 6th ed. University of Columbia Press. Available at: http://www.bartelby.com/65/. Accessed April 26, 2003.

15. Kasten FH. Paul Ehrlich: pathfinder in cell biology. 1. Chronicle of his life and accomplishments in immunology, cancer research, and chemotherapy. *Biotech Histochem.* 1996;71:2-37.

16. Nayler JH. Early discoveries in the penicillin series. *Trends Biochem Sci.* 1991;16:195-197.

17. Swann JP. Paul Ehrlich and the introduction of Salvarsan. *Med Herit.* 1985;1:137-138.

18. Money R. Early work on penicillin. *Med J Aust.* 1982;1:367.

19. McEwin R. Florey and Cairns—early work on penicillin. *Med J Aust.* 1982;1:12-13.

20. Wainwright M. Fleming's unfinished. *Perspect Biol Med.* 2002;45: 529-538.

21. Joklik WK. The story of penicillin: the view from Oxford in the early 1950s. *FASEB J.* 1996; 10:525-528.

22. Keifer DM. Chemistry chronicles. Miracle medicines–the advent of the sulfa drugs in the mid-1930s gave physicians a powerful weapon. *Today's Chemist at Work.* 2001;10:59-60. Available at: http://pubs.acs.org/subscribe/journals/tcaw/10/i06/html/06chemch. html. Accessed April 26, 2003.

23. Raju TN. The Nobel chronicles. 1939: Gerhard Domagk (1895-1964). *Lancet.* 1999;353:681.

24. Mandell GL, Petri WA Jr. Antimicrobial agents: sulfonamides, trimethoprim-sulfamethoxazole, quinolones, and agents for urinary tract infections. In: Hardman JG, Limbird LE, Molinoff PB, Ruddon RW, Goodman Gilman A, eds. *Goodman & Gilman's The Pharmacological Basis of Therapeutics.* 9th ed. New York, NY: McGraw-Hill Health Professions Division; 1996:1057-1072.

25. Raju TN. The Nobel chronicles. 1952: Selman Abraham Waksman (1888-1973). *Lancet.* 1999;353:1536.

26. Mandell GL, Petri WA Jr. Antimicrobial agents: penicillins, cephalosporins, and other β-lactam antibiotics. In: Hardman JG, Limbird LE, Molinoff PB, Ruddon RW, Goodman Gilman A, eds. *Goodman & Gilman's The Pharmacological Basis of Therapeutics.* 9th ed. New York, NY: McGraw-Hill Health Professions Division; 1996:1073-1101.

27. Mitsuhashi S. Drug resistance in bacteria: history, genetics and biochemistry. *J Int Med Res.* 1993;21:1-14.

28. Torok S. Howard Florey, the story: maker of the miracle mould. *Australian Broadcasting Corporation Online.* Available at: http://www.abc.net. au/science/slab/florey/story.htm. Accessed April 27, 2003.

29. Daniel TM. Selman A. Waksman and the first use of streptomycin. *J Lab Clin Med.* 1988;111:133-134.

30. Smith T. Antibiotics from soil bacteria. *Nat Struct Biol.* 2000;7: 189-190.

31. Wallgren A. The Nobel prize in physiology or medicine 1952 [presentation speech]. Nobel e-Museum Web site. Available at: http://www. nobel.se/medicine/laureates/1952/press.html. Accessed April 27, 2003.

32. Hamilton-Miller JM. Sir Edward Abraham's contribution to the development of the cephalosporins: a reassessment. *Int J Antimicrob Agents.* 2000;15:179-184.

33. Brotzu G. *Research on a New Antibiotic.* Cagliari, Italy: Cagliari Institute of Hygiene; 1948.

34. Abraham EP. A glimpse of the early history of the cephalosporins. *Rev Infect Dis.* 1979;1:99-105.

35. Iddon C. Famous old members: Sir Edward Penley Abraham (1913-1999), honorary fellow of Lincoln College. Lincoln College University of Oxford Web site. Available at: www.lincoln.ox.ac.uk/famous/abraham/. Accessed September 4, 2003.

36. Centers for Disease Control and Prevention. CDC Rocky Mountain spotted fever, introduction. Available at: http://www.cdc.gov/ncidod/ dvrd/rmsf/. Accessed December 18, 2003.

37. Kapusnik-Uner JE, Sande MA, Chambers HF. Antimicrobial agents: tetracyclines, chloramphenicol, erythromycin, and miscellaneous antibacterial agents. In: Hardman JG, Limbird LE, Molinoff PB, Ruddon RW, Goodman Gilman A, eds. *Goodman & Gilman's The Pharmacological Basis of Therapeutics.* 9th ed. New York, NY: McGraw-Hill Health Professions Division; 1996:1123-1153.

38. Mazzei T, Mini E, Novelli A, Periti P. Chemistry and mode of action of macrolides. *J Antimicrob Chemother.* 1993;31(suppl C):1-9.

39. Neu HC. The development of macrolides: clarithromycin in perspective. *J Antimicrob Chemother.* 1991;27(suppl A):1-9.

40. Johnson AP, Uttley AH, Woodford N, George RC. Resistance to vancomycin and teicoplanin: an emerging clinical problem. *Clin Microbiol Rev.* 1990;3:280-291.

41. Geraci JE, Hermans PE. Vancomycin. *Mayo Clin Proc.* 1983;58:88-91.

42. Griffith RS. Vancomycin use—an historical review. *J Antimicrob Chemother.* 1984;14(suppl D):1-5.

43. Ford CW, Zurenko GE, Barbachyn MR. The discovery of linezolid, the first oxazolidinone antibacterial agent. *Curr Drug Targets Infect Disord.* 2001;1:181-199.

44. Breithaupt H. The new antibiotics. *Nat Biotechnol.* 1999;17:1165-1169.

45. Ball P. The quinolones: history and overview. In: Andriole VT, ed. *The Quinolones.* 3rd ed. San Diego, Calif: Academic Press; 2000:2-24.

46. Fung HB, Kirshcenbaum HL, Ojofeitimi BO. Linezolid: an oxazolidinone antimicrobial agent. *Clin Ther.* 2001;23:356-391.

47. Todar K. Microbiology Web Textbook. University of Wisconsin-Madison. Department of Bacteriology Web site. Available at: http://www. bact.wisc.edu/microtextbook/. Accessed April 28, 2003.

48. Ouderkirck JP, Nord JA, Turett GS, Kislak JW. Polymyxin B nephrotoxicity and efficacy against nosocomial infections caused by multiresistant gram-negative bacteria. *Antimicrob Agents Chemother.* 2003;47:2659-2662.

49. Levy SB. *The Antibiotic Paradox.* 1st ed. New York, NY: Plenum Press; 1992:7, 10.

50. Jacobs MR. Emergence of antibiotic resistance in upper and lower respiratory tract infections. *Am J Manag Care.* 1999;5(suppl 11): S651-S661.

51. Murray BE. New aspects of antimicrobial resistance and resulting therapeutic dilemmas. *J Infect Dis.* 1991;163:1185-1194.

52. Gordon KA, Pfaller MA, Jones RN, and the SENTRY Participants Group. BMS284756 (formerly T-3811, a des-fluoroquinolone) potency and spectrum tested against over 10,000 bacterial bloodstream in-

fection isolates from the SENTRY antimicrobial surveillance programme (2000). *J Antimicrob Chemother.* 2002;49:851-855.

53. Doern GV, Heilmann KP, Huynh HK, Rhomberg PR, Coffman SL, Brueggemann AB. Antimicrobial resistance among clinical isolates of *Streptococcus pneumoniae* in the United States during 1999-2000, including a comparison of resistance rates since 1994-1995. *Antimicrob Agents Chemother.* 2001;45:1721-1729.

54. Murray BE. The life and times of the *Enterococcus. Clin Microbiol Rev.* 1990;3:46-65.

55. Pollack M. *Pseudomonas aeruginosa.* In: Mandell GL, Bennett JE, Dolin R, eds. *Mandell, Douglas, and Bennett's Principles and Practices of Infectious Diseases.* Vol 2. 5th ed. Philadelphia, Pa: Churchill Livingstone; 2000:2310-2335.

56. Murray BE. β-Lactamase-producing enterococci. *Antimicrobial Agents Chemother.* 1992;36:2355-2359.

57. Tran JH, Jacoby GA. Mechanism of plasmid-mediated quinolone resistance. *Proc Natl Acad Sci USA.* 2002;99:5638-5642.

58. Murray BE, Moellering RC Jr. Patterns and mechanisms of antibiotic resistance. *Med Clin North Am.* 1978;62:899-923.

59. Maraki S, Georgiladakis A, Tselentis Y, Samonis G. A 5-year study of the bacterial pathogens associated with acute diarrhoea on the island of Crete, Greece, and their resistance to antibiotics. *Eur J Epidemiol.* 2003;18:85-90.

60. Martin SJ, Jung R, Garvin CG. A risk-benefit assessment of levofloxacin in respiratory, skin and skin structure, and urinary tract infections. *Drug Saf.* 2001;24:199-222.

61. Dalhoff A, Schmitz FJ. In vitro antibacterial activity and pharmacodynamics of new quinolones. *Eur J Clin Microbiol Infect Dis.* 2003;22:203-221.

62. Davies TA, Goldschmidt R, Pfleger S, et al. Cross-resistance, relatedness and allele analysis of fluoroquinolone-resistant US clinical isolates of *Streptococcus pneumoniae* (1998-2000). *J Antimicrob Chemother.* 2003;52:168-175.

63. Lessard IA, Walsh CT. VanX, a bacterial D-alanyl-D-alanine dipeptidase: resistance, immunity, or survival function? *Proc Natl Acad Sci USA.* 1999;96:11028-11032.

64. Marshall CG, Broadhead G, Leskiw BK, Wright GD. D-Ala-D-Ala ligases from glycopeptide antibiotic-producing organisms are highly homologous to the enterococcal vancomycin-resistance ligases vanA and vanB. *Proc Natl Acad Sci USA.* 1997;94:6480-6483.

CHAPTER TWO CME QUESTIONS

1. True or False: Researchers have found that tempe, a fungal fermented soybean product, may inhibit adhesion of *Escherichia coli* to the brush-border membrane of the small intestine in piglets.

2. In 1908, what chemist synthesized *para*-aminobenzenesulfonamide, a compound that would eventually lead to the development of the sulfonamides or sulfa drugs?
   a. Paul Gelmo
   b. Gerhard Domagk
   c. Paul Ehrlich
   d. Ernest Chain

3. Alexander Fleming's discovery of the antibiotic properties of the mold *Penicillium* would not bear fruit until further work by a group of scientists in Britain isolated the active agent that Fleming had named penicillin. This group included:
   a. Howard Florey, Selman Waksman, and Ernest Chain
   b. Howard Florey, Ernest Chain, and Edward Abraham
   c. Edward Abraham, Howard Florey, and Giuseppe Brotzu
   d. None of the above

4. The synthetic classes of antibiotics include which of the following?
   a. Aminoglycosides, quinolones, and oxazolidinones
   b. Glycopeptides, quinolones, and oxazolidinones
   c. Quinolones, oxazolidinones, and sulfonamides
   d. Quinolones, sulfonamides, and aminoglycosides

5. Which of the following statements is true regarding antibacterial mechanisms of action?
   a. Erythromycin inhibits cell wall synthesis.
   b. The aminoglycosides bind to the 30S ribosomal subunit to alter protein synthesis.
   c. Tetracycline causes disruption of the cell membrane.
   d. Penicillin inhibits cell wall synthesis.
   e. Statements b and d are correct.
   f. All of the above are correct.

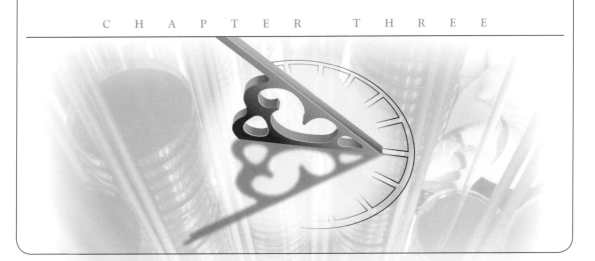

CREATION OF A NOVEL CLASS:

LINEZOLID AND THE OXAZOLIDINONES
A NEW CLASS OF ANTIBIOTICS

EDITOR

Donald H. Batts, MD, FACP

LEARNING OBJECTIVES

After completion of this chapter, readers should be able to:

1. Identify important individuals involved in the discovery and development of the oxazolidinones.

2. Discuss crucial developments in the early history of the oxazolidinones.

3. Develop an appreciation of the contribution of in vitro and in vivo data during the preclinical phase.

4. Characterize the activity of both linezolid and eperezolid against a broad spectrum of gram-positive and gram-negative pathogens.

5. Describe the mechanism of action of the oxazolidinones.

THE OXAZOLIDINONE ANTIBIOTICS

As is frequently true of scientific advances, many individuals contributed to the discovery and development of the oxazolidinone class of antibiotics. Additionally, over the course of the last 25 years, several chemical and pharmaceutical companies have been involved. Although listing all those involved in this effort is not possible, every attempt has been made to credit the persons most responsible for the development of this new antibiotic class.

The oxazolidinones were discovered in Delaware in the late 1970s by E. I. du Pont de Nemours and Company at the Wilmington Experimental Station and the Newark Stine Laboratory.[1-3] The initial research was performed in the agricultural division of the company, where Robert B. Fugitt and Raymond W. Luckenbaugh synthesized early versions of the oxazolidinones by building on the previous work of DuPont chemist Walter A. Gregory on chloramphenicol analogs such as thiamphenicol and tevenel.[3] Fugitt and Luckenbaugh were investigating the potential of the oxazolidinones for controlling fungal and bacterial plant pathogens[1,4] when the compounds were chosen by the antibacterial committee of the pharmaceutical department for routine antibacterial screening. Patricia Bartholomew, a microbiologist and DuPont research associate in charge of antimicrobial screening at the time, observed potent in vitro activity for one of the compounds (personal communication, May 2003). Although this initial finding proved to be erroneous, the consequence sparked interest in the oxazolidinones and prompted in vivo testing.[2-5] Subsequent testing conducted by Bartholomew on mice infected with gram-positive pathogens demonstrated clear evidence of an antimicrobial effect.

However, the in vitro activity proved to be poor when a purer sample was tested later (P. Bartholomew, personal communication, May 2003). Nevertheless, with the support of laboratory research manager Conrad E. Hoffman, Bartholomew continued testing the compounds, despite the disappointing in vitro findings. The anomaly surfaced repeatedly with the entire series, with the good efficacy in vivo in mice failing to correlate with the in vitro activity. An explanation was not apparent based on traditional pharmacokinetics. Although the DuPont team looked for active metabolites to explain the phenomenon, none was found. Nevertheless, despite these early inconsistencies, the researchers recognized immediately that no natural bacterial resistance to the compounds was evident, and although resistance could be induced by gradually exposing

pathogens to low concentrations of oxazolidinones, the bacteria reverted to susceptible strains when the agents were withdrawn.

Once the potential of this discovery was recognized, Walter Gregory, whose early endeavors had formed the basis for Fugitt and Luckenbaugh's work, began synthesizing compounds to increase the potency of the minimal inhibitory concentration (MIC) (personal communication, May 2003). Gregory, who was a research associate with what was then the pharmaceutical division of DuPont, had a wealth of experience working with chloramphenicol analogs and the expertise necessary to know what might enhance in vitro activity. Both he and Bartholomew were intrigued by this series of compounds and communicated frequently during the initial stages of development (C. Demos and P. Bartholomew, personal communications, May 2003). Gregory set about resolving the dextrorotatory and levorotatory characteristics of the compound and found that only one isomer demonstrated antibacterial activity, with a potency that was twice that of the racemate. Gregory felt this proved that these compounds were blocking an enzyme (personal communication, May 2003). He continued making modifications, eventually replacing a hydroxyl group with an amino and an acetamido group. The new acetamidomethyl compounds were decidedly more potent than the hydroxymethyl compounds. Gregory performed much of the work covered in the original patent; he was aided by technician Walter Meredith, who performed a significant portion of the laboratory work. In addition, Randall K. Carlson was hired to help Gregory with synthesizing new compounds. Patents for the oxazolidinones were granted to Gregory in 1984 and 1987[6,7] and to Carlson, Chung-Ho Park, and Gregory in 1993.[8] Toxicity was evident during the first animal experiments involving these compounds (P. Bartholomew, C. Demos, and W. Gregory, personal communications, May 2003). Although infections resolved with the new antibiotics, after prolonged treatment, the mice developed anorexia. This same phenomenon was observed in later tests with monkeys (C. Demos, personal communication, May 2003). Toxicity issues were resolved later in the development of the oxazolidinones, but the mechanisms involved were not determined.

In the 1980s, structure-activity relationship (SAR) research on the original compound yielded 2 oxazolidinones, DuP-721 and DuP-105, which were active with both oral and parenteral administration.[2,3,5,9] Their antibacterial spectrum included activity against staphylococci, streptococci, and *Bacteroides fragilis* strains.[9] The clinical research team was headed by Christopher H. Demos, who was director of Clinical Research Infectious Diseases at DuPont in the 1980s (personal communication, May 2003). Demos and clinical research associate Virginia Eberle worked with outside investigators to set up preclinical and phase I testing. Early investigators included Robert C. Moellering, Jr, and George M. Eliopoulos at New England Deaconess Hospital in Boston, Mass, who found in vitro evidence of antimicrobial activity.[10] DuP-721 in particular demonstrated strong in vitro and in vivo activity against a number of gram-positive pathogens, including methicillin-resistant *Staphylococcus aureus* (MRSA). DuP-721 and DuP-105 were introduced in 1987 at the 27th Interscience Conference on Antimicrobial Agents and Chemotherapy (ICAAC) in New York, NY, by the DuPont team. However, shortly thereafter, the program at DuPont was closed and research on the oxazolidinones was halted when liver toxicity occurred in rats after therapeutic use of DuP-721.[2-4,11]

The Early Years at Upjohn and Pharmacia

For a while, it appeared as if the promise of the first new class of antibiotics in decades might vanish. However, Steven J. Brickner, a scientist working at The Upjohn Company in the 1980s, had attended the 27th ICAAC in 1987 and was intrigued by this novel class of compounds (personal communication, May 2003). The oxazolidinones had a number of compelling attributes. They had potent activity against important gram-positive pathogens, including MRSA and *Mycobacterium tuberculosis*[10,12,13]; they were an entirely new class of antibacterial agents with a novel mechanism of action; they showed no cross-resistance with known antibiotics; attempts to induce resistance in vitro failed both at DuPont and subsequently, at Upjohn; and they had excellent pharmacokinetic properties, including oral activity. As a medicinal chemist, Brickner also found the fact that these were synthetic compounds with a low molecular weight very attractive because this property facilitated the quick initiation of an exploratory project (personal communication, May 2003).

At the time, Upjohn had a policy of allowing 10% of employee time to be spent as "free time" directed toward research in any area of personal interest (personal com-

munication, May 2003). Brickner decided to spend his free time researching oxazolidinone compounds. He began exploratory work in his laboratory as soon as he returned from the 27th ICAAC. He had little trouble convincing colleagues Charles Ford, an in vivo pharmacologist, and Gary Zurenko, a microbiologist, to support his laboratory in testing the new compounds because they also recognized the potential of the new antibiotic class. They soon had a number of novel compounds that exhibited in vitro and in vivo antibacterial activity equivalent to that of DuP-721.

Although Brickner initiated the Upjohn oxazolidinone project, it quickly became a team effort (personal communication, May 2003). For 5 years, he led the team as chair of the oxazolidinone discovery project. John Greenfield conducted the early pharmacokinetic studies on the first lead analogs, which were critical to demonstrating that good exposure of the compounds in rodents was maintained in toxicology and efficacy studies. For the sake of rapidity and ease of synthesis, Brickner decided that the team would first work in the racemic oxazolidinone series, with the knowledge that they would need to develop a viable method for asymmetric synthesis once they had discovered promising analogs. Peter Manninen made a critical contribution in this area, developing a novel approach to constructing the oxazolidinone ring. In an attempt to solve the asymmetric synthesis problem, Brickner had decided to use a strong base on a carbamate to close the oxazolidinone ring. He chose sodium hydride as the base, but the reaction did not work. Brickner was ready to reject the use of a strong base and was considering another approach when Manninen decided to try one more time but with another base, N-butyl lithium. The reaction proceeded successfully. Later, the lithium counter ion was demonstrated to play a pivotal role in the success of this very useful reaction. Upjohn chemists had long sought a way to produce optically active oxazolidinones that would avoid using isocyanates and the phosgene used to create the isocyanate intermediates. These intermediates are used to synthesize oxazolidinones in many of the DuPont published patents and scientific papers. Thus, Manninen's work resulted in a method to deliver oxazolidinones with high optical purity without using the extremely toxic reagent phosgene.[11]

Brickner served as chair of the Oxazolidinone Working Group and as chemistry team leader, and along with chemists Michael Barbachyn and Douglas Hutchinson, the 3 laboratories contributed to the rich SAR exploration that eventually led to the discovery of eperezolid and linezolid (S. Brickner, personal communication, May 2003). Richard Thomas and Paul Aristoff were key chemistry managers supporting the team. Gary Zurenko's laboratory did all of the in vitro MIC evaluations of the oxazolidinone compounds, and Charles Ford's laboratory did all of the in vivo antibacterial evaluation work. In 1994, Ford became co-chair of the Oxazolidinone Program Team along with Brickner.

Given the early experience at DuPont with this class of compounds, researchers quickly realized that solving the toxicity issue would be crucial to any further success (M. Barbachyn, personal communication, May 2003). Toxicologist Richard Piper played a very important role in the entire effort through his early demonstration of structure-toxicity relationships with several compounds developed in Brickner's laboratory. Rather than proceed using only the usual SAR studies for potency, the team at Upjohn placed additional emphasis on collecting early toxicological data. Thus, for each new "subclass" of oxazolidinones that demonstrated the desired antibacterial potency, the team had to synthesize sufficient quantities of representative analogs to perform multiday toxicology studies on animals to determine which were least toxic or nontoxic. In order to explore the potential of this new antibiotic class aggressively, the team also decided to synthesize scores of completely different subclasses of oxazolidinones to enhance the chance of capturing compounds with an acceptable safety profile.

This was a radically different discovery paradigm from the usual pharmaceutical research approach, which typically involves determining the most potent compounds, then testing for toxicity later in the process (S. Brickner, personal communication, May 2003). In this case, the entire project was based on the toxicology of the emerging antibacterially active compounds. Piper designed and performed the comparative 30-day toxicology studies of the lead compound, PNU-82965, alongside racemic DuP-721. In comparison with DuP-721, both PNU-82965 and a related indoline derivative, PNU-97456, performed very well. In the latter compound, a nitrogen on the phenyl group *para* to the oxazolidinone ring was demonstrated for the first time to confer potency and to be well tolerated. The usefulness of an N-hydroxyacetyl moiety also was

noted. These 2 discoveries led to the eventual incorporation of a nitrogen substituent on the phenyl ring in both linezolid and eperezolid and the N-hydroxyacetyl moiety in eperezolid.

Meanwhile, clinicians with expertise in infectious diseases and clinical pharmacology helped to provide the clinical perspective on development and guided the thinking early in the process (S. Brickner and D. Batts, personal communications, May 2003). Donald Batts supported the discovery team in this capacity from the outset; later, Batts, Charles Wajszczuk, and Steve Pawsey headed up the early clinical development and ran the initial clinical studies. Batts also was part of the later clinical development team. Dennis Stalker, Gail Jungbluth, Neil Duncan, Steve Cox, Ian Martin, and Robert Ings contributed to the pharmacokinetic studies of the compounds, and Dean Shinabarger conducted studies to characterize the mechanism of action for the oxazolidinones as a class.

Basing the project on toxicology rather than solely on potency not only was unusual but also required enormous effort. Bench-level synthesis of the requisite quantities of high-purity drug for so many different classes of oxazolidinones was a major undertaking (S. Brickner, personal communication, May 2003). David Houser supported the discovery effort by providing large quantities of oxazolidinone intermediates and efficiently increasing the supply of preclinical and clinical materials as needed. Although it was unorthodox, this novel discovery approach was ultimately worth the effort. Of the approximately 24 subclasses of oxazolidinones, 3 subclasses—the piperazines, indolines, and tropones—were found to have minimal toxicity (M. Barbachyn, personal communication, May 2003). A few chemists were then assigned to synthesize large numbers of congeners from those 3 classes to determine what side groups and 3-dimensional structures were associated with potent activity.

Ultimately, a decision was needed regarding which of the 3 subclasses should receive the focused attention of all the chemists.[14] The indolines generally exhibited an excellent safety profile, but they demonstrated somewhat lower levels of antibacterial activity. The tropone analogs were generally the most interesting compounds from an antibacterial activity standpoint, but they displayed poor water solubility and pharmacokinetic performance characteristics.[12,15] Selected piperazine derivatives exhibited excellent in vitro and in vivo activity while maintaining an acceptable safety profile, acceptable water solubility, and excellent pharmacokinetic parameters. As a bonus, the piperazine analogs were also the easiest compounds to synthesize. Because of these and other characteristics, the piperazine series became the principal focus of the ongoing chemistry effort (M. Barbachyn, personal communication, May 2003).

The chemists were cognizant of the alternative bioisosteric replacements for the piperazine moiety, primarily from literature on the quinolone antibacterial agents.[14] Systematic modification along these lines led to the identification of the interesting antimycobacterial thiomorpholine derivative, PNU-100480, and the morpholine analog PNU-100766, which subsequently became known as linezolid.[16]

Two patent applications covering the Upjohn piperazine, morpholine, and thiomorpholine oxazolidinone analogs were filed in 1992 and 1993 (M. Barbachyn, personal communication, May 2003). In addition, approximately 11 other applications were filed from 1988 to 1994, providing a strong intellectual property base for the emerging Upjohn oxazolidinone franchise. While other pharmaceutical companies also showed interest in the oxazolidinones, most presumably took the traditional route of SAR studies to determine the most potent drugs and tested those for toxicity (D. Batts, personal communication, May 2003). In many cases, by the time they found nontoxic subclasses of oxazolidinones, tested them, and attempted to file patents, they discovered that Upjohn had already filed conflicting patents.

When Upjohn merged with Pharmacia in 1995 to become Pharmacia & Upjohn Company, the oxazolidinone clinical development program was well under way. Chemical modification of the oxazolidinone nucleus had produced 2 derivatives, U-100592 (PNU-100592) and U-100766 (PNU-100766), that had in vitro activity similar to that of DuP-721, but without the acute toxicity observed in animal models with the earlier compounds.[3,4,11] PNU-100592 and PNU-100766 eventually became eperezolid and linezolid, respectively (Figure 1).

In September 1995 at the 35th ICAAC held in San Francisco, Calif, 25 separate presentations were made on the oxazolidinone agents by 11 academic collaborators.[17]

This meeting was considered extremely important to the oxazolidinone team, and the presentations generated considerable excitement because this was the first disclosure of the work performed with eperezolid and linezolid. The presentations covered studies in a number of areas, including the synthesis and SARs of the

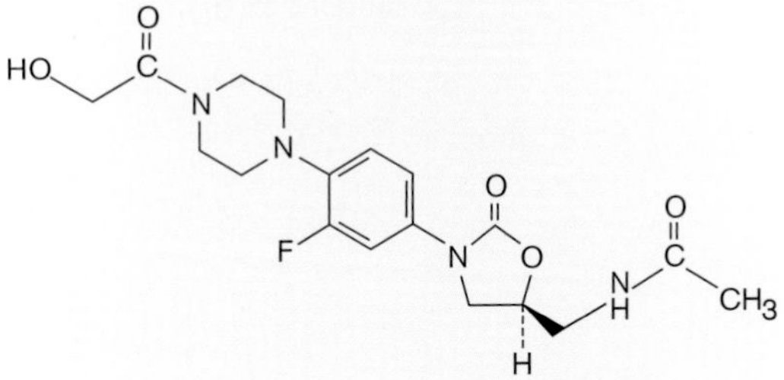

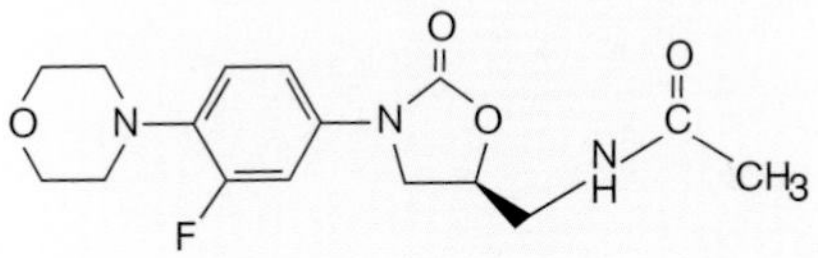

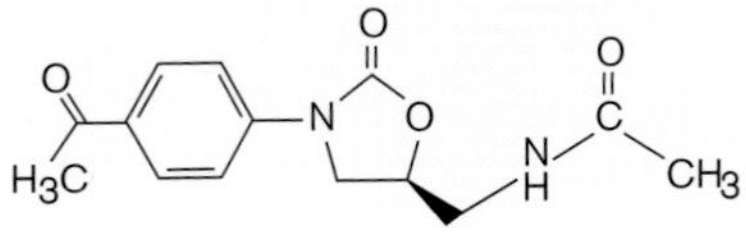

Figure 1. Chemical structures of eperezolid, linezolid, and DuP-721. Reprinted from Shinabarger DL, Marotti KR, Murray RW, et al. Mechanism of action of oxazolidinones: effects of linezolid and eperezolid on translation reactions. *Antimicrob Agents Chemother.* 1997;41:2132-2136, with permission from the American Society for Microbiology. Copyright © 1997, American Society for Microbiology. All rights reserved.

2 new compounds, data on in vitro and in vivo activity, drug safety, pharmacokinetics and metabolism, and the results of phase I human clinical studies performed with eperezolid.

Promising Results From in Vitro Studies

In 1996, a series of papers was published on the in vitro activities of the 2 new oxazolidinones. A study by Kaatz and Seo[18] at Wayne State University School of Medicine in Detroit, Mich, demonstrated good in vitro inhibitory activity for eperezolid and linezolid against *Staphylococcus aureus* and *Staphylococcus epidermidis*, regardless of methicillin resistance. Spontaneous development of resistance was negligible at 2-fold the MIC for both eperezolid and linezolid against all 12 strains of staphylococci evaluated. Comparisons of in vitro activity for the oxazolidinones with nafcillin and vancomycin showed that the latter agents were more active against methicillin-susceptible *Staphylococcus aureus* (MSSA) based on the MIC at which 90% of organisms are inhibited (MIC$_{90s}$: 0.78 µg/mL nafcillin, 1.56 µg/mL vancomycin) than the oxazolidinones (MIC$_{90s}$: 6.25 µg/mL eperezolid and linezolid). Results also showed that vancomycin was more active against MRSA (MIC$_{90s}$: 1.56 µg/mL vancomycin versus 3.13 µg/mL eperezolid and 6.25 µg/mL linezolid). However, no significant differences were noted for activity against *S epidermidis*. At the MIC$_{90}$, all of these agents were deemed to be of equal efficacy, with the exception of nafcillin against MRSA (MIC$_{90}$>100 µg/mL). As had proven true of the earlier oxazolidinones, both eperezolid and linezolid were bacteriostatic against these pathogens.[10,18]

In an effort to characterize the activity of these new oxazolidinones, Jones, Johnson, and Erwin of the University of Iowa College of Medicine, Iowa City, investigated the in vitro performance of eperezolid and linezolid against a broad spectrum of gram-positive and gram-negative organisms and compared it with the activity of glycopeptides, erythromycin, clindamycin, clinafloxacin, and chloramphenicol.[19] Complete inhibition by both compounds was achieved against oxacillin-resistant staphylococci, vancomycin-resistant enterococci, and gram-positive organisms from several species that had exhibited resistance to macrolides, aminoglycosides, and β-lactam antibiotics, including the clinically important pathogen penicillin-resistant *Streptococcus pneumoniae*. Again, consistent with other studies, both eperezolid and linezolid appeared to

be bacteriostatic rather than bactericidal for staphylococci and enterococci.[18,19]

Frequent exposure to antibiotic therapy for otitis media has resulted in some children serving as major reservoirs for resistant bacteria.[20-23] Consequently, serious otitis media caused by *S pneumoniae* has become increasingly difficult to treat on an outpatient basis. To test useful compounds for these infections, Mason et al[20] investigated the activity of eperezolid and linezolid against penicillin- and cephalosporin-resistant strains of *S pneumoniae* isolated from patients at the Texas Children's Hospital in Houston. Both oxazolidinones proved active against strains of *S pneumoniae* resistant to penicillin and ceftriaxone at MICs of 4 µg/mL or less. Interestingly, the MICs were lower for eperezolid than for linezolid. Other in vitro studies also showed excellent activity against pneumococci for both compounds, with MICs of 1 µg/mL or less.[24]

Enterococci are an important cause of nosocomial infection in the United States, and resistant strains pose a serious threat.[25-27] Eliopoulos, Wennersten, Gold, and Moellering of New England Deaconess Hospital and Harvard Medical School, explored the in vitro activity of both oxazolidinones against enterococci isolates, including strains that were resistant to vancomycin.[28] All enterococcal isolates were inhibited by eperezolid and linezolid at MICs between 1 µg/mL and 4 µg/mL. Both oxazolidinones were bacteriostatic against *Enterococcus faecalis*, and they exhibited bactericidal activity against one strain of *Enterococcus faecium*. A number of these strains were resistant to vancomycin, ampicillin, and minocycline.

Staphylococci are another group of pathogens that have become resistant to many commonly prescribed antibiotics and cause serious nosocomial and community-acquired infections.[29-31] Mulazimoglu of the Marmara University School of Medicine in Istanbul, Turkey, and Drenning and Yu of the Veterans Affairs Medical Center and University of Pittsburgh in Pennsylvania compared the in vitro activities of both oxazolidinones, the fluoroquinolone trovafloxacin, and quinupristin-dalfopristin against *S aureus* and *S epidermidis*.[32] At the time of the study, all 4 were research compounds, and comparable activity to vancomycin against both susceptible and resistant strains of *S aureus* and *S epidermidis* was found for all 4 compounds. The oxazolidinones and quinupristin-dalfopristin were the most potent compounds against methicillin-resistant S epidermidis, with MIC_{90s} of 1 µg/mL or less, whereas the MIC_{90s} for vancomycin and rifampin were 2 µg/mL and greater than 16 µg/mL, respectively. Trovafloxacin had an MIC_{90} of 4 µg/mL against methicillin-resistant S epidermidis. Results for MRSA showed that quinupristin-dalfopristin and rifampin were most active with MIC_{90s} of 0.5 µg/mL and 0.006 µg/mL, whereas eperezolid, linezolid, trovafloxacin, and vancomycin all had MIC_{90s} of 1 µg/mL. Ciprofloxacin was the only agent tested with an elevated MIC; its MIC_{90} was 16 µg/mL. Jones et al[33] also investigated the activity of the fluoroquinolones against S aureus, both ciprofloxacin-resistant and ciprofloxacin-susceptible strains, and compared them with the activity of quinupristin-dalfopristin, linezolid, gentamicin, and vancomycin. In this study, only quinupristin-dalfopristin and clinafloxacin had lower MIC_{90s} than linezolid against MRSA, and most fluoroquinolones had MIC_{90s} of 16 µg/mL or greater.

The findings of these earlier studies were corroborated by a number of subsequent in vitro studies.[34-36] A 1999 study of the in vitro activity of linezolid showed good activity against 37 clinical isolates of vancomycin-resistant enterococci, including organisms carrying resistance genes vanA, vanB, vanC-1, and vanC-2/3; 26 clinical isolates of MRSA; and 20 isolates of high-level penicillin-resistant S pneumoniae.[36] Vancomycin-resistant enterococci were inhibited by 4 µg/mL or less of linezolid; MRSA strains were inhibited by 8 µg/mL or less of linezolid; and penicillin-resistant S pneumoniae were inhibited by 2 µg/mL or less of linezolid.

Goldstein et al[37] explored the activity of linezolid compared with selected macrolides and other agents against both aerobic and anaerobic pathogens isolated from soft tissue bite infections in humans. Linezolid was active against all but 2 bite wound anaerobes at 2 µg/mL or less, including Fusobacterium, Prevotella, Porphyromonas, and Peptostreptococcus species.

At this time, the US Food and Drug Administration has approved linezolid for the treatment of vancomycin-resistant E faecium infections (including cases with concurrent bacteremia); nosocomial pneumonia caused by methicillin-susceptible and -resistant strains of S aureus or penicillin-susceptible strains of S pneumoniae; community-acquired pneumonia caused by S pneumoniae (penicillin-susceptible strains only), including cases with concurrent bacteremia, or S aureus (methicillin-susceptible strains only); uncomplicated skin and skin structure infections caused by S aureus (methicillin-susceptible strains only) or Streptococcus pyogenes; and complicated skin and skin structure infections, including diabetic foot infections without concomitant osteomyelitis, caused by S aureus (methicillin-susceptible and methicillin-resistant strains), S pyogenes, or Streptococcus agalactiae.[38]

Postantibiotic Effects and Protein Binding Characteristics

In combination with the pharmacokinetic profile, the postantibiotic effects (PAEs) of an agent help to determine the appropriate dose range. Rybak et al[39] of Wayne State University, Detroit, Mich, examined this issue for both oxazolidinone compounds versus vancomycin against S aureus, E faecalis, E faecium, and coagulase-negative staphylococci. As with past studies, Rybak and colleagues determined that both linezolid and eperezolid were bacteriostatic. The PAEs were similar in both compounds and were greater at 4 times the MIC (range, 0.2 to 1.4 hours) than at the MIC (0.1 to 0.8 hours) against all organisms tested. The PAEs appeared to be relatively short, but the investigators concluded that twice-a-day dosing might still be possible. Although the viability of twice-a-day dosing ultimately proved correct, human pharmacodynamic studies had yet to be concluded at that time.

The efficacy of an antibiotic in vivo can be affected by its protein-binding characteristics. An in vitro study by Zurenko et al[40] at Pharmacia & Upjohn, Inc., in Kalamazoo, Mich, examined the in vitro activity of both oxazolidinone compounds against 222 bacterial clinical isolates and explored the effect of pooled human serum on the broth microdilution MICs of the agents. Eperezolid and linezolid exhibited strong activity against corynebacteria, enterococci, staphylococci, and streptococci, and were not significantly affected by the presence of human serum for any of the cultures tested. Both compounds were also active against M tuberculosis and showed no evidence of cross-resistance with standard antitubercular agents.

Additive and synergistic effects are valuable antimicrobial characteristics, particularly when treating antibiotic-resistant infections. In 2003, Sweeney and Zurenko[41] examined the in vitro effects of linezolid alone and in combination with 35 antimicrobial agents against MSSA; MRSA; vancomycin-resistant enterococci; vancomycin-susceptible enterococci; *Klebsiella pneumoniae*; *Escherichia coli*; and penicillin-susceptible, penicillin-intermediate, and penicillin-resistant *S pneumoniae*. Although 99.2% (1369) of 1380 organism-drug combinations proved to be indifferent, synergy was discovered for 9 combinations of linezolid with 6 antibiotics: amoxicillin, erythromycin, imipenem, sparfloxacin, teicoplanin, and tetracycline. Antagonism occurred with only 2 combinations of linezolid and 2 drugs: ofloxacin and sparfloxacin. Some slight antagonism has been observed in an in vitro investigation of the bactericidal activities of linezolid in combination with either vancomycin or ciprofloxacin against *S aureus*. In this same study, when combined with fusidic acid, gentamicin, or rifampin, linezolid demonstrated no synergy but did prevent selection of resistant mutants.[42] Investigators in another in vitro study reported decreased antibacterial activity for both gentamicin and vancomycin and antagonism to the early bactericidal activity of gentamicin when linezolid was used in combination with either of these agents against MRSA.[43] Interestingly, additive activity was noted for the combination of rifampicin and linezolid against both rifampicin-resistant and -susceptible strains of the pathogen. However, the synergistic, additive, and antagonistic characteristics of linezolid have yet to be fully explored. In vitro activity does not always correlate with clinical success.[44] The antibiotic must reach the site of infection at adequate concentrations and be effective under local conditions, such as low or high pH and aerobic or anaerobic environments. Selective toxicity is of paramount importance. As experience with the earlier oxazolidinone compounds has shown, in vivo toxicity can eliminate otherwise propitious antibiotics.

Early Success in the Mouse Model

Results from early animal studies were also impressive. In the mid-1990s, Ford et al[5] reported that eperezolid and linezolid were effective in mouse models of systemic MRSA and methicillin-resistant *S epidermidis* infections using both oral and intravenous routes of administration. Both compounds exhibited activity comparable to that of vancomycin. Linezolid and eperezolid also exhibited in vivo activity against systemic infections with resistant and susceptible strains of *S pneumoniae*, *E faecalis*, and *E faecium*.

The capability of an antibiotic to penetrate and reach adequate concentrations can differ with the site of infection.[44] Thus, success in treating a systemic infection does not necessarily imply that there will be eradication of the infection at other sites. However, the data from Ford's study provided evidence that the oxazolidinones might be an effective treatment for skin, skin structure, and soft tissue infections.[5] Mouse models of soft tissue infections with *S aureus*, *E faecalis*, and *B fragilis* were cured with oral linezolid or eperezolid therapy. Host factors also play a tremendous role in the capability of an antibiotic to eradicate infection.[44] The increasing numbers of patients who have compromised immune systems pose a challenge to clinicians treating infections. However, the results of the Ford study were promising. An infection with a vancomycin-resistant strain of *E faecium* in an immunocompromised host was cured, demonstrating that the oxazolidinones might work on infections that fail to respond to powerful antibiotics such as vancomycin, even in patients with a minimal immune response.[5] Finally, serious infections are often treated empirically because definitive identification of the causative pathogen may involve unacceptable delays.[44] Combination therapy is common in such cases because, as in mixed infections, coverage for both gram-positive and gram-negative pathogens may be necessary. Thus, determining an antibiotic's antagonistic, additive, and synergistic effects when used in combination with other antibiotics in vivo is important. Once again, data from animal studies were promising. Ford et al[5] found that the oxazolidinones did not appear to be antagonistic and may have had additive effects when used in combination with vancomycin, imipenem-cilastatin, gentamicin, and rifampin. Both linezolid and eperezolid had activity equivalent to vancomycin when used in combination with gentamicin and aztreonam against a mixed gram-positive and gram-negative infection. In general, animal models of bacterial disease can be highly predictive of activity in humans (S. Brickner, personal communication, May 2003), and the results of this study were encouraging.

Another in vivo study evaluated oxazolidinone activity against a rat model of intra-abdominal abscess due to *E faecalis* or vancomycin-resistant *E faecium* because of the clinical importance of this site for enterococcal infections and the difficulty of treating these types of infections.[45] The data showed modest in vivo activity for both eperezolid and linezolid, although the latter reached higher peak levels in plasma with oral administration than eperezolid. However, these effects were comparable to those observed with subcutaneously administered vancomycin. The investigators concluded that further studies were necessary to determine the optimal dosage. The oxazolidinones also offered promise in one other crucial area, resistance.[18] Because they were an entirely synthetic class of antimicrobial, there were no known bacterial resistance mechanisms in nature, as had been the case with penicillin, for example, for which resistance emerged nearly simultaneously with the first therapeutic use.[46]

This lack of resistance to the oxazolidinones had been evident even during the earliest stages of development, in the work of Gregory and Bartholomew at DuPont (P. Bartholomew, personal communication, May 2003). Kaatz and Seo[18] later corroborated these findings. Furthermore, because these compounds were not a modification of any existing antibiotic class, cross-resistance with other antimicrobial classes was unlikely.[47] In 1995 at the 35th ICAAC in San Francisco, Calif, Pawsey, Harry, and Stalker[48] reported on the first administration of an oxazolidinone—eperezolid—to a healthy subject in a phase I study. However, linezolid was chosen for clinical development because of its far superior human pharmacokinetic properties (S. Brickner, personal communication, May 2003). Although in vitro and in vivo studies had found that eperezolid was 2- to 4-fold more potent than linezolid,[5,18-20,28] its short half-life meant that it would require dosing at 3 to 4 times per day to maintain adequate serum concentrations (D. Batts, personal communication, May 2003). In contrast, linezolid had very high serum concentration levels and a long half-life; therefore, it could be dosed twice a day.[38] Thus, linezolid was the first oxazolidinone chosen to enter phase II testing.[3] The clinical development team included Donald Batts, Barry Hafkin, Susan Cammarata, and Jon Bruss. Susan Speziale and Charles Hall provided project management and led the clinical development multidisciplinary team.

Mechanism of Action

The unique structure and activity of the oxazolidinones confer on them a distinct advantage against pathogens resistant to many common antibiotics because cross-resistance is unlikely.[49] Although oxazolidinone compounds were discovered in the late 1970s,[2] their mechanisms of action had yet to be fully characterized nearly 20 years later. As the project at Upjohn got under way, Dean

Shinabarger and a number of colleagues at the company's Infectious Disease Research and Molecular Biology Research Center in Kalamazoo set out to determine the mechanism of action of both linezolid and eperezolid.[50] Early work performed at DuPont on DuP-721 had revealed that this compound inhibited protein synthesis in vivo; however, RNA and DNA synthesis were not affected.

The Shinabarger study used a mutant strain of E coli that was sensitive to the oxazolidinones (eperezolid MIC=4 µg/mL) to examine the mechanism of action involved in the antibiotic effects of these compounds.[49] The investigators compared the activity of the original oxazolidinone compound, DuP-721, with that of streptomycin, eperezolid, and linezolid on protein synthesis in E coli UC6782 and discovered that the 2 newer oxazolidinones were 2.5 times more potent than DuP-721 and twice as potent as streptomycin (Figure 2). The addition of eperezolid to S30 extracts of E coli resulted in a 2.5-µM inhibitory concentration of 50% (IC_{50}), whereas linezolid proved to be somewhat more potent, with an IC_{50} of 1.8 µM. S aureus S30 transcription-translation was also sensitive to eperezolid, with an IC_{50} of 8 µM. Cell-free transcription-translation of either S aureus or E coli was highly sensitive to linezolid and eperezolid. However, when translation was uncoupled from transcription in the E coli system, 250 µM of DuP-721 was necessary to achieve 20% inhibition, whereas 20 µM of eperezolid accomplished 50% inhibition.

Studies using varying concentrations of MS2 RNA in the assay demonstrated an effect on the activity of these compounds. As MS2 RNA concentrations decreased, the potency of the oxazolidinones increased, indicating that this class of drug must affect binding of mRNA to the ribosome at the initiation phase of translation. Conversely, the potency of streptomycin, a peptidyl-tRNA inhibitor, was not greatly affected by changes in MS2 RNA levels. Shinabarger and colleagues also examined the effect of oxazolidinones on the elongation of the polypeptide chain, a common mechanism for protein inhibitor antibiotics, but found none. Likewise, no effect on ribosomal termination of translation was found for this drug class, and oxazolidinones did not appear to prevent the binding of a noninitiating message. A second paper was published by another group of research scientists at Pharmacia & Upjohn's Kalamazoo facility.[51] At the time, this class of drugs was believed to inhibit protein synthesis by acting at the step preceding the interaction between

N-formyl-methionine (fMet)-tRNA and the 30S ribosomal subunits with the initiator codon, possibly by inhibiting recognition of the 3' upstream ribosome-binding sequence of mRNA.[50] Lin et al[52] explored the activity of eperezolid on the 50S ribosomal subunit. A number of antibiotic agents were investigated to determine if they would compete for the oxazolidinone binding site, but only chloramphenicol, lincomycin, and clindamycin inhibited oxazolidinone binding to the 50S ribosomal subunit. Although chloramphenicol and to a certain extent, lincomycin, interfere with translation termination by inhibiting peptidyl transferase, the oxazolidinones do not; therefore, the mechanism of action of this new class of antibiotics appeared to be distinct, although the binding sites likely overlapped.

Interestingly, Lin and colleagues[52] found no evidence that eperezolid or linezolid binds to the 30S ribosomal subunit,

but they did find evidence of binding to the 50S ribosomal subunit. However, the binding property was determined to be relatively weak, which may account for these compounds being bacteriostatic rather than bactericidal. The investigators concluded that it was possible that the oxazolidinones may bind to a site on the 50S subunit closely related to the chloramphenicol and lincomycin binding site and near the 30S subunit interface. They postulated that the resulting distortion of the site could prevent proper positioning of the 30S initiation complex and prevent the formation of the 70S initiation complex, thereby inhibiting translation initiation.

In 1998, in a cooperative effort between the Pharmacia & Upjohn facility in Kalamazoo and the Department of Medical Research at the University of Toronto in Toronto, Ontario, Swaney et al[53] further explored the complex mechanisms involved in the inhibition of bacterial protein

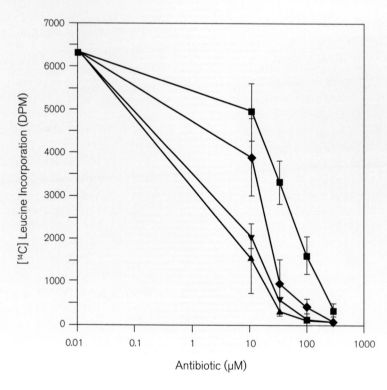

Figure 2. Effects of oxazolidinones on protein synthesis in *Escherichia coli* UC6782. Cells growing exponentially were labeled with [U-14C]leucine for 60 minutes at 37°C in the presence of various concentrations of either DuP-721 (■), eperezolid (▲), linezolid (▼), or streptomycin (◆). Error bars, standard errors of the means. DPM = disintegrations per minute. Reprinted from Shinabarger DL, Marotti KR, Murray RW, et al. Mechanism of action of oxazolidinones: effects of linezolid and eperezolid on translation reactions. *Antimicrob Agents Chemother.* 1997;41:2132-2136, with permission from the American Society for Microbiology. Copyright © 1997, American Society for Microbiology. All rights reserved.

synthesis by oxazolidinones. Results indicated that linezolid inhibited the formation of *E coli* 30S initiation complexes, and 70S complexes from either *E coli* or *S aureus*. Notably, the presence of initiation factors IF1, IF2, and IF3, essential for the in vivo formation of the preinitiation complex comprising the mRNA, the 30S subunit, and fMet-tRNA, was not required for linezolid to inhibit protein synthesis in *E coli*. No determination could be made on *S aureus* initiation factors. The investigators noted that because translation initiation is a complex interaction of dynamic forces, in vitro assays detect increasing IC_{50} as the processes examined become further removed

More recently, Aoki et al[56] presented evidence that supported the findings of prior studies and further elucidated the exact binding site for the oxazolidinones. In an article published in 2002, the researchers reported on antibacterial activity and translation inhibition of *E coli* using 3 oxazolidinones—linezolid, PNU-140693, and PNU-176798. The potency of the 3 compounds correlated well with their ability to inhibit cell-free translation, and PNU-176798 was approximately 9-fold more potent than linezolid (PNU-10076). Dose-dependent inhibition of fMet-tRNA binding to 70S ribosomes also was reported (Table).

Table. Antibacterial Activity and Translation Inhibition by Oxazolidinones

Oxazolidinone	MIC for *E coli* (µM)*	IC_{50} (µM) Translation	70S Initiation	Translocation
PNU-100766 (linezolid)	24	4.7	152	110
PNU-140693	6	1.74	NA†	41
PNU-176798	1.4	0.53	32	8

MIC = minimal inhibitory concentration; IC_{50} = inhibitory concentration needed to inhibit 50% of organisms.
E coli tolC knockout.
†NA = not applicable.
Adapted from Aoki H, Ke L, Poppe SM, et al. Oxazolidinone antibiotics target the P site on *Escherichia coli* ribosomes. *Antimicrob Agents Chemother*. 2002;46:1080-1085, with permission from the American Society for Microbiology. Copyright © 2002, American Society for Microbiology. All rights reserved.

from intact, coupled transcription-translation. The linezolid IC_{50} for coupled transcription-translation is 1.8 µM, whereas the IC_{50} is 15 µM for translation alone and 110 µM for 70S initiation complex inhibition. When considered with evidence from previous studies, the results of this study demonstrated that the oxazolidinones inhibit the formation of the initiation complex in bacterial translation systems by preventing the formation of the fMet-tRNA-ribosome-mRNA ternary complex. Kloss et al,[54] using resistance mutations in *Halobacterium halobium*, presented evidence that linezolid binds to the 50S subunit within domain V of the 23S rRNA peptidyl transferase center. Seven strains of *H halobium* with mutations affecting 6 different positions in the central loop of domain V of the 23S rRNA peptidyl transferase center proved to be resistant to linezolid, suggesting this area as a potential binding site. This was subsequently corroborated by Xiong et al.[55]

The authors felt the evidence indicated that the oxazolidinones had effects in addition to inhibiting initiation.[56] They reasoned that the simplest interpretation of the data from their own study and previous studies suggested that the oxazolidinones principally targeted the ribosomal P site and possibly inhibited translocation into this site; thus, they exerted pleiotropic effects on several intermediate steps of translation.

Pharmacokinetics and Metabolism

Although the pharmacokinetics and metabolism of linezolid are addressed in greater detail in Chapter 4, the contributions made in this area by J. Greg Slatter and colleagues and the Pharmacia research facility in Kalamazoo are important to note. First in a presentation at the 38th ICAAC in 1998, and then subsequently in greater detail in an article published in 2001, Slatter et al[57] characterized the metabolic pathways, plasma and blood concentration levels, and pharmacokinetic parameters for linezolid. The researchers compared metabolism of the agent in humans, rats, and dogs and found intriguing differences. Metabolism in humans occurred primarily through the lactone pathway, but metabolism in dogs occurred nearly equally through the lactone and lactam pathways. This relationship was reversed in rats, with the greatest degree of metabolism occurring through the lactam pathway. These differences were suggested to account for the lower areas under the curve found in dogs and rats relative to humans. The rate-limiting step in humans was PNU-142586 formation, whereas in rats it was PNU-142300 formation. Urinary excretion was the major elimination route; linezolid was demonstrated to circulate in the plasma primarily as the parent drug.

Summary

The discovery period and early in vitro and in vivo experience with the oxazolidinones showed that this new class of antibiotics had a unique mechanism of action with no known cross-resistance with other antibiotic classes. The early exploratory period revealed the value of a toxicity-based model of pharmaceutical development. In vitro and in vivo experience indicated that both eperezolid and linezolid had potent activity against major gram-positive pathogens, including both susceptible and resistant strains of staphylococci, streptococci, enterococci, and a number of important anaerobic organisms. The mechanism of action was determined to be bacterial protein synthesis inhibition during the initiation phase. Binding was determined to occur on the ribosomal P site of the 50S subunit, affecting both transcription, translation, and possibly translocation, and blocking the formation of the fMet-tRNA-ribosome-mRNA ternary complex. Eperezolid was chosen for the first phase I clinical studies, quickly followed by linezolid. Linezolid was chosen by the research team at Pharmacia & Upjohn for the first phase II clinical trials in humans because of its superior pharmacokinetics in humans. Thus, with a very promising start, linezolid entered into phase II and III testing.

References

1. Fugitt RB, Luckenbaugh RW, inventors; E.I. du Pont de Nemours and Company, assignee. 5-Halomethyl-3-phenyl-2-oxazolidinones. US patent 4 128 654. December 5, 1978.

2. Fung HB, Kirschenbaum HL, Ojofeitimi BO. Linezolid: an oxazolidinone antimicrobial agent. Clin Ther. 2001;23:356-391.

3. Moellering RC Jr. A novel antimicrobial agent joins the battle against resistant bacteria. Ann Intern Med. 1999;130:155-157.

4. Brickner SJ. Oxazolidinone antibacterial agents. Curr Pharm Des. 1996;2:175-194.

5. Ford CW, Hamel JC, Wilson DM, et al. In vivo activities of U-100592 and U-100766, novel oxazolidinone antimicrobial agents, against experimental bacterial infections. Antimicrob Agents Chemother. 1996;40:1508-1513.

6. Gregory WA, inventor; E.I. du Pont de Nemours and Company, assignee. P-Oxooxazolidinylbenzene compounds as antibacterial agents. US patent 4 461 773. July 24, 1984.

7. Gregory WA, inventor; E. I. du Pont de Nemours and Company, assignee. Aminomethyl oxooxazolidinyl benzenes useful as antibacterial agents. US patent 4 705 799. November 10, 1987.

8. Carlson RK, Park C-H, Gregory WA, inventors; The du Pont Merck Pharmaceutical Company, assignee. Aminomethyloxooxazolidinyl arylbenzene derivatives useful as antibacterial agents. US patent 5 254 577. October 19, 1993.

9. Slee AM, Wuonola MA, McRipley RJ, et al. Oxazolidinones, a new class of synthetic antibacterial agents: in vitro and in vivo activities of DuP 105 and DuP 721. Antimicrob Agents Chemother. 1987;31: 1791-1797.

10. Daly JS, Eliopoulos GM, Reiszner E, Moellering RC Jr. Activity and mechanism of action of DuP 105 and DuP 721, new oxazolidinone compounds. J Antimicrob Chemother. 1988;21:721-730.

11. Brickner SJ, Hutchinson DK, Barbachyn MR, et al. Synthesis and antibacterial activity of U-100592 and U-100766, two oxazolidinone antibacterial agents for the potential treatment of multidrug-resistant gram-positive bacterial infections. J Med Chem. 1996;39:673-679.

12. Barbachyn MR, Toops DS, Grega KC, et al. Synthesis and antibacterial activity of new tropone-substituted phenyloxazolidinone antibacterial agents. 2. Modification of the phenyl ring-the potentiating effect of fluorine substitution on in vivo activity. Bioorg Med Chem Lett. 1996;6:1009-1014.

13. Barbachyn MR, Hutchinson DK, Brickner SJ, et al. Identification of a novel oxazolidinone (U-100480) with potent antimycobacterial activity. J Med Chem. 1996;39:680-685.

14. Ford CW, Zurenko GE, Barbachyn MR. The discovery of linezolid, the first oxazolidinone antibacterial agent. Curr Drug Targets Infect Disord. 2001;1:181-199.

15. Barbachyn MR, Toops DS, Ulanowicz DA, et al. Synthesis and antibacterial activity of new tropone-substituted phenyloxazolidinone antibacterial agents. 1. Identification of leads and importance of the tropone substitution pattern. Bioorg Med Chem Lett. 1996;6: 1003-1008.

16. Barbachyn MR, Brickner SJ, Gadwood RC, et al. Design, synthesis, and evaluation of novel oxazolidinone antibacterial agents active against multidrug-resistant bacteria. In: Rosen BP, Mobashery S, eds. Resolving the Antibiotic Paradox. New York, NY: Kluwer Academic/Plenum Publishers; 1998:219-238.

17. Upjohn Oxazolidinone Antibacterial Agents. Paper presented at: 35th Interscience Conference on Antimicrobial Agents and Chemotherapy, September 17-20, 1995; San Francisco, Calif.

18. Kaatz GW, Seo SM. In vitro activities of oxazolidinone compounds U100592 and U100766 against Staphylococcus aureus and Staphylococcus epidermidis. Antimicrob Agents Chemother. 1996;40:799-801.

19. Jones RN, Johnson DM, Erwin ME. In vitro antimicrobial activities and spectra of U-100592 and U-100766, two novel fluorinated oxazolidinones. *Antimicrob Agents Chemother.* 1996;40:720-726.

20. Mason EO Jr, Lamberth LB, Kaplan SL. In vitro activities of oxazolidinones U-100592 and U-100766 against penicillin-resistant and cephalosporin-resistant strains of *Streptococcus pneumoniae*. *Antimicrob Agents Chemother.* 1996;40:1039-1040.

21. McCaig LF, Hughes JM. Trends in antimicrobial drug prescribing among office-based physicians in the United States. *JAMA.* 1995;273:214-219.

22. Block SL, Harrison CJ, Hedrick JA, et al. Penicillin-resistant *Streptococcus pneumoniae* in acute otitis media: risk factors, susceptibility patterns and antimicrobial management. *Pediatr Infect Dis J.* 1995;14:751-759.

23. Duchin JS, Breiman RF, Diamond A, et al. High prevalence of multidrug-resistant *Streptococcus pneumoniae* among children in a rural Kentucky community. *Pediatr Infect Dis J.* 1995;14:745-750.

24. Spangler SK, Jacobs MR, Appelbaum PC. Activities of RPR 106972 (a new oral streptogramin), cefditoren (a new oral cephalosporin), two new oxazolidinones (U-100592 and U-100766), and other oral and parenteral agents against 203 penicillin-susceptible and -resistant pneumococci. *Antimicrob Agents Chemother.* 1996;40:481-484.

25. Moellering RC Jr. *Enterococcus* species, *Streptococcus bovis*, and *Leuconostoc* species. In: Mandell GL, Bennett J Dolin R, eds. *Mandell, Douglas and Bennett's Principles and Practice of Infectious Diseases*. Vol 1. 4th ed. Philadelphia, Pa: Churchill Livingstone; 1995:2147-2156.

26. Centers for Disease Control and Prevention. Recommendations for preventing the spread of vancomycin resistance. Recommendations of the Hospital Infection Control Practices Advisory Committee (HICPAC). *MMWR Morb Mortal Wkly Rep.* 1995;44:1-14.

27. Centers for Disease Control and Prevention. Nosocomial enterococci resistant to vancomycin—United States, 1989-1993. *MMWR Morb Mortal Wkly Rep.* 1993;42:597-599.

28. Eliopoulos GM, Wennersten CB, Gold HS, Moellering RC Jr. In vitro activities of new oxazolidinone antimicrobial agents against enterococci. *Antimicrob Agents Chemother.* 1996;40:1745-1747.

29. National Nosocomial Infections Surveillance System. National Nosocomial Infections Surveillance (NNIS) System report, data summary from January 1992-June 2001, issued August 2001. *Am J Infect Control.* 2001;29:404-421.

30. Centers for Disease Control and Prevention. *Staphyloccous aureus* resistant to vancomycin—United States, 2002. *MMWR Morb Mortal Wkly Rep.* 2002;51:565-567.

31. Centers for Disease Control and Prevention. Public health dispatch: outbreaks of community-associated methicillin-resistant *Staphylococcus aureus* skin infections—Los Angeles County, California, 2002—2003. *MMWR Morb Mortal Wkly Rep.* 2003;52:88.

32. Mulazimoglu L, Drenning SD, Yu VL. In vitro activities of two novel oxazolidinones (U100592 and U100766), a new fluoroquinolone (trovafloxacin), and dalfopristin-quinupristin against *Staphylococcus aureus* and *Staphylococcus epidermidis*. *Antimicrob Agents Chemother.* 1996;40:2428-2430.

33. Jones ME, Visser MR, Klootwijk M, Heisig P, Verhoef J, Schmitz FJ. Comparative activities of clinafloxacin, grepafloxacin, levofloxacin, moxifloxacin, ofloxacin, sparfloxacin, and trovafloxacin and non-quinolones linezelid [sic], quinupristin-dalfopristin, gentamicin, and vancomycin against clinical isolates of ciprofloxacin-resistant and -susceptible *Staphylococcus aureus* strains. *Antimicrob Agents Chemother.* 1999;43:421-423.

34. Noskin GA, Siddiqui F, Stosor V, Hacek D, Peterson LR. In vitro activities of linezolid against important gram-positive bacterial pathogens including vancomycin-resistant enterococci. *Antimicrob Agents Chemother.* 1999;43:2059-2062.

35. Jorgensen JH, McElmeel ML, Trippy CW. In vitro activities of the oxazolidinone antibiotics U-100592 and U-100766 against *Staphylococcus aureus* and coagulase-negative *Staphylococcus* species. *Antimicrob Agents Chemother.* 1997;41:465-467.

36. Patel R, Rouse MS, Piper KE, Steckelberg JM. In vitro activity of linezolid against vancomycin-resistant enterococci, methicillin-resistant *Staphylococcus aureus* and penicillin-resistant *Streptococcus pneumoniae*. *Diagn Microbiol Infect Dis.* 1999;34:119-122.

37. Goldstein EJ, Citron DM, Merriam CV. Linezolid activity compared to those of selected macrolides and other agents against aerobic and anaerobic pathogens isolated from soft tissue bite infections in humans. *Antimicrob Agents Chemother.* 1999;43:1469-1474.

38. Zyvox [package insert]. Kalamazoo, Mich: Pharmacia & Upjohn Company; 2003.

39. Rybak MJ, Cappelletty DM, Moldovan T, Aeschlimann JR, Kaatz GW. Comparative in vitro activities and postantibiotic effects of the oxazolidinone compounds eperezolid (PNU-100592) and linezolid (PNU-100766) versus vancomycin against *Staphylococcus aureus*, coagulase-negative staphylococci, *Enterococcus faecalis*, and *Enterococcus faecium*. *Antimicrob Agents Chemother.* 1998;42:721-724.

40. Zurenko GE, Yagi BH, Schaadt RD, et al. In vitro activities of U-100592 and U-100766, novel oxazolidinone antibacterial agents. *Antimicrob Agents Chemother.* 1996;40:839-845.

41. Sweeney MT, Zurenko GE. In vitro activities of linezolid combined with other antimicrobial agents against staphylococci, enterococci, pneumococci, and selected gram-negative organisms. *Antimicrob Agents Chemother.* 2003;47:1902-1906.

42. Grohs P, Kitzis MD, Gutmann L. In vitro bactericidal activities of linezolid in combination with vancomycin, gentamicin, ciprofloxacin, fusidic acid, and rifampin against *Staphylococcus aureus*. *Antimicrob Agents Chemother.* 2003;47:418-420.

43. Jacqueline C, Caillon J, Le Mabecque V, et al. In vitro activity of linezolid alone and in combination with gentamicin, vancomycin or rifampicin against methicillin-resistant *Staphylococcus aureus* by time-kill curve methods. *J Antimicrob Chemother.* 2003;51:857-864.

44. Chambers HF, Sande MA. Antimicrobial agents. General considerations. In: Hardman JG, Limbird LE, Molinoff PB, Ruddon RW, Goodman Gilman A, eds. *Goodman & Gilman's The Pharmacological Basis of Therapeutics*. 9th ed. New York, NY: McGraw-Hill Health Professions Division; 1996:1029-1056.

45. Schulin T, Thauvin-Eliopoulos C, Moellering RC Jr, Eliopoulos GM. Activities of the oxazolidinones linezolid and eperezolid in experimental intra-abdominal abscess due to *Enterococcus faecalis* or vancomycin-resistant *Enterococcus faecium*. *Antimicrob Agents Chemother.* 1999;43:2873-2876.

46. Levy SB. *The Antibiotic Paradox*. 1st ed. New York, NY: Plenum Press; 1992.

47. Fines M, Leclercq R. Activity of linezolid against Gram-positive cocci possessing genes conferring resistance to protein synthesis inhibitors. *J Antimicrob Chemother.* 2000;45:797-802.

48. Pawsey SD, Harry JD, Stalker DJ. 1st administration of a new oxazolidinone antibiotic (U-100592) to man. In: Program and Abstracts of the 35th Interscience Conference on Antimicrobial Agents and Chemotherapy; September 17-20, 1995; San Francisco, Calif. Abstract 152.

49. Shinabarger DL, Marotti KR, Murray RW, et al. Mechanism of action of oxazolidinones: effects of linezolid and eperezolid on translation reactions. *Antimicrob Agents Chemother.* 1997;41:2132-2136.

50. Eustice DC, Feldman PA, Zajac I, Slee AM. Mechanism of action of DuP 721: inhibition of an early event during initiation of protein synthesis. *Antimicrob Agents Chemother.* 1988;32:1218-1222.

51. Nicas TI, Zeckel ML, Braun DK. Beyond vancomycin: new therapies to meet the challenge of glycopeptide resistance. *Trends Microbiol.* 1997;5:240-249.

52. Lin AH, Murray RW, Vidmar TJ, Marotti KR. The oxazolidinone eperezolid binds to the 50S ribosomal subunit and competes with binding of chloramphenicol and lincomycin. *Antimicrob Agents Chemother.* 1997;41:2127-2131.
53. Swaney SM, Aoki H, Ganoza MC, Shinabarger DL. The oxazolidinone linezolid inhibits initiation of protein synthesis in bacteria. *Antimicrob Agents Chemother.* 1998;42:3251-3255.
54. Kloss P, Xiong L, Shinabarger DL, Mankin AS. Resistance mutations in 23 S rRNA identify the site of action of the protein synthesis inhibitor linezolid in the ribosomal peptidyl transferase center. *J Mol Biol.* 1999;294:93-101.
55. Xiong L, Kloss P, Douthwaite S, et al. Oxazolidinone resistance mutations in 23S rRNA of *Escherichia coli* reveal the central region of domain V as the primary site of drug action. *J Bacteriol.* 2000;182:5325-5331.
56. Aoki H, Ke L, Poppe SM, et al. Oxazolidinone antibiotics target the P site on *Escherichia coli* ribosomes. *Antimicrob Agents Chemother.* 2002;46:1080-1085.
57. Slatter JG, Stalker DJ, Feenstra KL, et al. Pharmacokinetics, metabolism, and excretion of linezolid following an oral dose of [14C]linezolid to healthy human subjects. *Drug Metab Dispos.* 2001;29:1136-1145.

CHAPTER THREE CME QUESTIONS

1. True or False: The team at DuPont involved in the discovery of the oxazolidinone class of antibiotics included Walter Gregory, Patricia Bartholomew, and Christopher Demos.

2. True or False: After attending the 27th ICAAC, Steven Brickner, then at Upjohn, decided to pursue research of the oxazolidinone compounds and convinced colleagues Charles Ford and Gary Zurenko to support his endeavor.

3. Which of the 3 subclasses of oxazolidinones became the principal focus of the ongoing chemistry effort at Upjohn?
   a. Indolines
   b. Piperazines
   c. Tropones

4. In early in vitro studies, both eperezolid and linezolid, the first 2 oxazolidinones developed, showed good activity against what gram-positive pathogens?
   a. Staphylococci
   b. Enterococci
   c. *Streptococcus pneumoniae*
   d. All of the above
   e. None of the above

5. Which of the following statements is correct regarding the mechanism of action of the oxazolidinone class?
   a. This class of drug affects binding of mRNA to the ribosome at the initiation phase of translation.
   b. This class of drugs affects elongation of the polypeptide chain, a common mechanism for protein inhibitor antibiotics.
   c. This class of drugs affects ribosomal termination of translation.
   d. This class of drugs prevents the binding of a noninitiating message.

CREATION OF A NOVEL CLASS:

A PHARMACOLOGIC PROFILE OF LINEZOLID

EDITOR

David P. Nicolau, PharmD, FCCP

LEARNING OBJECTIVES

After completion of this chapter, readers should be able to:

1. Describe the absorption characteristics of linezolid and discuss how its bio-availability affects its efficacy.

2. Discuss the possibility of interactions between linezolid and other drugs.

3. Describe the metabolic pathways of linezolid and how these differ between men and women and between humans and different animal species.

4. Identify possible adverse reactions associated with linezolid.

5. Summarize the tissue penetration characteristics of linezolid and discuss the impact tissue penetration has on the treatment of infection.

THE OXAZOLIDINONE ANTIBIOTICS

The results of the early in vitro testing left little doubt that linezolid held great promise. However, antimicrobial efficacy is far more than in vitro activity. The interactions of host, pathogen, and antimicrobial agent are complex, and an understanding of the general pharmacologic profile of an antibiotic is essential to effective therapeutic use of the agent.

The goals of treating any infection are to optimize antibiotic therapy and eradicate the organism as quickly as possible while minimizing adverse effects. Recent insight into the activity of antimicrobial agents has brought about a more precise methodology for creating dosing regimens. Antimicrobial dosing regimens should exploit the pharmacodynamic profile of the class under consideration. When selecting the optimal antimicrobial regimen and appropriate dose, both the pharmacokinetic profile and microbiological activity of the drug should be considered. Pharmacodynamics integrates patient-specific pharmacokinetic characteristics (ie, absorption, distribution, metabolism, elimination) with the critical interaction between the antibiotic and the pathogen.

Pharmacokinetic Profile

Data from preclinical animal studies indicate that linezolid is completely absorbed after oral administration, with an absolute bioavailability of approximately 100%.[1,2] As a result, linezolid may be given orally or intravenously without dose adjustment,[2] a benefit for patients who have been on intravenous medication during a hospital stay and must continue the antibiotic after their release. Notably, linezolid is sufficiently water soluble to permit an intravenous formulation; however, it maintains the proper physicochemical properties to facilitate high oral bioavailability (S. Brickner, personal communication, 2003). Linezolid is available as 400- or 600-mg tablets, as an oral suspension (100 mg/5 mL in 240-mL bottle), or as an isotonic solution (100-, 200-, or 300-mL bag, 2 mg of linezolid per mL) for intravenous administration.[2]

Maximum plasma concentrations (C_{max}) are achieved within 1 to 2 hours after the oral administration of linezolid as a result of the rapid absorption of this antimicrobial.[2] The high rate of oral absorption of linezolid appears to be a class characteristic; similar observations have been made with previously studied DuPont compounds (ie, DuP-721, DuP-105) and eperezolid.[3] Because the interaction with food is not clinically significant (time to maximum concentration is delayed from 1.5 to 2.2 hours and C_{max} is reduced by 17% when given with a high-fat meal), oral linezolid may be given without regard to the timing of meals.[2] Moreover, additional pharmacologic advantages of this compound are the rapid attainment of high serum concentrations after oral or intravenous administration and the maintenance of these concentrations above the minimum concentration at which 90% of organisms are inhibited (MIC_{90}) for the entire 24-hour period with the 600-mg twice-daily dose (S. Brickner, personal communication, 2003).

Tissue Penetration

Failure to achieve adequate concentrations at the site of infection is a major cause of therapeutic failure. Because of limited tissue penetration to the site, an antibiotic may be very effective against a pathogen in one site (eg, the bloodstream in cases of septicemia), while it may have no effect in another (eg, the central nervous system in cases of meningitis).[4] In well-perfused tissue, the volume of distribution has a significant impact,[5] but local factors also may affect this.[4] The large amount of hemoglobin found in an infected hematoma can reduce the effectiveness of an agent that is highly protein-bound, whereas the low pH found in an undrained abscess may interfere with the antimicrobial activity of some agents but enhance the activity of others.[4] This interplay of host and local factors and antibiotic pharmacokinetics determines to a large extent the amount of active compound that can reach the pathogenic target. In particular, protein binding can play a major role in the capability of an agent to penetrate tissue.[6] Although protein binding may adversely affect the distribution of some antimicrobials, the plasma protein binding of linezolid is low (~31%) and therefore does not hinder this agent's tissue penetration profile.[2]

Studies have indicated that linezolid distributes readily into well-perfused tissues, and the volume of distribution at steady state averaged 40 L to 50 L in healthy human volunteers.[2] The distribution of linezolid into a variety of body fluids has been determined from volunteers participating in phase I studies. The ratio of linezolid in saliva to plasma is 1.2:1, and the ratio of sweat to plasma is 0.55:1.

Gee et al[5] assessed the adequacy of tissue penetration in human volunteers after multiple oral doses of linezolid. Because blister fluid mimics inflammatory exudate, a blister technique was used to create a site on the forearm from which fluid could be drawn to assess tissue penetration. Volunteers were given 600-mg doses of linezolid twice a day for 2.5 days, after which linezolid concentrations in both plasma and blister fluid were evaluated.

Mean penetration of linezolid into inflammatory fluid was 104%, and the 12-hour concentration was 4.9 mg/L.[5] The MIC_{90s} for *Staphylococcus aureus* (susceptible strains), streptococci, and enterococci are 4 µg/mL or less,[7] suggesting that for this infection site, penetration of linezolid is more than sufficient.[5] Table 1 presents the pharmacokinetic parameters for linezolid in plasma and inflammatory fluid.

centrations in alveolar macrophages were less than those noted for either plasma or epithelial lining fluid, suggesting that the drug was either excluded or rapidly removed from the intracellular space. While these intracellular concentrations appear low, this agent is generally used for extracellular pathogens such as staphylococci, and as such, this finding is of little clinical importance.

In a recent study, the penetration of linezolid into bone, fat, muscle, and hematoma was evaluated during hip replacement surgery in 12 patients.[9] Conventional prophylaxis with 1 g of cefamandole was given along with a 600-mg intravenous infusion of linezolid immediately before surgery. As hip arthroplasty was performed, samples of fat, muscle, and bone were taken at timed intervals and assayed for evidence of linezolid. Penetra-

Table 1. Pharmacokinetic Parameters for Linezolid in Plasma and Inflammatory Fluid After 5 Doses of 600-mg Tablets at 12-Hour Intervals

Source of Fluid	Mean ± SD (range [minimum-maximum])					
	C_{max} (µg/mL)	T_{max} (h)	$t_{1/2}$ (h)	AUC_{last} (µg h/mL)	$AUC_{0-\infty}$ (µg h/mL)	Penetration (%)
Plasma	18.3 ± 6.0 (12.2-27.5)	0.7 ± 0.3 (0.5-1.0)	4.9 ± 1.8 (2.9-7.9)	107.5 ± 40.6 (64.5-271.4)	140.3 ± 73.1 (60.3-171.6)	
Blister	16.4 ± 10.6 (6.8-36.8)	3.0 ± 0.6 (2.0-4.0)	5.7 ± 1.7 (4.6-8.6)	101.6 ± 63.0 (57.4-224.5)	155.3 ± 80.1 (79.5-283.8)	104 ± 20.7 (80-130)

SD = standard deviation; C_{max} = maximal drug concentration; T_{max} = time of maximal concentration; $t_{1/2}$ = elimination half-life; AUC_{last} = area under the curve up to the last measurable concentration; $AUC_{0-\infty}$ = area under the curve extrapolated to infinity. Reprinted from Gee T, Ellis R, Marshall G, et al. Pharmacokinetics and tissue penetration of linezolid following multiple oral doses. *Antimicrob Agents Chemother.* 2001;45:1843-1846, with permission from the American Society for Microbiology. Copyright © 2001, American Society for Microbiology. All rights reserved.

In 2002, Conte et al[8] reported on the intrapulmonary disposition of linezolid. Twenty-five healthy male volunteers were given 600-mg doses of linezolid every 12 hours for 5 doses. Subjects were divided into 5 subgroups of 5 and then underwent bronchoscopy and bronchoalveolar lavage 4, 8, 12, 24, or 48 hours after the administration of the last dose.

The concentration profile of linezolid in plasma, epithelial lining fluid, and alveolar macrophages is displayed in Figures 1, 2, and 3.[8] In plasma and epithelial lining fluid, linezolid concentrations remained above the MIC_{90} for 100% of the 12-hour dosing interval, indicating likely efficacy against common pulmonary pathogens. However, con-

tion into bone was rapid, with a mean concentration of 9.1 mg/L achieved 10 minutes after the infusion. This decreased to 6.3 mg/L at 30 minutes. Corresponding values were 4.5 mg/L and 4.1 mg/L for fat and 10.4 mg/L and 12.0 mg/L for muscle. The percentage of penetration for bone was 51% at 10 minutes and 47% at 30 minutes. For fat, it was 27% at 10 minutes and 31% at 30 minutes. For muscle, it was 58% at 10 minutes and 93% at 30 minutes. Drainage of hematoma fluid showed linezolid concentrations of 8.2 mg/L at 6 to 8 hours, 5.6 mg/L at 10 to 12 hours after the initial infusion, and 7.0 mg/L at 2 to 4 hours following a second 600-mg infusion given 12 hours postoperatively. Linezolid demonstrated rapid penetration of all 3 tissue types, the capability to maintain levels above the MIC_{90}

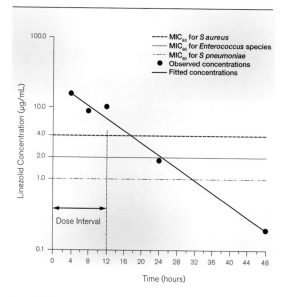

Figure 1. Mean concentrations of linezolid in plasma at the times of bronchoscopy. The MIC_{90s} for *Staphylococcus aureus, Enterococcus* species, and *Streptococcus pneumoniae* are included for comparison. MIC_{90} = minimum concentration needed to inhibit 90% of organisms. Reprinted from Conte JE Jr, Golden JA, Kipps J, Zurlinden E. Intrapulmonary pharmacokinetics of linezolid. *Antimicrob Agents Chemother.* 2002;46:1475-1480, with permission from the American Society for Microbiology. Copyright © 2002, American Society for Microbiology. All rights reserved.

for susceptible pathogens, and maintenance of therapeutic concentrations in the hematoma fluid surrounding the surgical site.

Although the complete pharmacokinetic profile of linezolid in the cerebrospinal fluid of patients being treated for central nervous system infections has not been described, preliminary data suggest that 600 mg given twice daily produces cerebrospinal fluid concentrations that should be sufficient for adequate treatment of susceptible pathogens.[10]

Metabolism

The pharmacokinetic nature of linezolid was explored in 2001 by Slatter et al.[11] The group reported on the disposition of linezolid in 16 healthy volunteers in a randomized, open-label, parallel group study. In the first group, a single 500-mg oral dose of linezolid labeled with radioactive carbon (^{14}C) was given on day 1, while in the second (steady-state) group, subjects received two 250-mg tablets of linezolid twice daily on days 1 through 3. On day 4, sub-

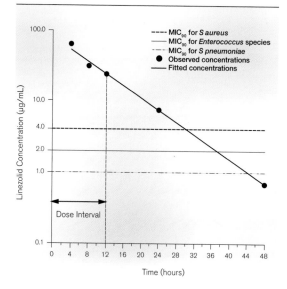

Figure 2. Mean concentrations of linezolid in eELF. The MICs for *Staphylococcus aureus, Enterococcus* species, and *Streptococcus pneumoniae* are included for comparison. eELF = epithelial lining fluid; MIC_{90} = minimum concentration needed to inhibit 90% of organisms. Reprinted from Conte JE Jr, Golden JA, Kipps J, Zurlinden E. Intrapulmonary pharmacokinetics of linezolid. *Antimicrob Agents Chemother.* 2002;46:1475-1480, with permission from the American Society for Microbiology. Copyright © 2002, American Society for Microbiology. All rights reserved.

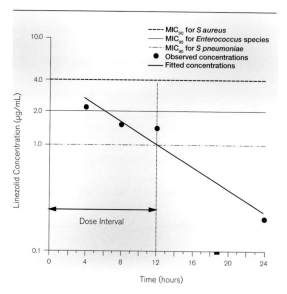

Figure 3. Mean concentrations of linezolid in AC. The MIC_{90s} for *Staphylococcus aureus, Enterococcus* species, and *Streptococcus pneumoniae* are included for comparison. AC = alveolar cells; MIC_{90} = minimum concentration needed to inhibit 90% of organisms. Reprinted from Conte JE Jr, Golden JA, Kipps J, Zurlinden E. Intrapulmonary pharmacokinetics of linezolid. *Antimicrob Agents Chemother.* 2002;46:1475-1480 with permission from the American Society for Microbiology. Copyright © 2002, American Society for Microbiology. All rights reserved.

jects in the steady-state group were given a 500-mg dose of [14C]-linezolid in the morning, followed by two 250-mg tablets of linezolid in the evening. On days 5 through 10, subjects in the steady-state group were again given two 250-mg tablets of linezolid twice daily.

Linezolid circulates primarily as the parent drug.[11] The compound is metabolized chiefly through oxidation of the morpholine ring, producing 2 inactive, morpholine ring–oxidized metabolites, PNU-142586 and PNU-142300. The formation of PNU-142300 is presumed to be enzymatic, whereas the formation of PNU-142586 appears to be nonenzymatic, the result of a slow oxidation step that may occur throughout the body. Lactone-to-lactam metabolic pathway ratios were 4.5:1 in all groups except the single-dose female group, in which the ratio was 2.5:1. The primary metabolite of the lactone pathway was PNU-142586; the lactam pathway metabolites included PNU-142300. In contrast, dogs metabolize linezolid equally by these 2 pathways, and rats favor the lactam pathway by a ratio of 4:1. These findings suggest subtle but interesting pharmacokinetic differences in linezolid metabolism

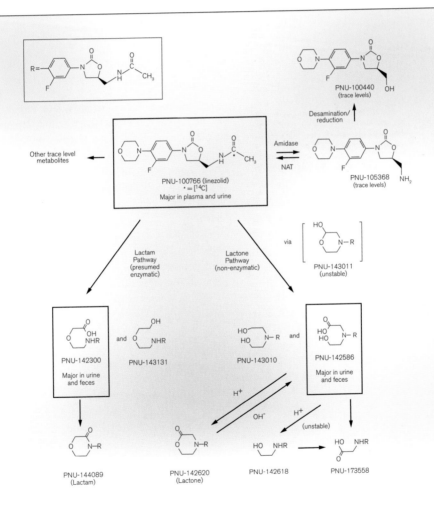

Figure 4. Linezolid metabolic pathways in mouse, dog, and human. Reprinted with permission from Slatter JG, Stalker DJ, Feenstra KL, et al. Pharmacokinetics, metabolism, and excretion of linezolid following an oral dose of [14C] linezolid to healthy human subjects. *Drug Metab Dispos.* 2001;29:1136-1142. The statements and opinions contained in the articles of *Drug Metabolism and Disposition* are solely those of the individual authors and contributors and not of the American Society for Pharmacology and Experimental Therapeutics. The American Society for Pharmacology and Experimental Therapeutics disclaims responsibility for any injury to persons or property resulting from any ideas or products referred to in the articles or advertisements.

between humans and animals. The higher lactam pathway metabolism noted in animals may account for the lower area under the curve (AUC) relative to humans observed in these other species, with dogs having a greater AUC of linezolid than rats but a lower AUC than humans. Furthermore, whereas the rate-limiting step in the clearance of linezolid in humans is the formation of PNU-142586, in rats it appears to be the formation of PNU-142300 (Figure 4).

Linezolid does not induce cytochrome P-450 (CYP-450) in rats, and no evidence indicates that it does so in humans.[2,12] Additionally, it does not inhibit the clinically important human CYP isozymes 1A2, 2C9, 2C19, 2D6, 2E1, or 3A4. Thus, CYP-450–related drug interactions are not anticipated with the use of this agent.[12]

Mean total recovery of radioactivity in urine and feces was 93.0%±0.9% of the dose in the single-dose group and 94.5%±0.8% in the steady-state group.[11] Excretion in urine was the predominant route of elimination, accounting for 83.9%±3.3% of the dose. Approximately 30% of the dose appears in the urine as linezolid, 40% as PNU-142586, and 10% as PNU-142300.[2] Fecal excretion of linezolid accounts for less than 1% of the dose, which conforms with the compound's 100% bioavailability; in contrast, fecal excretion of PNU-142586 and PNU-142300 account for 6% and 3% of the dose, respectively.[1,12] Fecal excretion was lower in females in the single-dose group. This is in agreement with findings from prior studies that indicate less metabolism of linezolid to PNU-142586 in females; however, this difference was not observed in the steady-state group.[11] Approximately 80% of the radioactive dose was recovered within the first 24 hours, and recovery was essentially complete within 48 hours. The authors suggested that the remaining 5% to 7% of the dose may have been exhaled as radioactive-labeled carbon dioxide ($^{14}CO_2$). The elimination half-life with a 600-mg, twice-daily dose is 5.4 hours.[2]

Older age does not affect the pharmacokinetics of linezolid, and no dose adjustments are necessary for elderly persons.[2] Likewise, mild-to-moderate impairment in renal function does not alter these pharmacokinetic parameters; however, a significant increase in clearance does occur in patients undergoing hemodialysis, and the dose should be given after dialysis. In patients with severe renal impairment, the metabolites PNU-142586 and PNU-142300 may accumulate, although the clinical significance of this accumulation is not known. Mild-to-moderate hepatic insufficiency does not alter the pharmacokinetics of linezolid; however, this agent has not been evaluated in patients with severe hepatic insufficiency.

Pediatric patients have C_{max} and volume of distribution values similar to those found in adults, but clearance in younger patients is increased.[2] Thus, the half-life is shorter and the AUC is lower than in adults. As children grow older, clearance decreases; by adolescence, values approach those found in adults. The dose in children aged 11 years or younger is 10 mg/kg every 8 hours. In patients aged 12 through 17 years, the dose is 600 mg or 10 mg/kg, not to exceed 600 mg every 12 hours.

Interactions

Because linezolid does not induce or inhibit the cytochrome system, CYP-450–related drug interactions are not anticipated with the use of this agent.[2]

As a reversible, nonselective monoamine oxidase inhibitor, linezolid has the potential to interact with adrenergic and serotonergic agents.[2] A pressor response has been noted in healthy adults receiving linezolid concomitantly with tyramine, although the response occurred only when extremely high doses of tyramine were administered.[2,13] Healthy volunteers were given 625 mg of linezolid twice daily at steady state and increasing doses of tyramine until a 30–mm Hg rise in systolic blood pressure was noted. A minimum of 100 mg of tyramine was required before this effect was observed.[13] This was judged to be similar to or less than the pressor effects noted with the concomitant administration of moclobemide and tyramine.

Although no restrictions were suggested regarding normal dietary intake of tyramine-containing foods,[13] patients should be advised to avoid consuming large amounts of foods or beverages with a high tyramine content, such as cheese, red wine, tofu, miso soup, or smoked meats or fish, when taking this agent.[2]

A reversible enhancement of the pressor response of pseudoephedrine hydrochloride and phenylpropanolamine hydrochloride has also been observed in healthy adults.[2,13] These effects include increases in the maximum positive change in systolic and diastolic blood pressures and in the mean increase in the maximum blood pressure attained.[13] No statistically significant effect on heart rate was noted, and the increases in blood pressure were transient. However, this study was conducted on a healthy, uncompromised population. Patients sensitive to the effects of increased blood pressure may respond differently.

The potential for serotonergic interactions has also been studied in healthy volunteers.[13] Interactions between monoamine oxidase inhibitors and compounds that inhibit the reuptake of serotonin can have potentially serious clinical consequences. Linezolid had no effect on any dextromethorphan pharmacodynamic variables, and no serotonin syndrome effects were noted in a study conducted on 14 volunteer subjects. The study assessed both autonomic functioning and mentation. However, recent reports indicate that in some patients, concomitant administration of linezolid and selective serotonin-reuptake inhibitors may cause serotonin syndrome.[14] This is discussed in greater detail in Chapter 9.

Pharmacodynamic Profile

As established by a number of time-kill studies, linezolid has a bacteriostatic effect against staphylococci and enterococci and a bactericidal effect against streptococci, regardless of resistance patterns.[1,7,15,16] This bacteriostatic rather than bactericidal effect may result from a lack of inhibition during the peptide elongation phase.[17] Linezolid relies on time-dependent killing and has a moderate postantibiotic effect (PAE) that has been documented by Rybak et al.[18]

In the study by Rybak et al,[18] the in vitro PAE of linezolid against staphylococci and enterococci was determined to be greater at 4 times the minimal inhibitory concentration (MIC), with a range of 0.2 to 1.4 hours, than at the MIC (0.1 to 0.8 hours). This was true of both oxazolidinones tested—eperezolid and linezolid. As a point of comparison, that study found that the PAE of vancomycin against staphylococci was 1.1 to 2.9 hours at 4 times the MIC, but 0 to 1.9 hours at the MIC. However, note that vancomycin is bactericidal against staphylococci. Interestingly, the PAE for both oxazolidinones was considerably shorter against Enterococcus faecalis than against Enterococcus faecium and staphylococci isolates. The study also found that the MICs tended to be slightly higher for the E faecalis isolates than for E faecium.

Munckhof et al[19] examined the in vitro PAE of linezolid using various concentrations of the agent against strains of streptococci, staphylococci, and enterococci and confirmed the findings of Rybak et al.[18] Eight different concentrations of linezolid were used, from 0.5 times the MIC to 64 times the MIC. Mean maximal PAEs were 2.2 hours for S aureus, 1.8 hours for Staphylococcus epidermidis, 2.8 hours for E faecalis, 2.0 hours for E faecium, and 3.0 hours for Streptococcus pneumoniae. No reduced effect was noted for E faecalis.

Pharmacodynamic parameters are becoming increasingly important for predicting clinical outcomes and establishing effective antibiotic dosing schedules.[20] In a recent pharmacodynamic study of linezolid, Andes et al[21] experimentally induced infections in the thighs of mice with 2 methicillin-susceptible Staphylococcus aureus (MSSA) strains, 2 methicillin-resistant Staphylococcus aureus (MRSA) strains, 1 penicillin-susceptible strain of S pneumoniae, 2 penicillin-intermediate-resistant strains of S pneumoniae, and 5 penicillin-resistant S pneumoniae strains. As was true in the in vitro studies, PAEs were minimal to modest in vivo. Similar to the β-lactam and macrolide antibiotic classes, linezolid does not achieve enhanced antimicrobial activity with increased drug concentrations. The duration that the serum concentration exceeded the MIC should have been the pharmacodynamic parameter that best correlated with clinical success; however, the investigators determined that it was the 24-hour AUC-to-MIC ratio that best predicted efficacy against S pneumoniae and was also important in establishing in vivo activity against S aureus. These data reveal that the 24-hour AUC-to-MIC ratio required for a bacteriostatic effect varied from 22 to 97 (mean, 48) for S pneumoniae and from 39 to 167 (mean, 83) for S aureus. With a goal of achieving a 24-hour AUC-to-MIC ratio of 50 to 100, Andes and colleagues concluded that a linezolid regimen of 600 mg given twice daily would be successful against pathogens with MICs of 4 μg/mL (Figure 5).[5,21]

A rat model of pneumococcal pneumonia provided additional information on the pharmacodynamics of low-dose (50 mg/kg/d) and high-dose (100 mg/kg/d) oral linezolid compared with subcutaneous ceftriaxone (100 mg/kg/d) for treating penicillin-susceptible S pneumoniae.[22] The linezolid regimens were chosen to help provide information on what might constitute an effective dose versus a substandard dose.

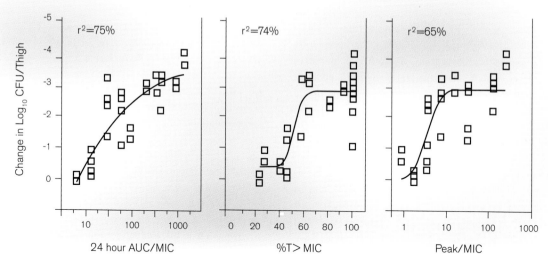

Figure 5. Relationships between the percentage of the dosing interval that levels in serum remained above the MIC for *Staphylococcus aureus* ATCC 6538p, the 24-hour AUC/MIC, and the peak/MIC and the $\log_{10}$ number of CFU/thigh after 24 hours of therapy. Each symbol represents the data for 2 mice. The lines represent the best-fit line. CFU = colony-forming units; AUC = area under the curve; MIC = minimal inhibitory concentration; r^2 = coefficient of determination; %T>MIC = percentage of time above the MIC. Reprinted from Andes D, van Ogtrop ML, Peng J, Craig WA. In vivo pharmacodynamics of a new oxazolidinone (linezolid). *Antimicrob Agents Chemother.* 2002;46;3484-3489, with permission from the American Society for Microbiology. Copyright © 2002, American Society for Microbiology. All rights reserved.

By the time antibiotic therapy was initiated 18 hours postinfection, bacteremia was noted in 90% of the rats.[22] The ceftriaxone pharmacodynamic parameters of free-fraction AUC-to-MIC and C_{max}-to-MIC ratios were significantly higher than those observed with either low-dose or high-dose linezolid (P<.001). However, the low ceftriaxone MIC for this *S pneumoniae* strain may have accounted for much of this; furthermore, this may not be representative of the more resistant strains commonly encountered in patients with pneumonia. Additionally, in the face of higher MICs, the high protein-binding levels found with ceftriaxone might be expected to contribute to diminished clinical efficacy.

In contrast, the free-fraction pharmacodynamic parameter of the percentage of time above the MIC (%T>MIC) was significantly higher for high-dose linezolid (39.0%) than for either low-dose linezolid (31.1%) (P<.01) or ceftriaxone (31.3%) (P<.01).[22] This latter parameter reflects the antibiotic half-life of the agent, the concentration in serum, and the MIC against the organism. The investigators noted that the use of serum free-fraction values to calculate pharmacodynamic parameters appeared to better characterize the in vivo antibiotic response.

Because linezolid is a slowly bactericidal drug against *S pneumoniae* at low AUC-to-MIC ratios, the authors expected the poor performance at low doses.[22] They further stated that when free-fraction AUC-to-MIC, C_{max}-to-MIC, and %T>MIC values of 147.0, 24.3, and 39.0, respectively, are achieved for linezolid, the resulting efficacy is similar to that of ceftriaxone. At the standard linezolid dose of 600 mg twice daily, these values should be exceeded. However, the authors cautioned that in infections caused by pneumococci that are very susceptible to β-lactams, agents such as ceftriaxone would be the better choice because the slowly bactericidal nature of linezolid could result in a slower resolution of the infection. They suggested reserving linezolid for patients with infections caused by *S pneumoniae* isolates known or suggested to be resistant to penicillin or for patients in whom β-lactam therapy has failed.

In a murine model of hematogenous pulmonary infection, Yanagihara et al[23] noted the efficacy of linezolid within lung tissue. Lung infection with either MRSA or vancomycin-intermediate-resistant *Staphylococcus aureus* (VISA) was established in mice via an intravenous injection of bacteria. The effects on the survival rate of linezolid, vancomycin, and teicoplanin (100 mg/kg/d each) were assessed, and the pharmacodynamic parameters were evaluated. Survival rates were twice as high (85%) in the linezolid group for MRSA as they were in the vancomycin or teicoplanin groups (40% and 45%, respectively; $P<.05$). No survival effect was noted for VISA infections with either vancomycin or teicoplanin, but treatment with linezolid decreased mortality. In the MRSA infection, the parameter for when the AUC is greater than the MIC was highest for linezolid, whereas in the VISA infection, the %T>MIC was the longest for linezolid. Fewer abscesses and less inflammation were noted in linezolid-treated mice with VISA infections than in mice treated with either vancomycin or teicoplanin.

Additive and Synergistic Effects in Vitro

Combination therapy is often necessary with multidrug-resistant infections, and characterizing the additive or synergistic effects of newer compounds is an important part of establishing the pharmacologic profile. The additive and synergistic effects of the new antibiotics quinupristin-dalfopristin and linezolid were explored in combination with each other and with cefepime, ampicil-

lin, doxycycline, and vancomycin in an in vitro study by Allen et al.[24] Various combinations were tested against 5 strains of staphylococci (ie, methicillin-susceptible *S epidermidis* R387, methicillin-resistant *S epidermidis* R444, methicillin-susceptible *S aureus* 1199, MRSA 494, glycopeptide-intermediate-resistant *Staphylococcus aureus* [GISA] 992), 1 strain of vancomycin-resistant *E faecium* (strain 12311), and 1 strain of vancomycin-resistant *E faecalis* (strain SF11848).

The authors established the MICs and minimum bactericidal concentrations for the antibiotics against each bacterial strain.[24] These are presented in Table 2. For MRSA 494, quinupristin-dalfopristin was initially bactericidal; however, regrowth to the starting level occurred after 8 hours. Cefepime, linezolid, and vancomycin were bacteriostatic when administered alone, but improvement was noted when cefepime was combined with either quinupristin-dalfopristin or linezolid. The combination of quinupristin-dalfopristin and linezolid proved to be bactericidal, as was quinupristin-dalfopristin and vancomycin. Against methicillin-resistant *S epidermidis* R444, both cefepime and linezolid were bacteriostatic; however, in combination, their effects were bactericidal.[24] For entero-

Table 2. Susceptibility Testing Results

Agent	MIC (mg/L) (MBC [mg/L]) for:						
	MSSE R387	MRSE R444	MSSA 1199	MRSA 494	GISA 992	VREF 12311	VREFc SF11848
Q-D	0.03 (0.125)	0.06 (0.25)	0.25 (0.5)	0.5 (1)	0.125 (0.25)	0.25 (0.5)	4 (4)
Cefepime	0.5 (0.5)	8 (8)	2 (2)	8 (16)	1.6 (32)	>8192 (>8192)	>8192 (>8192)
Linezolid	1 (2)	1 (2)	2 (4)	4 (8)	1 (32)	2 (32)	2 (32)
Ampicillin	0.5 (1)	32 (32)	0.5 (1)	512 (1024)	512 (1024)	128 (1024)	1 (32)
Doxycycline	0.06 (2)	0.5 (4)	0.06 (2)	4 (64)	4 (64)	0.125 (8)	0.125 (8)
Vancomycin	1 (1)	1 (2)	1 (1)	0.25 (0.5)	4 (8)	512 (>8192)	512 (>8192)

MIC = minimal inhibitory concentration; MBC = minimal bactericidal concentration; Q-D = quinupristin-dalfopristin; MSSE = methicillin-susceptible *Staphylococcus epidermidis*; MRSE = methicillin-resistant *Staphylococcus epidermidis*; MSSA = methicillin-susceptible *Staphylococcus aureus*; MRSA = methicillin-susceptible *Staphylococcus aureus*; GISA = glycopeptide-intermediate-resistant *Staphylococcus aureus*; VREF = vancomycin-resistant *Enterococcus faecium*; VREFc = vancomycin-resistant *Enterococcus faecalis*. Reprinted from Allen GP, Cha R, Rybak MJ. In vitro activities of quinupristin-dalfopristin and cefepime, alone and in combination with various antimicrobials, against multidrug-resistant staphylococci and enterococci in an in vitro pharmacodynamic model. *Antimicrob Agents Chemother.* 2002;46;2606-2612, with permission from the American Society for Microbiology. Copyright © 2002, American Society for Microbiology. All rights reserved.

coccal isolates, enhancement or improvement was observed with the combination of doxycycline and linezolid versus vancomycin-resistant *E faecalis* and vancomycin-resistant *E faecium*, respectively, and quinupristin-dalfopristin and linezolid together had improved activity against vancomycin-resistant *E faecalis*.[24] The authors concluded that although these results need corroboration before such combinations are used in clinical practice, they appear promising.

More recently, Sweeney and Zurenko[25] examined the synergistic and antagonistic effects of linezolid alone and in combination with 35 antimicrobial agents against a number of susceptible and resistant gram-positive pathogens, including staphylococci, streptococci, and enterococci. Of the 1380 organism-drug combinations tested, 1369 (99.2%) with 28 antibiotic agents were indifferent, while 9 combinations with 6 drugs (ie, amoxicillin, erythromycin, imipenem, sparfloxacin, teicoplanin, tetracycline) were synergistic. Antagonism occurred with only 2 combinations of linezolid involving ofloxacin and sparfloxacin.

Adverse Reactions

Data on adverse reactions are from 7 comparator-controlled phase III clinical trials. Safety was evaluated in 2046 adult patients who were treated for up to 28 days. Most (85%) adverse events reported with linezolid were described as mild to moderate in intensity.[2] Diarrhea was the most commonly reported adverse event in patients treated with linezolid, with an incidence across studies that ranged from 2.8% to 11%, with a mean of 8.3%. Headache, which occurred in 6.5% (range across studies, 0.5% to 11.3%), and nausea, which occurred in 6.2% (range across studies, 3.4% to 9.6%), were the next 2 most frequently reported adverse reactions in patients on linezolid therapy. Other reported adverse effects include taste alteration, vaginal moniliasis, fungal infection, abnormal liver function tests, vomiting, tongue discoloration, dizziness, and oral moniliasis.

Pediatric safety was evaluated in 215 patients ranging in age from birth through 11 years and in 248 patients aged 5 through 17 years enrolled in 2 phase III comparator-controlled clinical trials and treated for up to 28 days.[2] In these 2 studies, 83% and 99%, respectively, of adverse events reported in patients taking linezolid were considered mild or moderate in intensity. In the first study, in

patients hospitalized with gram-positive infections and ranging in age from birth through 11 years, the mortality rate was 6% in the linezolid group and 3% in the vancomycin group. Thrombocytopenia has been noted to occur in 2.4% of adult patients (range across studies, 0.3% to 10%) on linezolid therapy compared with 1.5% (range across studies, 0.4% to 7%) of those taking a comparator.[2] In hospitalized pediatric patients, the incidence was 12.9% with linezolid therapy, compared with 13.4% with vancomycin. The incidence in pediatric outpatients was 0% with linezolid, compared with 0.4% with cefadroxil.

Thrombocytopenia is associated with the duration of therapy, primarily occurring in those treated for longer than 2 weeks. Platelet counts returned to normal in most patients after cessation of therapy.[2] No related clinical adverse events were associated with thrombocytopenia in phase III clinical trials; however, bleeding events were noted patients with thrombocytopenia in the compassionate use program, although the role of linezolid was not determined.

Postmarketing experience has revealed a number of adverse events associated with or possibly associated with linezolid therapy. Myelosuppression has been noted, including anemia, leukopenia, pancytopenia, and thrombocytopenia.[2] Neuropathy, both peripheral and optic, also has been reported in patients treated with linezolid. Although this primarily occurred in patients who were treated for more than the recommended maximum treatment period of 28 days, it sometimes occurred in patients who received shorter courses of therapy.

Pharmacologic Profile and Biofilm-Related Infection

The increasing use of indwelling medical devices, such as central venous catheters, has contributed to a rise in biofilm-related infection.[26] Pathogens found in biofilms often exhibit higher MICs than planktonic microbes and therefore, reduced sensitivity to many antibiotics.[26-28] Several factors contribute to the difficulty of eradicating these infections. The presence of a polysaccharide matrix (glycocalyx) enveloping the bacterial colony inhibits the diffusion of antimicrobials into the biofilm.[28,29] To reach and kill biofilm pathogens, the antibiotic must penetrate the glycocalyx. A slower metabolic state in biofilm bacteria compared with planktonic bacteria also may retard the efficacy of antimicrobials because many agents depend on bacterial growth to facilitate killing.[28-30]

Two recent studies explored the issue of antimicrobial efficacy and the penetration of biofilms. In the first, Wilcox et al[31] performed in situ measurements of linezolid and vancomycin concentrations in intravascular catheter–associated biofilms. Concentrations of vancomycin varied considerably, but even extremely high levels did not eradicate the biofilm bacteria. In only one case were biofilm-associated bacteria eliminated, despite concentrations thousands of times higher than the probable MICs of the gram-positive cocci. Experience with linezolid proved more disappointing. Killing of biofilm bacteria was generally greater with vancomycin than with linezolid, and lower concentrations of linezolid were achieved than had been hoped. Given the good tissue penetration reported elsewhere,[5,8,9] this finding was surprising. Vancomycin had a mean biofilm concentration of 6.8 mg (vancomycin concentration 0.2 to 89 mg/g biofilm); in comparison, the mean biofilm concentration of linezolid was 5.9 mg (linezolid concentration 0.9 to 6.1 mg/g biofilm).[31] Nonetheless, linezolid did show activity against biofilm-associated pathogens, which included coagulase-negative staphylococci, S aureus, and enterococci, reducing biofilm-associated bacterial counts by 0% to 98% (median, 91%). Comparable figures for vancomycin were 84% to 100% (median, 95%).

These findings underscore the difficulty of treating infections in certain sites and in particular, the complex nature of catheter-associated infection. The second study yielded more promising results, particularly for linezolid.[26] In this study, MRSA, MSSA, a coagulase-negative S epidermidis, and 3 GISA strains were exposed to either a constant concentration of antibiotic for 2 hours or 3 doses of exponentially decreasing concentrations of the drug. The constant level simulates in vivo administration of the drug by infusion, and the decreasing concentrations simulate administration of antibiotics at 12-hour intervals. The agents investigated were linezolid, quinupristin-dalfopristin, vancomycin, teicoplanin, and ciprofloxacin.

This unusual in vitro dosing regimen provided some surprising findings.[26] Ciprofloxacin kills in a concentration-dependent manner and would therefore be expected to have a greater effect in the constant-concentration exposure experiments. This proved to be the case with all 3 GISA strains and the coagulase-negative S epidermidis, but not for the MRSA and MSSA strains, which responded better to the exponentially decreasing concentration experiments. Vancomycin had the greatest effect on 1 of the GISA strains during the constant-concentration experiment. However, with time-dependent killing, linezolid performed as expected; the best response was observed with the exponentially decreasing concentrations. Linezolid was also the only antibiotic to demonstrate a reduction in the number of viable bacteria eluted from the biofilms throughout the experiment. Although these results are considerably more positive than those of Wilcox et al[31], that study was conducted in vivo. This study was conducted in vitro; thus, the findings may not be clinically relevant.[26]

Summary

Linezolid offers a number of advantages in the treatment of serious gram-positive infections. It has 100% bioavailability, good tissue penetration, and a low rate of protein binding, which allow it to achieve concentration levels above the MIC_{90} for a number of infection sites.[2] In addition, it remains a potent therapeutic weapon against the major gram-positive pathogens S aureus, S epidermidis, S pneumoniae, E faecium, and E faecalis. To date, little resistance has been reported, and MICs remain within an easily achieved range. Pharmacodynamic studies have indicated that a linezolid regimen of 600 mg given twice daily would be successful against pathogens with MICs of 4 µg/mL or less.[5,8,21]

Adverse events are mostly mild to moderate, with diarrhea, headache, and nausea being the most common.[2] However, as with most antimicrobials, serious reactions are a possibility. Thrombocytopenia occurs in 2.4% of adults and in up to 12.9% of children and is most often associated with therapy lasting longer than 2 weeks. However, the very serious nature of the infections being treated with this agent outweighs the risks associated with treatment. Linezolid has become a highly valuable therapy, and in the case of some multidrug-resistant strains, one of the only effective agents left in the antibiotic armamentarium.

References

1. Fung HB, Kirschenbaum HL, Ojofeitimi BO. Linezolid: an oxazolidinone antimicrobial agent. *Clin Ther.* 2001;23:356-391.

2. Zyvox [package insert]. Kalamazoo, Mich: Pharmacia & Upjohn Company; 2003.

3. Brickner SJ. Oxazolidinone antibacterial agents. *Curr Pharm Des.* 1996;2:175-194.

4. Chambers HF, Sande MA. Antimicrobial agents: general considerations. In: Hardman JG, Limbird LE, Molinoff PB, Ruddon RW, Goodman Gilman A, eds. *Goodman & Gilman's The Pharmacological Basis of Therapeutics.* 10th ed. New York, NY: McGraw-Hill Health Professions Division; 2001:1143-1170.

5. Gee T, Ellis R, Marshall G, Andrews J, Ashby J, Wise R. Pharmacokinetics and tissue penetration of linezolid following multiple oral doses. *Antimicrob Agents Chemother.* 2001;45:1843-1846.

6. Hyatt JM, McKinnon PS, Zimmer GS, Schentag JJ. The importance of pharmacokinetic/pharmacodynamic surrogate markers to outcome. Focus on antibacterial agents. *Clin Pharmacokinet.* 1995;28:143-160.

7. Zurenko GE, Yagi BH, Schaadt RD, et al. In vitro activities of U-100592 and U-100766, novel oxazolidinone antibacterial agents. *Antimicrob Agents Chemother.* 1996;40:839-845.

8. Conte JE Jr, Golden JA, Kipps J, Zurlinden E. Intrapulmonary pharmacokinetics of linezolid. *Antimicrob Agents Chemother.* 2002;46:1475-1480.

9. Lovering AM, Zhang J, Bannister GC, et al. Penetration of linezolid into bone, fat, muscle and haematoma of patients undergoing routine hip replacement. *J Antimicrob Chemother.* 2002;50:73-77.

10. Villani P, Regazzi MB, Marubbi F, et al. Cerebrospinal fluid linezolid concentrations in postneurosurgical central nervous system infections. *Antimicrob Agents Chemother.* 2002;46:936-937.

11. Slatter JG, Stalker DJ, Feenstra KL, et al. Pharmacokinetics, metabolism, and excretion of linezolid following an oral dose of [¹⁴C]linezolid to healthy human subjects. *Drug Metab Dispos.* 2001;29:1136-1145.

12. Wynalda MA, Hauer MJ, Wienkers LC. Oxidation of the novel oxazolidinone antibiotic linezolid in human liver microsomes. *Drug Metab Dispos.* 2000;28:1014-1017.

13. Hendershot PE, Antal EJ, Welshman IR, Batts DH, Hopkins NK. Linezolid: pharmacokinetic and pharmacodynamic evaluation of coadministration with pseudoephedrine HCl, phenylpropanolamine HCl, and dextromethorpan HBr. *J Clin Pharmacol.* 2001;41:563-572.

14. Bernard L, Stern R, Lew D, Hoffmeyer P. Serotonin syndrome after concomitant treatment with linezolid and citalopram. *Clin Infect Dis.* 2003;36:1197.

15. Jorgensen JH, McElmeel ML, Trippy CW. In vitro activities of the oxazolidinone antibiotics U-100592 and U-100766 against *Staphylococcus aureus* and coagulase-negative *Staphylococcus* species. *Antimicrob Agents Chemother.* 1997;41:465-467.

16. Mulazimoglu L, Drenning SD, Yu VL. In vitro activities of two novel oxazolidinones (U100592 and U100766), a new fluoroquinolone (trovafloxacin), and dalfopristin-quinupristin against *Staphylococcus aureus* and *Staphylococcus epidermidis. Antimicrob Agents Chemother.* 1996;40:2428-2430.

17. Wise R, Andrews JM, Boswell FJ, Ashby JP. The in-vitro activity of linezolid (U-100766) and tentative breakpoints. *J Antimicrob Chemother.* 1998;42:721-728.

18. Rybak MJ, Cappelletty DM, Moldovan T, Aeschlimann JR, Kaatz GW. Comparative in vitro activities and postantibiotic effects of the oxazolidinone compounds eperezolid (PNU-100592) and linezolid (PNU-100766) versus vancomycin against *Staphylococcus aureus,* coagulase-negative staphylococci, *Enterococcus faecalis,* and *Enterococcus faecium. Antimicrob Agents Chemother.* 1998;42:721-724.

19. Munckhof WJ, Giles C, Turnidge JD. Post-antibiotic growth suppression of linezolid against Gram-positive bacteria. *J Antimicrob Chemother.* 2001;47:879-883.

20. Rodvold KA. Pharmacodynamics of antiinfective therapy: taking what we know to the patient's bedside. *Pharmacotherapy.* 2001;21 (11 pt 2): 319S-330S.

21. Andes D, van Ogtrop ML, Peng J, Craig WA. In vivo pharmacodynamics of a new oxazolidinone (linezolid). *Antimicrob Agents Chemother.* 2002;46:3484-3489.

22. Gentry-Nielsen MJ, Olsen KM, Preheim LC. Pharmacodynamic activity and efficacy of linezolid in a rat model of pneumococcal pneumonia. *Antimicrob Agents Chemother.* 2002;46:1345-1351.

23. Yanagihara K, Kaneko Y, Sawai T, et al. Efficacy of linezolid against methicillin-resistant or vancomycin-insensitive *Staphylococcus aureus* in a model of hematogenous pulmonary infection. *Antimicrob Agents Chemother.* 2002;46:3288-3291.

24. Allen GP, Cha R, Rybak MJ. In vitro activities of quinupristin-dalfopristin and cefepime, alone and in combination with various antimicrobials, against multidrug-resistant staphylococci and enterococci in an in vitro pharmacodynamic model. *Antimicrob Agents Chemother.* 2002;46:2606-2612.

25. Sweeney MT, Zurenko GE. In vitro activities of linezolid combined with other antimicrobial agents against staphylococci, enterococci, pneumococci, and selected gram-negative organisms. *Antimicrob Agents Chemother.* 2003;47:1902-1906.

26. Gander S, Hayward K, Finch R. An investigation of the antimicrobial effects of linezolid on bacterial biofilms utilizing an in vitro pharmacokinetic model. *J Antimicrob Chemother.* 2002;49:301-308.

27. Desai M, Buhler T, Weller PH, Brown MR. Increasing resistance of planktonic and biofilm cultures of *Burkholderia cepacia* to ciprofloxacin and ceftazidime during exponential growth. *J Antimicrob Chemother.* 1998;42:153-160.

28. Ashby MJ, Neale JE, Knott SJ, Critchley IA. Effect of antibiotics on nongrowing planktonic cells and biofilms of *Escherichia coli. J Antimicrob Chemother.* 1994;33:443-452.

29. Brooun A, Liu S, Lewis K. A dose-response study of antibiotic resistance in *Pseudomonas aeruginosa* biofilms. *Antimicrob Agents Chemother.* 2000;44:640-646.

30. Costerton JW, Stewart PS, Greenberg EP. Bacterial biofilms: a common cause of persistent infection. *Science.* 1999;284:1318-1322.

31. Wilcox MH, Kite P, Mills K, Sugden S. In situ measurement of linezolid and vancomycin concentrations in intravascular catheter-associated biofilm. *J Antimicrob Chemother.* 2001;47:171-175.

CHAPTER FOUR CME QUESTIONS

1. What is the absolute bioavailability of linezolid after oral administration?
   a. 50%
   b. 75%
   c. 93%
   d. 100%

2. True or False: Studies have indicated that linezolid penetrates well into bone, fat, and muscle tissue as well as plasma and epithelial lining fluid; however, the penetration into alveolar macrophages is poorer.

3. Which of the following statements is true regarding the metabolism of linezolid?
   a. Linezolid circulates primarily in the form of its metabolites, PNU-142586 and PNU-142300.
   b. Humans metabolize linezolid primarily via the lactam pathway.
   c. Humans have a greater area under the curve of linezolid than either dogs or rats.
   d. The rate-limiting step in the clearance of linezolid in humans is the formation of PNU-142300.

4. Which of the following statements is true regarding linezolid?
   a. Older age does not affect the pharmacokinetics of linezolid.
   b. Mild-to-moderate impairment of renal function does not alter the pharmacokinetic parameters.
   c. In patients on hemodialysis, the dose should be given after dialysis.
   d. All of the above statements are true.
   e. None of the above statements is true.

5. Which of the following statements is correct regarding the microbiology of linezolid?
   a. Linezolid has a bacteriostatic effect against staphylococci and enterococci and a bactericidal effect against streptococci.
   b. Linezolid is bacteriostatic against staphylococci, enterococci, and streptococci.
   c. Linezolid is bactericidal against staphylococci, enterococci, and streptococci.
   d. Linezolid has a bactericidal effect against staphylococci and enterococci and a bacteriostatic effect against streptococci.

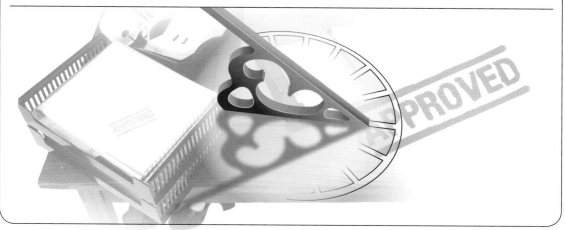

CREATION OF A NOVEL CLASS:

R E G U L A T O R Y   H I S T O R Y
THE PHASE I, II, AND III CLINICAL TRIAL EXPERIENCE

EDITOR

Donald H. Batts, MD, FACP

LEARNING OBJECTIVES

After completion of this chapter, readers should be able to:

1. Understand the clinical trial process necessary for FDA approval.

2. Recognize important resistant pathogens that respond to linezolid.

3. Identify diseases most likely to respond to treatment with linezolid.

4. Discuss the advantages of intravenous and oral dosing equivalency possible with linezolid.

5. Describe the effects of various antibiotics treatments on the length of hospital stay and subsequent morbidity and mortality.

THE OXAZOLIDINONE ANTIBIOTICS

The preclinical phase of development produced data from in vitro and in vivo animal studies indicating that linezolid had favorable pharmacokinetics and pharmacodynamics. The work of Dean Shinabarger and others, such as Lin, Swaney, Kloss, Xiong, and Aoki, provided evidence of the mechanism involved in the activity of the oxazolidinones against bacteria.[1-6] The early work of Zurenko, Kaatz, Eliopoulos, Jones, Mason, Mulazimoglu, and others helped determine pathogenic targets, document in vitro antimicrobial efficacy, and establish tentative breakpoints.[7-12] Experimental animal models of infection developed by Charles Ford and, more recently, researchers such as Gentry-Nielsen and Schulin, provided valuable information not only on in vivo efficacy but also on the pharmacokinetics and pharmacodynamics of linezolid.[13-15]

As illustrated in Table 1, the early in vitro studies showed that linezolid had minimum concentrations at which 90% of organisms are inhibited ($MIC_{90}s$) of between 1 μg/mL and 4 μg/mL against major gram-positive pathogens, including both resistant and susceptible strains.[7-10,16-19] Look-

Table 1. MIC_{90} Values for Linezolid From Early in Vitro Studies Against Select Gram-Positive Pathogens[7-10,16-19]

	MIC_{90} (μg/mL)							
	Zurenko	Eliopoulos	Jones	Kaatz	Spangler	Rybak	Noskin	Wise
MSSA	4	NA	2*	6.25	NA	4	4*	1
MRSA	4	NA	2*	6.25	NA	4	4*	1
MSSE	2	NA	2*	3.13	NA	2	4*	0.5
MRSE	2	NA	2*	3.13	NA	2	4*	NA
Penicillin-susceptible *Streptococcus pneumoniae*	1	NA	NA	NA	1	NA	1	NA
Penicillin-resistant *S pneumoniae*	1	NA	2†	NA	1	NA	NA	2
Streptococcus pyogenes	2	NA	4	NA	NA	NA	NA	1
Enterococcus faecalis	4	2 vanB	1*	NA	NA	4‡	4‡	1
Enterococcus faecium	NA	2	2	NA	NA	2‡	4‡	1
VR *E faecalis*	4	4	1	NA	NA	NA	NA	NA
VR *E faecium*	NA	2 vanA	2	NA	NA	NA	NA	NA
		4 vanB						
Bacteroides fragilis	4	NA	NA	NA	NA	NA	NA	4

MIC_{90} = minimum concentration needed to inhibit 90% of organisms; MSSA = methicillin-susceptible *Staphylococcus aureus;* MRSA = methicillin-resistant *Staphylococcus aureus;* MSSE = methicillin-susceptible *Staphylococcus epidermidis;* MRSE = methicillin-resistant *Staphylococcus epidermidis;* VR = vancomycin-resistant.
*Oxacillin-resistant.
†Includes penicillin-intermediate and -resistant strains.
‡Includes vancomycin-resistant isolates.

ing at the earlier studies by Zurenko et al,[7] Eliopoulos et al,[9] Jones et al,[10] Kaatz et al,[8] and Spangler et al,[16] all published in 1996, and comparing them with the Rybak et al[17] and Wise et al[18] studies published in 1998 and the Noskin et al[19] study published in 1999, little or no increase in minimal inhibitory concentrations (MICs) is evident for these major pathogens. In a study designed to evaluate tentative breakpoints for linezolid, Wise et al[18] of the Department of Medical Microbiology at City Hospital National Health Service Trust in Birmingham, England, found activity for the compound to be comparable with that of vancomycin against staphylococci and streptococci, whereas activity against enterococci was less with linezolid than with either vancomycin or quinupristin-dalfopristin. These investigators set a tentative breakpoint of 2 µg/mL,[18] which was one 2-fold dilution less, and more conservative, than that proposed by Jones et al[10] in 1996. Noskin et al[19] of Northwestern University in Chicago, Ill, reported that of the more than 10 agents tested, including levofloxacin, trovafloxacin, vancomycin, chloramphenicol, penicillin, and ampicillin-sulbactam, linezolid was the most active agent tested and exhibited activity comparable with that of vancomycin.

Another in vitro study in 1999 by a group of researchers at the Eijkman-Winkler Institute for Clinical Microbiology at University Hospital Utrecht in the Netherlands compared the activity of 8 fluoroquinolones and linezolid, quinupristin-dalfopristin, gentamicin, and vancomycin against ciprofloxacin-resistant and ciprofloxacin-susceptible strains of *Staphylococcus aureus*.[20] Linezolid showed activity that was equal to or greater than that of vancomycin, with MIC_{90s} of 2 µg/mL for linezolid and 1 µg/mL to 2 µg/mL for vancomycin for both resistant and susceptible strains, underscoring the clinically important role of this newer compound. Of the fluoroquinolones, only clinafloxacin and moxifloxacin had an MIC_{90} that was 2 µg/mL or less against ciprofloxacin-resistant, methicillin-resistant *Staphylococcus aureus* (MRSA).

Phase I trial results were also promising. Schaadt et al[21] demonstrated that in human subjects given doses of either linezolid or eperezolid, steady-state samples of sera drawn at the projected peak time points were generally inhibitory against *S aureus* and *Enterococcus faecalis*, although no bactericidal activity was noted for either drug. Inhibitory activity against *Streptococcus pneumoniae* was observed for both drugs at projected peak and trough times. Moreover,

for patients on higher-dose regimens, this activity proved to be bactericidal, an observation consistent with previous findings.[7,21] By 1997, phase I clinical trials were completed, and phase II trials of linezolid had begun.[1] These trials, conducted in small numbers of patients, found linezolid to be effective in the treatment of gram-positive skin and soft tissue infections (SSTIs) and pneumonia.[22,23]

The Approval Process— Trial and Evidence

With solid preclinical and phase I and II evidence of strong activity against a distinct group of common gram-positive pathogens as support, Pharmacia & Upjohn Company took the unusual approach of seeking US Food and Drug Administration (FDA) approval of linezolid for the treatment of specific resistant pathogens and for bacterial infections of specific sites.[24] Thus, some trials dealt with several different infection sites, including skin and skin structures, urinary tract, respiratory tract (pneumonia), as well as any site with associated bacteremia and bacteremia of unknown origin. Seven randomized, multicenter, comparative trials and an open-label noncomparative study were conducted on more than 2000 patients treated for up to 28 days with linezolid at 400 mg or 600 mg twice a day. In addition, data were gathered from a compassionate use program initiated in 1997.[25] Other double-blind and open-label studies provided corroborating evidence to support the application. Several of these trials are reviewed herein.

Vancomycin-Resistant Enterococcal Infections

Enterococci are commonly found in the intestinal tract of humans and rarely cause infections in otherwise healthy individuals. But these bacteria may become pathogenic in the weakened immune systems of elderly or immunocompromised patients. Others are at risk because of indwelling devices such as central venous catheters.

The incidence of nosocomial vancomycin-resistant enterococci (VRE) infections has risen dramatically in recent years, both in the ICU and in other areas of the hospital.[26] An urgent need exists to maintain the effectiveness of the current antibiotic arsenal against this pathogen and to discover new and effective agents to eradicate infections caused by resistant pathogens. One of the phase III trials of linezolid against resistant pathogens was aimed at establishing the efficacy of the new agent against VRE infections.

A randomized, double-blind, multicenter, dose-comparison trial was conducted on 145 patients with infections caused by VRE to determine the most effective dose of linezolid.[24] A dose-comparison trial design was used because an FDA-approved comparator was not available. Of the patients enrolled in the study, 79 were randomized to a high-dose regimen of linezolid (600 mg BID) and 66 to a low-dose regimen of linezolid (200 mg BID), to be taken for 7 to 28 consecutive days. Patients were given either oral or intravenous linezolid, depending on their condition, and those requiring gram-negative coverage were given intravenous aztreonam or an aminoglycoside. A follow-up evaluation was conducted 15 to 20 days after the end of treatment.

Of the total of 110 patients who completed the treatment (60 in the high-dose group, 50 in the low-dose group), only 48 and 40, respectively, were clinically evaluable; 36 and 29, respectively, were microbiologically evaluable.[24] Death was the most common reason for discontinuation, occurring in 7.6% of patients overall during the treatment period and in 22.8% of patients in the high-dose group and 31.8% of those in the low-dose group during the follow-up period. Lack of efficacy caused 2 discontinuations in the low-dose group but none in the high-dose group.

Among evaluable patients, urinary tract infection was the most common diagnosis in both groups, occurring in 29.2% of those in the high-dose group and 47.5% of those in the low-dose group ($P=.0769$), whereas SSTIs occurred in 20.8% and 17.5% ($P=.6933$), respectively, and bacteremia of unknown origin occurred in 18.8% and 7.5% ($P=.1257$), respectively.[24] Other diagnoses included pneumonia and bacteremia in combination with other infections.

Forty-four clinically evaluable patients were assessed in the high-dose group, and 38 were assessed in the low-dose group.[24] Thirty-seven patients (84.1%) in the high-dose group were considered cured, whereas 26 (68.4%) patients in the low-dose group were considered cured. An additional 7 patients in each group improved, constituting 15.9% and 18.4% of the high- and low-dose groups,

respectively. Treatment failure occurred in 5 patients (13.2%) in the low-dose group but in no patients in the high-dose group. At the follow-up visit 7 to 10 days later, of 43 assessed patients in the high-dose group, 39 remained cured (90.7%, $P=.6914$), and treatment failed in 4 (9.3%). Five patients had an indeterminate finding. In the low-dose group, of 33 patients assessed, 29 (87.9%, $P=.6914$) were cured, and treatment failed in 4 (12.1%). Four patients had indeterminate findings, and 3 patients were lost to follow-up.

At follow-up, an analysis of cure rates by primary source of VRE infection indicated that 100% of those with pneumonia were cured (high-dose group only).[24] In patients with SSTIs, 88.9% in the high-dose group and 100% of those in the low-dose group were cured ($P=.3980$). For urinary tract infections, the cure rates for patients in the high- and low-dose groups were 92.3% and 81.3% ($P=.3904$), respectively. For the category of other, the cure rates were 100% and 88.9% ($P=88.9$), respectively, and for bacteremia of unknown origin, the cure rates were 75% and 100% ($P=.4292$), respectively. None of these differences was statistically significant.

When analyzed by sex or age, cure rates were higher for patients receiving linezolid 600 mg twice a day. Interestingly, cure rates in the high-dose group were comparable with or without concomitant use of an aminoglycoside.[24] Linezolid had equal activity in both *Enterococcus faecium* and *E faecalis* infections, and although both doses were judged by the investigators to be clinically effective, greater efficacy was found for the higher dose. The results of a microbiologic evaluation indicated that cure rates at the follow-up visit for urinary tract infections caused by *E faecium* were 90% for the high-dose group and 73.3% for the low-dose group. For other primary sources of infection, cure rates were significantly higher in the high-dose group (100%) compared with the low-dose group (62.5%) ($P=.0339$).

The investigators concluded that the evidence supported the efficacy of the 600-mg dose of linezolid in the treatment of VRE infections, including *E faecium*.[24] Other than reversible thrombocytopenia, adverse events did not appear to be dose-related. The frequency of patients experiencing at least one adverse event was significantly higher in the low-dose group (98.5%, 65/66, $P=.0323$) than in the high-dose group (89.9%, 71/79).

Another noteworthy finding was that a statistically significant dose response was not observed among female patients.[24] This may be explained in part by the different pharmacokinetics for linezolid that have been noted in female subjects.[24,27] With a lower volume of distribution than male subjects and a lower clearance of the compound, female subjects appear to have a 30% higher maximal clearance than males.

Methicillin-Resistant Staphylococcal Infections

Staphylococci, particularly MRSA, are of great concern as a cause of nosocomial infection. Vancomycin-intermediate-resistant *Staphylococcus aureus* (VISA) and vancomycin-resistant *Staphylococcus aureus* (VRSA) remain exceedingly rare, with only 8 VISA and 2 VRSA infections documented in the United States.[26,28-31] However, vancomycin often proves to be less than optimal therapy against MRSA.[32] Establishing effective treatment for MRSA is critical. In another phase III, resistant-pathogen trial, 460 patients participated in a randomized, open-label, multicenter trial designed to compare the use of linezolid (600 mg BID) with vancomycin (1 g IV BID) in the treatment of methicillin-resistant *Staphylococcus* species infections.[24] Linezolid was started as intravenous treatment and either continued intravenously for the duration of therapy or switched to oral therapy. The linezolid intent-to-treat (ITT) group included 240 patients, and the vancomycin ITT group had 220. The patients treated with linezolid were slightly older on average, with a mean age of 63.9 years, compared with 59.8 years for the vancomycin group (*P*=.0157). The linezolid group had 124 clinically and 64 microbiologically evaluable patients, and the vancomycin group had 130 clinically and 70 microbiologically evaluable patients.

Linezolid and vancomycin proved to be equally effective in treating MRSA and methicillin-resistant *Staphylococcus epidermidis* (MRSE) infections, including pneumonia, SSTIs, urinary tract infections, other infections, and bacteremia of unknown origin.[24] The cure rate was 94.2% (97/103) in linezolid-treated patients and 87.3% (96/110) in those who received vancomycin in the clinically evaluable population. At the follow-up assessment, the cure rate for clinically evaluable patients was 77.0% (94/122) in the linezolid group and 74.4% (87/117) in the vancomycin group.

Microbiological success was somewhat less than clinical cure for each group, as is often the case. The microbiological success rate was 59.4% (38/64) for patients treated with linezolid and 64.2% (43/67) for those treated with vancomycin.[24] The cure rate overall was 57.8% (37/62) for patients in the linezolid group and 60.9% (39/64) for those treated with vancomycin. No differences were observed in cure rates related to the primary site of infection or the pathogen, and in general the effectiveness of the 2 agents among the various subanalysis results was similar and comparable to those noted for the overall analysis.

A significantly greater percentage of patients treated with linezolid (18.3%, 44/240) than with vancomycin (8.2%, 18/220) reported drug-related adverse events.[24] However, the percentage of patients who experienced drug-related adverse events resulting in discontinuation was comparable in the 2 groups. Ten patients in each study group (4.2% linezolid, 4.5% vancomycin) experienced adverse events of a severity sufficient to cause withdrawal from the study. However, most events were mild to moderate in intensity and were common to antibiotic therapy. Of the patients treated with linezolid, 16.7% (40/240) died; 13.6% (30/220) of patients treated with vancomycin died. Death was not judged to be related to the study medication in any patient.

The investigators concluded that linezolid was as safe and effective as vancomycin for eradicating resistant strains of *S aureus* and *S epidermidis*.[24]

Nosocomial Pneumonia

Nosocomial pneumonia is the most common cause of death from nosocomial infection, and discovering effective antibiotics is a major priority for critical care specialists.[33] Thus, a third phase III, double-blind, multicenter study provided valuable comparative data on the treatment of this illness.[34] This international study was conducted in 90 centers in North America, South America, Israel, South Africa, Australia, and Europe. Because resistance patterns can vary greatly with location,[35] the diverse distribution of trial centers afforded useful data on the efficacy of both linezolid and vancomycin against a wide variety of potentially resistant pathogens.

A total of 396 adult patients with documented nosocomial pneumonia were randomized to receive either linezolid (600 mg IV BID) plus aztreonam (n=203) or vancomycin (1 g IV BID) plus aztreonam (n=193).[34] Aztreonam 1 g to 2 g was given every 8 hours to provide coverage for gram-negative pathogens. Patients treated with linezolid received the medication for a mean duration of 9.6±4.4 days, whereas those on vancomycin were treated for a mean duration of 8.9±4.4 days. Discontinuations were similar between treatment groups, and the most common cause for discontinuing treatment was lack of efficacy in 10 (4.9%) patients in the linezolid group and 11 (5.7%) in the vancomycin group. The percentage of patients who discontinued treatment because of an adverse event was slightly higher in the vancomycin group (14/193, 7.3%) than in the linezolid group (9/203, 4.4%), but the difference was not statistically significant.

Consistent with other trial results, most adverse events in both treatment groups ranged from mild to moderate in intensity, were of limited duration, and did not require discontinuation of the study drug.[34] Although a greater percentage of patients assigned to the vancomycin group died (49/193, 25.4%) compared with the linezolid group (36/203, 17.7%, P=.06), the deaths were considered unrelated to the study medications. In 83.3% of the 36 patients who died in the linezolid group, death was deemed the result of complications of an underlying disease. The cause of death was also deemed the result of complications of an underlying disease in 73.4% of the 49 patients who died in the vancomycin group. Overall, the data suggested that linezolid was well tolerated compared with vancomycin.

Pathogen eradication rates and clinical and microbiological cure rates are presented in tables 2 and 3.[34] The study results indicate that linezolid and vancomycin were equally effective in treating nosocomial pneumonia, with respect to both clinical cure rates (66.4% and 68.1%, respectively; P=.79; 95% confidence interval [CI], −14.9 to 11.3) and microbiological cure rates (67.9% and 71.8%, respectively; P=.69; 95% CI, −22.8 to 15.0). No statistically significant differences were found between the 2 treatment groups for either clinical or microbiological cure rates, as is shown in Table 2. As Table 3 indicates, eradication rates were highest for S pneumoniae (100%, both regimens) and lowest for S aureus (61.0% linezolid, 65.2% vancomycin).

Table 2. Assessment of Efficacy in Clinically Evaluable and Microbiologically Evaluable Populations From a Phase III Trial of Linezolid Versus Vancomycin in the Treatment of Nosocomial Pneumonia

Assessment at TOC	Linezolid Recipients	Vancomycin Recipients	P Value	95% CI
Clinical outcome*	107	91	.79	−14.9 to 11.3
Cure	71 (66.4%)	62 (68.1%)		
Failure	36 (33.6%)	29 (31.9%)		
Indeterminate	1	5		
Microbiological outcome[†]	53	39	.69	−22.8 to 15
Success	36 (67.9%)	28 (71.8%)		
Failure	17 (32.1%)	11 (28.2%)		
Indeterminate	1	1		

Data are number (%) of patients assessed, unless otherwise indicated. Percentages are based on number of assessed patients, excluding missing and indeterminate patients. Percentages may not total 100 because of rounding.
TOC = test of cure; CI = confidence interval.
*Among clinically evaluable subjects.
[†]Among microbiologically evaluable subjects.
Reprinted from Rubinstein E, Cammarata SK, Oliphant TH, Wunderink RG, and the Linezolid Nosocomial Pneumonia Study Group. Linezolid (PNU-100766) versus vancomycin in the treatment of hospitalized patients with nosocomial pneumonia: a randomized, double-blind, multicenter study. Clin Infect Dis. 2001;32:402-412, with permission from the University of Chicago Press. © 2001 by the Infectious Diseases Society of America. All rights reserved.

Table 3. Eradication Rates at Follow-up by Pathogen Among Microbiologically Evaluable Patients in a Phase III Trial of Linezolid Versus Vancomycin in the Treatment of Nosocomial Pneumonia*

Pathogen	Linezolid Recipients (%)	Vancomycin Recipients (%)
Staphylococcus aureus	25/41 (61)	15/23 (65.2)
Documented	3/41 (7.3)	5/23 (21.7)
Presumed	22/41 (53.7)	10/23 (43.5)
Methicillin-resistant *Staphylococcus aureus*	15/23 (65.2)	7/9 (77.8)
Documented	1/23 (4.3)	2/9 (22.2)
Presumed	14/23 (60.9)	5/9 (55.6)
Streptococcus pneumoniae	9/9 (100)	9/9 (100)
Documented	3/9 (33.3)	6/9 (66.7)
Presumed	6/9 (66.7)	3/9 (33.3)

*Eradication was presumed in infections in which clinical cure had been achieved but specimens had not been obtained.

Reprinted from Rubinstein E, Cammarata SK, Oliphant TH, Wunderink RG, and the Linezolid Nosocomial Pneumonia Study Group. Linezolid (PNU-100766) versus vancomycin in the treatment of hospitalized patients with nosocomial pneumonia: a randomized, double-blind, multicenter study. *Clin Infect Dis.* 2001;32:402-412, with permission from the University of Chicago Press. © 2001 by the Infectious Diseases Society of America. All rights reserved.

Complicated Skin and Skin Structure Infections in Adults

Gram-positive bacteria are a major cause of SSTIs.[36] Infections involving deeper tissues, such as the subcutaneous tissues, fascia, and underlying muscle, or those requiring surgical intervention are considered complicated. The rise of bacterial resistance to commonly available antibiotics has made treating these infections a clinical challenge. Thus, finding effective antimicrobials to treat these infections is of critical concern.

A phase III randomized, double-blind equivalence study was conducted at 133 sites and involved 826 hospitalized adults.[37] The ITT population consisted of 819 patients, 400 randomized to the linezolid group and 419 randomized to the oxacillin-dicloxacillin group. Patients received initial intravenous therapy for gram-positive SSTIs with either linezolid (600 mg BID) or oxacillin (2 g QID) plus intravenous aztreonam (1-2 g TID/QID) as appropriate for empiric coverage of gram-negative pathogens. When patients showed clinical improvement, they could be switched to either oral linezolid at 600 mg twice a day or dicloxacillin at 500 mg 4 times a day.

Clinically relevant pathogens isolated at baseline were *S aureus* in 140 linezolid and 143 oxacillin-dicloxacillin

patients, *Streptococcus pyogenes* in 41 linezolid and 46 oxacillin-dicloxacillin patients, and *Streptococcus agalactiae* in 10 linezolid and 12 oxacillin-dicloxacillin patients. Patients from whom MRSA was isolated were excluded from the trial.

The mean duration of treatment was 13.4±5.4 days in the linezolid group and 13.4±6.0 days in the oxacillin-dicloxacillin group.[37] Similar percentages of patients in each group completed the study medication—84% among patients treated with linezolid and 78% among those treated with oxacillin-dicloxacillin. Among those who discontinued the study, the most common reason reported, regardless of study medication, was lack of efficacy. This included 2.3% of patients randomized to receive linezolid and 3.6% of those randomized to receive oxacillin-dicloxacillin.

Clinical cure rates in the ITT population were comparable in both treatment groups at the test-of-cure visit, with 279 (69.8%) of 400 in the linezolid group demonstrating clinical cure and 272 (64.9%) of 419 in the oxacillin-dicloxacillin group achieving clinical cure (*P*=.141; 95% CI, −1.58 to 11.25).[37] In clinically evaluable patients, cure rates were 88.6% and 85.8% of patients in the linezolid and oxacillin-dicloxacillin groups, respectively (*P*=.3; 95% CI, −2.5 to 8.2). A subgroup analysis of clinical outcome based on race, age, sex, or diagnosis revealed no statistically significant differences except for the male ITT population, in which the cure rate in the linezolid group was 85.3% versus 76.7% in the oxacillin-dicloxacillin group (*P*=.024; 95% CI, 1.2-16.5).

Microbiologically evaluable patients demonstrated similar success rates in both groups at the test-of-cure visit, with 88.1% of patients treated with linezolid and 86.1% of those treated with oxacillin-dicloxacillin achieving micro-

biological cure (*P*=.606; 95% CI, –5.6 to 9.7).[37] Again, no significant differences were found after subanalysis related to age, sex, race, or causative pathogen. Efficacy data are presented in Table 4, and eradication rates are presented in Table 5.

Adverse events were similar in the 2 treatment groups, with 67 (16.8%) of 400 patients in the linezolid group and 72 (17.2%) of 419 in the oxacillin-dicloxacillin group

Table 4. Phase III Trial of the Treatment of Complicated Skin and Soft Tissue Infections: Assessment of Efficacy in ITT, Clinically Evaluable, and Microbiologically Evaluable Subjects

Subject Group	Treatment	Total Subjects Assessed*	Subjects With Assessment		*P* (95% CI[†] [point estimate])
			Cure	Failure[‡]	
ITT	LNZ	400 (100%)	279 (69.8%)	121 (30.8%)	.141(–1.58 to11.25 [4.9])
	OXA-DCL	419 (100%)	272 (64.9%)	147 (35.1%)	
Clinically evaluable	LNZ	298 (100%)	264 (88.6%)	34 (11.4%)	.3 (–2.5 to 8.2 [2.8])
	OXA-DCL	302 (100%)	259 (85.8%)	43 (14.2%)	
Microbiologically evaluable	LNZ	143 (100%)	126 (88.1%)	17 (11.9%)	.606 (–5.6 to 9.7 [2])
	OXA-DCL	151 (100%)	130 (86.1%)	21 (13.9%)	

ITT = intent-to-treat; CI = confidence interval; LNZ = linezolid; OXA-DCL = oxacillin-dicloxacillin.
*Percentages based on number of assessed subjects.
[†]Confidence interval based on normal approximation, expressed as a percentage.
[‡]Includes subjects with missing or indeterminate outcomes.
Reprinted from Stevens DL, Smith LG, Bruss JB, et al, for the Linezolid Skin and Soft Tissue Infections Study Group. Randomized comparison of linezolid (PNU-100766) versus oxacillin-dicloxacillin for treatment of complicated skin and soft tissue infection. *Antimicrob Agents Chemother.* 2000;44:3408-3413, with permission from the American Society for Microbiology. Copyright © 2000, American Society for Microbiology. All rights reserved.

Table 5. Phase III Trial of the Treatment of Complicated Skin and Soft Tissue Infections: Eradication Rates of Selected Baseline Pathogens*

Pathogen	Eradication Rate (%)[†]		*P* (95% CI[‡] [point estimate])
	Linezolid	Oxacillin-Dicloxacillin	
Staphylococcus aureus	85/93 (91.4)	87/103 (84.5)	.139 (–2.1 to 16.0 [6.9])
Streptococcus pyogenes	23/29 (79.3)	27/32 (84.4)	.607 (–24.4 to 14.3 [5.1])
Streptococcus agalactiae	7/7 (100)	4/6 (66.7)	.097 (–4.4 to 71.1 [33.3])

CI = confidence interval.
*In microbiologically evaluable subjects.
[†]Eradication rate is the number of eradicated pathogens divided by the total of eradicated and noneradicated pathogens.
[‡]Confidence interval based on normal approximation, expressed as a percentage.
Reprinted from Stevens DL, Smith LG, Bruss JB, et al, for the Linezolid Skin and Soft Tissue Infections Study Group. Randomized comparison of linezolid (PNU-100766) versus oxacillin-dicloxacillin for treatment of complicated skin and soft tissue infection. *Antimicrob Agents Chemother.* 2000;44:3408-3413, with permission from the American Society for Microbiology. Copyright © 2000, American Society for Microbiology. All rights reserved.

reporting at least one adverse event.[37] Nausea was the most commonly reported adverse event in both groups, occurring in 3.5% of patients treated with linezolid and 2.9% of those treated with oxacillin-dicloxacillin. Serious adverse events were observed in 5.5% (22/400) of patients in the linezolid group and 4.5% (19/419) in the oxacillin-dicloxacillin group. No adverse events in the linezolid group were considered drug related, whereas 4 events in the oxacillin-dicloxacillin group were possibly or probably drug related. Three patients treated with linezolid died, and 1 treated with oxacillin-dicloxacillin died. However, no deaths were considered related to the treatment drugs. Of 12 patients receiving linezolid in whom hypertension was noted during the trial, 5 were normotensive at baseline.

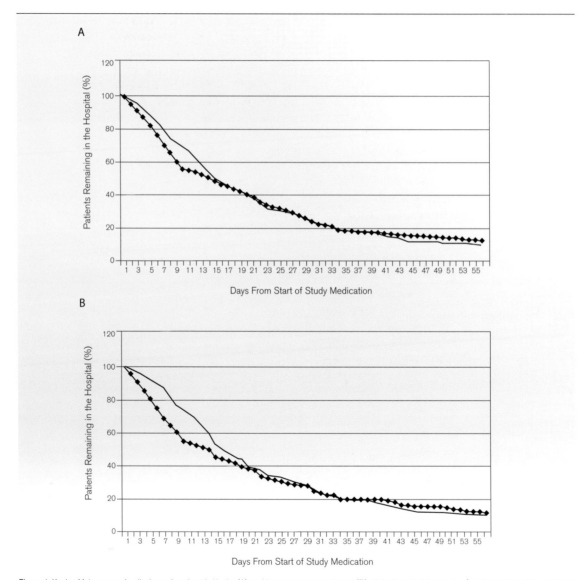

Figure 1. Kaplan-Meier curves for discharge from hospital in the (A) total intent-to-treat sample and (B) clinically evaluable sample. ◆ indicates linezolid; − indicates vancomycin. Reprinted with permission from Li Z, Willke RJ, Pinto LA, et al. Comparison of length of hospital stay for patients with known or suspected methicillin-resistant *Staphylococcus* species infections treated with linezolid or vancomycin: a randomized, multicenter trial. *Pharmacotherapy*. 2001;21:263-274. Copyright © 2001 Pharmacotherapy Publications. All rights reserved.

Four of these had intermittently elevated blood pressure during treatment, but it returned to normal in 3 patients at follow-up. One patient had a single transient episode of elevated blood pressure. Hypertension was noted in only one patient in the oxacillin-dicloxacillin group.

The investigators concluded that linezolid was as effective and well tolerated as oxacillin-dicloxacillin for the treatment of SSTIs.[37] They further suggested that the high level of linezolid tissue penetration[38] and the capability of linezolid to inhibit the formation of bacterial virulence factor and produce toxin in S aureus and S pyogenes at concentrations below the MICs may have contributed to its efficacy.[37,39]

Effect of Treatment on Length of Hospital Stay for Patients With MRSA Infections

Li et al[40] compared the length of stay (LOS) for hospitalized patients with MRSA or possible MRSA infections in a multinational, randomized phase III trial. Infections with MRSA contribute considerably to the LOS in hospitalized patients and increase medical costs dramatically.[41] Hospitals in North America, Latin America, and Europe participated; 460 hospitalized patients with infections known or suspected to be caused by MRSA were randomized to either intravenous linezolid (600 mg BID) or intravenous vancomycin (1 g BID).[40] At the discretion of the investigators, patients on linezolid could be switched to oral medication or continued on intravenous medication for the entire length of therapy. Those on vancomycin received intravenous therapy for the entire course of treatment.

Patients who received linezolid were significantly older than those randomized to receive vancomycin—63.9 years versus 59.8 years ($P=.0157$).[40] Patients with SSTIs constituted nearly 50% of the study population, whereas 22% had pneumonia, 6% had urinary tract infections, and 11% had bacteremia of unknown origin. While MRSA was isolated from 49% of patients, other staphylococci were found in 17%. No pathogen could be isolated from the remaining 34%. Although no statistically significant differences were noted in the primary site of infection, pathogen, or proportion of patients with MRSA infection for either treatment cohort, the number of patients enrolled from the ICU or step-down units was higher (20.8% and 6.3%, respectively) in the linezolid group than in the vancomycin group (19.1% and 1.4%, respectively). More patients randomized to vancomycin than to linezolid came from medical-surgical units (79.5% versus 72.9%, respectively). These differences were statistically significant ($P=.02$). A greater proportion of patients (32.9%) in the linezolid treatment group had 7 or more comorbid medical conditions compared with those in the vancomycin treatment group (25.9%) ($P=.10$).

In the ITT population, the median LOS was 14 days (95% CI, 9-17 days) for those receiving linezolid, compared with 15 days (95% CI, 13-17 days) for those receiving vancomycin ($P=.19$).[40] Analysis of the clinically evaluable population revealed greater differences for LOS, with a median of 14 days (95% CI, 9-18 days) for the linezolid cohort and a median of 16 days (95% CI, 14-19 days) for those treated with vancomycin ($P=.08$) (Figure 1). Among patients with complicated SSTIs, the median LOS was significantly shorter for those receiving linezolid than for those receiving vancomycin—5 days shorter in the ITT analysis ($P=.05$) and 8 days shorter in the clinically evaluable sample ($P=.003$). In the overall population, the mean and median duration of intravenous therapy was significantly shorter in the linezolid group than in the vancomycin cohort ($P<.001$); however, this was expected because some patients were switched to oral therapy. When oral therapy was taken into account, antibiotic treatment was 1 to 2 days shorter in the vancomycin group than in the linezolid group.

The availability of an oral formulation of linezolid provides a distinct advantage in allowing patients to continue therapy at home without the complications involved in home intravenous treatment. The investigators hypothesized that although the overall duration of treatment was actually slightly longer in the linezolid group, oral therapy may have led to reductions in hospital LOS and an increased number of patients being discharged in the first and second weeks of therapy.[40]

Overview of Safety Analysis

Of the total population of 2046 patients treated with linezolid in phase III clinical trials, 839 (41%) began therapy on the intravenous formulation of linezolid and then were switched to the oral dose; 822 (40.2%) were treated with oral medication alone; and 385 (18.8%) received intravenous medication alone.[24] The majority of patients (1498,

73.2%) received a linezolid dosage of 600 mg twice a day, whereas the others (548, 26.8%) received linezolid at 400 mg twice a day. Most were also treated for SSTIs (1070, 52.3%), some (908, 44.4%) were treated for pneumonia and the remainder (68, 3.3%) were treated for other infections. Of adverse events reported with linezolid treatment, 85% were mild to moderate in intensity; the most commonly reported adverse events were diarrhea (4.0%), nausea (3.3%), and headache (1.9%).[42] Other adverse events reported in phase II and III studies included oral moniliasis, vaginal moniliasis, hypertension, dyspepsia, localized abdominal pain, pruritus, and tongue discoloration.

The incidence of patients receiving the 600-mg dose and reporting at least one adverse event was 20.4% compared with 14.3% in the combined-comparator group.[42] Discontinuations due to drug-related adverse events were comparable between the linezolid group and the combined-comparator group (2.1% versus 1.7%, respectively). The most commonly cited drug-related adverse events resulting in discontinuation were nausea, headache, diarrhea, and vomiting.

Pediatric Trials

Pharmacia & Upjohn Company pursued approval for the pediatric use of linezolid in 2002 under the leadership of Jon Bruss and Donald Anderson, 2 years after receiving approval for use in adults for nosocomial and community-acquired pneumonia, complicated and uncomplicated skin and skin structure infections, and VRE infections.[24] Gram-positive pathogens are a major cause of pneumonia, (both nosocomial and community-acquired), complicated SSTIs, bacteremia, and sepsis in children.

Treatment of Gram-Positive Bacterial Infections in Patients From Birth Through Age 11 Years

A phase III, randomized, comparator-controlled, multicenter pediatric study was performed in hospitalized children from birth through age 11 years.[24] Patients with known or probable antibiotic-resistant gram-positive bacterial infections caused by methicillin-resistant *Staphylococcus* species (including MRSA), VRE, and penicillin-resistant *S pneumoniae*, were treated with either intravenous or oral linezolid or intravenous vancomycin. A total of 321 patients were enrolled and randomized to the study medications, although children with documented VRE infections were switched to linezolid. During the first 3 days, treatment was administered intravenously; a patient in the linezolid group could then be switched to oral medication at the discretion of the investigator if the patient was aged at least 91 days. Patients in the vancomycin group aged at least 91 days could be switched to an oral step-down medication if a susceptible pathogen had been isolated.

The ITT population consisted of 215 patients in the linezolid group and 101 in the vancomycin group.[24] The linezolid group had 151 clinically evaluable patients, and the vancomycin group had 73 clinically evaluable patients; 93 and 46 microbiologically evaluable patients were in the linezolid and vancomycin groups, respectively. As with the first pediatric study, the percentages and reasons for patients discontinuing were similar in both treatment groups with one exception: a higher percentage of patients randomized to receive vancomycin were lost to follow-up compared with those treated with linezolid (9.9% versus 3.3%). Overall, 21.9% of patients in the linezolid cohort and 24.8% in the vancomycin group discontinued treatment. The most commonly cited reason for discontinuation in the linezolid group was adverse events (16 patients, 7.4%). Although "lost to follow-up" was the most common reason reported in the vancomycin group (9.9%), nearly as high a percentage of patients (6.9%) in this group discontinued because of adverse events. Lack of efficacy was reported as the reason in 2 patients (0.9%) in the linezolid group and one subject (1%) in the vancomycin group.

This was a very young population.[24] The mean age was 2.91±3.16 years (range 0 to 11.7 years) for the linezolid group. Although the linezolid group included a larger proportion of preterm infants, the distribution of subject characteristics between the 2 treatment groups was otherwise similar.

The most commonly treated infection in both treatment groups was skin and skin structure infections, which occurred in 80 (37.2%) patients in the linezolid cohort and 40 (39.6%) in the vancomycin group.[24] The baseline diagnoses of other primary infections were hospital-acquired pneumonia in 23 (10.7%) patients treated with linezolid and 16 (15.8%) treated with vancomycin; vascular catheter-associated bacteremia in 48 (22.3%) and 13 (12.9%), respectively; bacteremia of unknown origin in 33 (15.3%) and 19 (18.8%), respectively; and other infections in 31 (14.4%) and 13 (12.9%), respectively.

The mean duration of treatment was 11.3±5 days in the linezolid group and 12.2±6.4 days in the vancomycin group.[24] Fifty-three percent of patients in the linezolid group were switched to oral medication at some point during their treatment. The mean number of days on intravenous linezolid was 7.7±4.8 days and on oral medication was 7.8±3 days. Of patients in the vancomycin group, 31% were able to switch to oral medication during their treatment. The mean number of days on intravenous vancomycin was 9.8±6.2 days, whereas the mean duration for oral medication was 8.8±4.1 days.

The cure rate for the ITT population was 95.9% (164/215) in the linezolid group and 93.5% (72/101) in the vancomycin group (P=.415; 95% CI, −3.9 to 8.7).[24] In the clinically evaluable population, 97.2% (140/151) were cured in the linezolid group and 95.6% (65/73) were cured in the vancomycin group (P=.534; 95% CI, −3.9 to 7.2).

Statistically significant differences for clinical cure based on selected pathogens were not noted for either treatment group.[24] However, investigators noted that among neonates (age 0 to 90 days), cure rates were higher in the linezolid group than in the vancomycin group.

Pathogen eradication rates were high at the follow-up visit in both treatment groups.[24] Microbiological success was observed in 79.7% of patients treated with linezolid and 82.4% treated with vancomycin in the modified ITT population (P=.685; 95% CI, −15.4 to 10.0). Among the microbiologically evaluable patients, success rates in the linezolid and vancomycin groups were 88% and 87%, respectively (P=.855; 95% CI, −10.7 to 12.9). Comparisons with a similar adult study found consistent results. High clinical and microbiological cure rates were achieved with linezolid and vancomycin in both adults and children with infections caused by resistant gram-positive pathogens. Higher cure and success rates were found among pediatric patients, which is noteworthy since both the adult and pediatric populations were severely ill.

The investigators determined that linezolid and vancomycin are equally effective for treating infections in children caused by possible or proven resistant gram-positive

pathogens.[24] The response was similar in all age groups, including neonates. Linezolid was also deemed to be as effective as vancomycin, both clinically and microbiologically, in patients infected with S aureus (including MRSA), coagulase-negative staphylococci (including MRSE), S pyogenes, and enterococci.

Summary of Findings From Pediatric Trials

The application for a pediatric indication for linezolid included not only the results from phase III trials but also data from several phase II trials on pediatric patients, and data on pediatric patients treated in the compassionate use program.[24] Phase I data indicated that the clearance of linezolid is faster in children than in adults; thus, the elimination half-life in these patients is shorter. Phase II trials suggested that children younger than 12 years should be given 10 mg/kg (maximum 600 mg/dose) of linezolid 3 times a day, and that those aged 12 years or older should be given 600 mg twice a day. Phase II trials demonstrated that linezolid was effective in all pediatric age groups and for all indications tested. Linezolid was as effective as vancomycin for treating complicated skin and skin structure infections, hospital-acquired pneumonia, community-acquired pneumonia, and VRE infections. Furthermore, linezolid could be used safely with concomitant aztreonam or aminoglycosides and could be switched safely and effectively from an intravenous to an oral formulation in patients as young as 91 days.

Compassionate Use

Linezolid was first made available for compassionate use in December 1997.[43] Although linezolid is not indicated for the treatment of endocarditis and osteomyelitis, the patients included in this program had infections that had failed to respond to currently available antibiotics, so it was deemed necessary to provide them with alternative therapy.

Patients who were older than 28 days and had a serious infection caused by a resistant gram-positive pathogen or who could not tolerate therapy with approved agents were eligible for the compassionate use program. Data were collected by the State University of New York at Buffalo Pharmacy Department on a total of 796 patients who experienced 828 episodes of infection and were presented by investigators in a number of different analyses.[44]

Early in the program, Birmingham et al[45] assessed the tolerability and efficacy of linezolid in 386 patients. The average age of the 369 adults was 55.4 years, while the average age of the 17 children was 9.4 years. Given the serious nature of these infections, the fact that 91% of the adult patients were hospitalized at the time of treatment was not surprising; additionally, 39% had been in the ICU. Bacteremia was the most common infection, occurring in 43.3% of patients, followed by SSTIs (20.4%), urinary tract infections (17.0%), gastrointestinal abscess and peritonitis (16.1%), lower respiratory tract infections (16.0%), endocarditis (5.8%), osteomyelitis (5.1%), and unspecified infections (4.0%). Vancomycin-resistant enterococci were identified in 72.8% of infections, and methicillin-resistant *Staphylococcus* species were the identified pathogen in 20.7%. The adult dosage was 600 mg of linezolid twice a day, administered orally or intravenously. However, children or adults weighing less than 40 kg received linezolid 10 mg/kg twice a day.

Clinical outcome was assessable in 185 patients; 78.9% were cured, but treatment failed in 5.9%.[45] In 15.2% of patients, the clinical outcome was indeterminate, most often because of a negative culture result before the initiation of linezolid therapy and death as the result of the underlying disease. In the 109 patients for whom microbiological outcome was available, 78.9% were cured, and 20.2% experienced treatment failure. Indeterminate outcomes occurred in 0.9% of patients. Adverse events occurred in 32.9% of patients and resulted in discontinuation of treatment in 9.3%. The most serious adverse event observed was thrombocytopenia.

A more recent analysis of the compassionate use program was performed by Birmingham et al[25] and published in 2003. This study examined data from 796 patients who had 828 episodes of infection and incorporated data from patients included in earlier reports. Consistent with earlier findings, the most common form of infection was bacteremia, occurring in 46% of infections. Line-related infections occurred in 31.1% of infections, and endocarditis was present in 10.6%. Other infections treated included intraabdominal infections (15.1%), complicated skin and skin structure infections (13.3%), and osteomyelitis (10.7%). Vancomycin-resistant enterococci were determined to be the cause of infection 66.4% of the time, while methicillin-resistant staphylococci caused 22.1%. Again, this is consistent with earlier findings by Birmingham et al.[45]

Clinical cure was achieved in 73.3% of evaluable patients, treatment failure occurred in 6.8%, and indeterminate outcomes occurred in 19.9%.[25] Microbiological cure was achieved in 83.6% of evaluable patients, failure occurred in 13.8%, and indeterminate outcomes occurred in 2.6%. Gastrointestinal disturbances were the most common adverse events reported, occurring in 9.8% of cases, whereas thrombocytopenia was observed in 7.4%. This incidence is at the high end of the range found with linezolid and compares with an average incidence of thrombocytopenia of 2.4% (range across studies: 0.3% to 10%) as determined from phase III trials.[42] Other adverse events reported in this study were decreased hemoglobin/hematocrit levels (4.1%) and cutaneous reactions (4.0%).[25]

Moise et al[44] analyzed a subset of 183 patients with 191 infections caused by S aureus, 92.7% of which were MRSA. Forty of these infections had failed to respond to previous therapy with vancomycin. In 11 infections, a concurrent infection with VRE or vancomycin-dependent enterococci precluded the use of vancomycin, whereas vancomycin intolerance, due to either allergy or prior adverse reaction, was the reason for inclusion in the compassionate use program for 112 persons. The inability to tolerate long-term intravenous treatment was the reason for inclusion in 28 persons.

The average age of patients was 57 years.[44] Because of the inclusion criteria for compassionate use, patients entering the program were debilitated and had multiple underlying medical problems. Despite this, the clinical cure rate was 83.9% and the microbiological cure rate was 76.9% in the evaluable population,[44] which is similar to findings from the 2 studies by Birmingham et al.[25,45] This demonstrates consistency between the results obtained in the total patient population and the subgroup of patients with S aureus infections.

The lowest clinical success rates were observed in patients with bone or joint infections; however, at least some of these patients may have had chronic osteomyelitis, a disease that necessitates surgical intervention.[44] The clinical success rates according to site of infection are presented in Table 6. Patients with indeterminate outcomes were considered treatment failures for the purpose of analysis. Although only 27.2% of patients had bone or joint infections and only 4.7% had infective endocarditis, the median duration of linezolid therapy was 28 days. Bacteremias and lower respiratory tract infections, which constituted 20.9% and 12.6% of the infections, respectively, had more typical course durations, with 16.5 days for bacteremia and 13 days for lower respiratory tract infections. Prolonged courses of treatment were used in many of the patients with skin and skin structure infections because a substantial proportion of these were actually deep wound infections and were complicated in some patients by severe peripheral vascular disease. Many of these patients did not respond to previous treatment, and the prolonged duration of their linezolid therapy was deemed necessary by their attending physicians.

Given the complicated nature of treating serious resistant infections, the 70% clinical success rate achieved with linezolid in patients in whom previous treatment with vancomycin had failed was encouraging.[44] Rates were even higher in patients who had been included in the program because they were intolerant to vancomycin (85.7%) or unable to endure intravenous access (93.8%). Adverse events may also somewhat reflect the difficulties involved in treating debilitated patients. The incidence of thrombo-

cytopenia was 10.5% in this patient cohort,[44] higher than the average of 2.4% observed with linezolid treatment in the combined clinical trials.[42] In most of these patients, assigning causation to the presence of thrombocytopenia was confounded by the presence of other potential causes. Additionally, some of these patients had serious underlying diseases that precluded accurate assessment.

Multidrug-resistant gram-positive infections were reviewed by Chien et al[46] in a small subset of patients from the compassionate use trial. Seventeen patients—15 with serious vancomycin-resistant *Enterococcus faecium* infections, 1 with a methicillin-resistant coagulase-negative staphylococcal infection, and another with an MRSA infection— were included in the analysis. All patients with VRE infections were debilitated and had multiple preexisting medical conditions. The majority (73.3%) had undergone a recent major surgical procedure, including 5 patients (33.3%) who had received an orthotopic liver transplant. Twelve (80%) patients were in an ICU when the infection was diagnosed.

Many of these patients had multiple sites of infection, with an average of 2.6 per patient.[46] Bacteremia was the most common form of VRE infection and occurred in 66.7% of patients; the second most common source of VRE iso-

Table 6. Clinical Success Rates for Linezolid Treatment Episodes According to Type of Infection From a Compassionate Use Study of *Staphylococcus aureus* Infection

Infection	Success Rate*	
	Clinically Evaluable	All Treated[†]
Bone or joint	18/26 (69.2%)	18/46 (39.1%)
Infective endocarditis	3/4 (75.0%)	3/5 (60.0%)
Lower respiratory tract	11/14 (78.6%)	11/19 (57.9%)
Bacteremia	18/21 (85.7%)	18/24 (75%)
Skin and skin structure	32/35 (91.4%)	32/44 (72.7%)
Upper respiratory tract	5/5	5/5
Central nervous system	2/2	2/2
Urinary tract	2/2	2/2
Intra-abdominal	2/2	2/3
Device-related	1/1	1/1

*Assessed at the test-of-cure (follow-up) visit.
[†]Includes clinically evaluable episodes and those for which the responses were categorized as indeterminate, but excludes nonevaluable episodes. The success rate was calculated by dividing the number of successful responses by the sum of the number of successful responses, the number of failures, and the number of episodes for which the responses were indeterminate.
Reprinted from Moise PA, Forrest A, Birmingham MC, Schentag JJ. The efficacy and safety of linezolid as treatment for *Staphylococcus aureus* infections in compassionate use patients who are intolerant of, or who have failed to respond to, vancomycin. *J Antimicrob Chemother.* 2002;50:1017-1026, by permission of Oxford University Press. Copyright © 2002 The British Society for Antimicrobial Chemotherapy. All rights reserved.

lates was urine, documented in 6 patients. Five of these 6 patients also had bacteremia; the sixth patient had VRE peritonitis. Five of the surgical patients developed wound infections involving VRE, 2 with concurrent VRE peritonitis and 2 with concurrent VRE bacteremia. Peritonitis due to VRE also developed in 4 of 5 orthotopic liver transplant recipients, and 3 of these patients had concurrent VRE bacteremia. In 4 of the liver transplant patients, intra-abdominal abscesses formed from which VRE could be isolated.

At the end of the intended treatment period, 66.7% of the VRE patients were alive; microbiological cure had been achieved in all 10.[46] Short-term follow-up revealed that 8 patients (53.3%) had survived and all were clinically cured, including one case of VRE endocarditis. Seven patients (46.6%) were alive at long-term follow-up and still showed no sign of VRE infection. Among patients who died, 5 (66.7%) died before completing the course of linezolid, and none of the deaths was attributed to VRE infection; clearance of the original VRE infection was demonstrated for all but one of the patients who died before long-term follow-up. During the course of treatment, 2 patients developed adverse reactions that were attributed to the study drug; 1 developed leukopenia and the other developed nausea. In neither case did this necessitate withdrawal from linezolid therapy. Both patients with staphylococcal infections were clinically and microbiologically cured after a 3-week course of linezolid and were alive at the long-term follow-up evaluation. However, it is important to emphasize that linezolid is not indicated in the treatment of peritonitis caused by VRE.

The successful cure rate observed in this cohort of patients must be considered noteworthy in light of the debilitated condition and multiple underlying medical problems in these patients.[46] In all cases, persistent infection was documented after conventional therapeutic options, including multiple wound debridements, abscess drainages, and prosthetic device removals, failed to result in a cure. Without effective antimicrobial therapy, all of these patients would have died.

Summary

On April 17, 2000, Pharmacia & Upjohn Company received FDA approval for the use of linezolid in the United States to treat nosocomial infections involving gram-positive organisms, including MRSA, multidrug-resistant S pneumoniae, and vancomycin-resistant E faecium. In 2002, following the submission of clinical trial data involving the pediatric population, Pharmacia received FDA approval for linezolid use in the United States in patients from birth through age 17 years. The results of phase II and III trials and the compassionate use program indicated that cure rates for infections caused by staphylococcal, streptococcal, and enterococcal organisms were comparable to those of vancomycin. High rates of cure were found in patients with resistant infections such as with MRSA, MRSE, methicillin-resistant Staphylococcus species, VRE, and penicillin-resistant S pneumoniae. Many of the patients enrolled in these trials were debilitated and had serious comorbid conditions, yet clinical and microbiological cure was achieved in the overwhelming majority of them. Adverse reactions generally ranged from mild to moderate, with the most common being diarrhea, headache, and nausea. Laboratory tests showed reversible hematologic effects after prolonged use. No significant monoamine oxidase inhibitory effects were observed.

References

1. Shinabarger DL, Marotti KR, Murray RW, et al. Mechanism of action of oxazolidinones: effects of linezolid and eperezolid on translation reactions. Antimicrob Agents Chemother. 1997;41:2132-2136.
2. Lin AH, Murray RW, Vidmar TJ, Marotti KR. The oxazolidinone eperezolid binds to the 50S ribosomal subunit and competes with binding of chloramphenicol and lincomycin. Antimicrob Agents Chemother. 1997;41:2127-2131.
3. Swaney SM, Aoki H, Ganoza MC, Shinabarger DL. The oxazolidinone linezolid inhibits initiation of protein synthesis in bacteria. Antimicrob Agents Chemother. 1998;42:3251-3255.
4. Kloss P, Xiong L, Shinabarger DL, Mankin AS. Resistance mutations in 23 S rRNA identify the site of action of the protein synthesis inhibitor linezolid in the ribosomal peptidyl transferase center. J Mol Biol. 1999;294:93-101.
5. Xiong L, Kloss P, Douthwaite S, et al. Oxazolidinone resistance mutations in 23S rRNA of Escherichia coli reveal the central region of domain V as the primary site of drug action. J Bacteriol. 2000;182: 5325-5331.
6. Aoki H, Ke L, Poppe SM, et al. Oxazolidinone antibiotics target the P site on Escherichia coli ribosomes. Antimicrob Agents Chemother. 2002;46:1080-1085.
7. Zurenko GE, Yagi BH, Schaadt RD, et al. In vitro activities of U-100592 and U-100766, novel oxazolidinone antibacterial agents. Antimicrob Agents Chemother. 1996;40:839-845.
8. Kaatz GW, Seo SM. In vitro activities of oxazolidinone compounds U100592 and U100766 against Staphylococcus aureus and Staphylococcus epidermidis. Antimicrob Agents Chemother. 1996;40:799-801.
9. Eliopoulos GM, Wennersten CB, Gold HS, Moellering RC Jr. In vitro activities of new oxazolidinone antimicrobial agents against enterococci. Antimicrob Agents Chemother. 1996;40:1745-1747.
10. Jones RN, Johnson DM, Erwin ME. In vitro antimicrobial activities and spectra of U-100592 and U-100766, two novel fluorinated oxazolidinones. Antimicrob Agents Chemother. 1996;40:720-726.

11. Mason EO Jr, Lamberth LB, Kaplan SL. In vitro activities of oxazolidinones U-100592 and U-100766 against penicillin-resistant and cephalosporin-resistant strains of *Streptococcus pneumoniae*. *Antimicrob Agents Chemother*. 1996;40:1039-1040.

12. Mulazimoglu L, Drenning SD, Yu VL. In vitro activities of two novel oxazolidinones (U100592 and U100766), a new fluoroquinolone (trovafloxacin), and dalfopristin-quinupristin against *Staphylococcus aureus* and *Staphylococcus epidermidis*. *Antimicrob Agents Chemother*. 1996;40:2428-2430.

13. Gentry-Nielsen MJ, Olsen KM, Preheim LC. Pharmacodynamic activity and efficacy of linezolid in a rat model of pneumococcal pneumonia. *Antimicrob Agents Chemother*. 2002;46:1345-1351.

14. Schulin T, Thauvin-Eliopoulos C, Moellering RC Jr, Eliopoulos GM. Activities of the oxazolidinones linezolid and eperezolid in experimental intra-abdominal abscess due to *Enterococcus faecalis* or vancomycin-resistant *Enterococcus faecium*. *Antimicrob Agents Chemother*. 1999;43:2873-2876.

15. Ford CW, Hamel JC, Wilson DM, et al. In vivo activities of U-100592 and U-100766, novel oxazolidinone antimicrobial agents, against experimental bacterial infections. *Antimicrob Agents Chemother*. 1996;40:1508-1513.

16. Spangler SK, Jacobs MR, Appelbaum PC. Activites of RPR 106972 (a new oral streptogramin), cefditoren (a new oral cephalosporin), two new oxazolidinones (U-100592 and U-100766), and other oral and parenteral agents against 203 penicillin-susceptible and -resistant pneumococci. *Antimicrob Agents Chemother*. 1996;40:481-484.

17. Rybak MJ, Cappelletty DM, Moldovan T, Aeschlimann JR, Kaatz GW. Comparative in vitro activities and postantibiotic effects of the oxazolidinone compounds eperezolid (PNU-100592) and linezolid (PNU-100766) versus vancomycin against *Staphylococcus aureus*, coagulase-negative staphylococci, *Enterococcus faecalis*, and *Enterococcus faecium*. *Antimicrob Agents Chemother*. 1998;42:721-724.

18. Wise R, Andrews JM, Boswell FJ, Ashby JP. The in-vitro activity of linezolid (U-100766) and tentative breakpoints. *J Antimicrob Chemother*. 1998;42:721-728.

19. Noskin GA, Siddiqui F, Stosor V, Hacek D, Peterson LR. In vitro activities of linezolid against important gram-positive bacterial pathogens including vancomycin-resistant enterococci. *Antimicrob Agents Chemother*. 1999;43:2059-2062.

20. Jones ME, Visser MR, Klootwijk M, Heisig P, Verhoef J, Schmitz FJ. Comparative activities of clinafloxacin, grepafloxacin, levofloxacin, moxifloxacin, ofloxacin, sparfloxacin, and trovafloxacin and nonquinolones linezolid [sic], quinupristin-dalfopristin, gentamicin, and vancomycin against clinical isolates of ciprofloxacin-resistant and -susceptible *Staphylococcus aureus* strains. *Antimicrob Agents Chemother*. 1999;43:421-423.

21. Schaadt RD, Batts DH, Daley-Yates PT, Pawsey SD, Stalker DJ, Zurenko GE. Serum inhibitory titers and serum bactericidal titers for human subjects receiving multiple doses of the antibacterial oxazolidinones eperezolid and linezolid. *Diagn Microbiol Infect Dis*. 1997;28:201-204.

22. Cammarata SK, Hafkin B, Todd WM, Batts DH. Efficacy of linezolid in community-acquired S pneumoniae pneumonia [abstract]. *J Respir Crit Care Med*. 1999;159(suppl pt 2[3]):A844.

23. Cammarata SK, Hafkin B, Demke D, Eckert SM, Batts DH. Efficacy of linezolid in skin and soft tissue infections [abstract]. *Clin Microbiol Infect*. 1999;5(suppl 3):133.

24. Data on file. Pfizer Inc. New York, NY.

25. Birmingham MC, Rayner CR, Meagher AK, Flavin SM, Batts DH, Schentag JJ. Linezolid for the treatment of multidrug-resistant, gram-positive infections: experience from a compassionate-use program. *Clin Infect Dis*. 2003;36:159-168.

26. Centers for Disease Control and Prevention. Summary of notifiable diseases, United States, 1998. *MMWR Morb Mortal Wkly Rep*. 1999;47:ii-92.

27. Slatter JG, Stalker DJ, Feenstra KL, et al. Pharmacokinetics, metabolism, and excretion of linezolid following an oral dose of [^{14}C]linezolid to healthy human subjects. *Drug Metab Dispos*. 2001;29:1136-1145.

28. Centers for Disease Control and Prevention. VISA/VRSA fact sheet. Available at: http://www.cdc.gov/ncidod/hip/ARESIST/visa.htm. Accessed December 23, 2003.

29. National Nosocomial Infections Surveillance System. National Nosocomial Infections Surveillance (NNIS) System report, data summary from January 1992-June 2001, issued August 2001. *Am J Infect Control*. 2001;29:404-421.

30. Centers for Disease Control and Prevention. Staphylococcus aureus resistant to vancomycin—United States, 2002. *MMWR Morb Mortal Wkly Rep*. 2002;51:565-567.

31. Centers for Disease Control and Prevention. Public health dispatch: outbreaks of community-associated methicillin-resistant *Staphylococcus aureus* skin infections—Los Angeles County, California, 2002—2003. *MMWR Morb Mortal Wkly Rep*. 2003;52:88.

32. Gonzalez C, Rubio M, Romeo-Vivas J, Gonzalez M, Picazo JJ. Bacteremic pneumonia due to *Staphylococcus aureus*: a comparison of disease caused by methicillin-resistant and methicillin-susceptible organisms. *Clin Infect Dis*. 1999;29:1171-1177.

33. American Thoracic Society. Hospital-acquired pneumonia in adults: diagnosis, assessment of severity, initial antimicrobial therapy, and preventive strategies. A consensus statement, American Thoracic Society, November 1995. *Am J Respir Crit Care Med*. 1996;153:1711-1725.

34. Rubinstein E, Cammarata S, Oliphant T, Wunderink R, Linezolid Nosocomial Pneumonia Study Group. Linezolid (PNU-100766) versus vancomycin in the treatment of hospitalized patients with nosocomial pneumonia: a randomized, double-blind, multicenter study. *Clin Infect Dis*. 2001;32:402-412.

35. Felmingham D, Gruneberg RN. The Alexander Project 1996-1997: latest susceptibility data from this international study of bacterial pathogens from community-acquired lower respiratory tract infections. *J Antimicrob Chemother*. 2000;45:191-203.

36. Nichols RL. Optimal treatment of complicated skin and skin structure infections. *J Antimicrob Chemother*. 1999;44(suppl A):19-23.

37. Stevens DL, Smith LG, Bruss JB, et al, for the Linezolid Skin and Soft Tissue Infections Study Group. Randomized comparison of linezolid (PNU-100766) versus oxacillin-dicloxacillin for treatment of complicated skin and soft tissue infections. *Antimicrob Agents Chemother*. 2000;44:3408-3413.

38. Lovering AM, Zhang J, Bannister GC, et al. Penetration of linezolid into bone, fat, muscle and haematoma of patients undergoing routine hip replacement. *J Antimicrob Chemother*. 2002;50:73-77.

39. Gemmell CG, Ford CW. Expression of virulence factors by gram-positive cocci exposed to sub-MIC levels of linezolid [abstract]. Paper presented at: 39th Interscience Conference on Antimicrobial Agents and Chemotherapy; September 26-29, 1999; San Francisco, Calif. Abstract 1537.

40. Li Z, Willke RJ, Pinto LA, et al. Comparison of length of hospital stay for patients with known or suspected methicillin-resistant *Staphylococcus* species infections treated with linezolid or vancomycin: a randomized, multicenter trial. *Pharmacotherapy*. 2001;21:263-274.

41. Chaix C, Durand-Zaleski I, Alberti C, Brun-Buisson C. Control of endemic methicillin-resistant *Staphylococcus aureus*: a cost-benefit analysis in an intensive care unit. *JAMA*. 1999;282:1745-1751.

42. Zyvox [package insert]. Kalamazoo, Mich: Pharmacia & Upjohn Company; 2003.

43. Fung HF, Kirschenbaum HL, Ojofeitimi BO. Linezolid: an oxazolidinone antimicrobial agent. *Clin Ther*. 2001;23:356-391.

44. Moise PA, Forrest A, Birmingham MC, Schentag JJ. The efficacy and safety of linezolid as treatment for *Staphylococcus aureus* infections in compassionate use patients who are intolerant of, or who have failed to respond to, vancomycin. *J Antimicrob Chemother*. 2002;50:1017-1026.

45. Birmingham MC, Zimmer GS, Hafkin B, et al. Outcomes with linezolid from an ongoing compassionate use trial of patients with significant resistant gram-positive infections. Paper presented at: 39th Interscience Conference on Antimicrobial Agents and Chemotherapy; September 26-29, 1999; San Francisco, Calif. Abstract 1098.

46. Chien JW, Kucia ML, Salata RA. Use of linezolid, an oxazolidinone, in the treatment of multidrug-resistant gram-positive bacterial infections. *Clin Infect Dis.* 2000;30:146-151.

CHAPTER FIVE CME QUESTIONS

1. What is the tentative breakpoint for linezolid set by Wise et al in 1998?
   a. 1 μg/mL
   b. 1.5 μg/mL
   c. 2 μg/mL
   d. 0.5 μg/mL

2. Which of the following statements regarding the metabolism of linezolid in women is true and might account for the lack of a significant dose response in this group?
   a. With a higher volume of distribution than males and a higher clearance of the compound, females appear to have a 30% lower maximal clearance(C_{max}) than males.
   b. With a lower volume of distribution than males and a lower clearance of the compound, females appear to have a 30% higher C_{max} than males.
   c. No metabolic differences have been noted between the sexes.

3. True or False: In a phase III clinical trial, linezolid and vancomycin proved to be equally effective in treating infections caused by methicillin-resistant *Staphylococcus aureus* and methicillin-resistant *Staphylococcus epidermidis*, including pneumonia, skin and soft tissue infections, urinary tract infections, other infections, and bacteremia of unknown origin.

4. What were the most common adverse reactions observed in phase III clinical trials of linezolid?
   a. Dyspepsia and tongue discoloration
   b. Diarrhea, nausea, and headache
   c. Pruritus and headache
   d. Tongue discoloration and pruritus

5. What year did the FDA approve linezolid for use in nosocomial infections involving gram-positive organisms, including methicillin-resistant *Staphylococcus aureus*, multidrug-resistant *Streptococcus pneumoniae*, and vancomycin-resistant *Enterococcus faecium*?
   a. 1999
   b. 2000
   c. 2001
   d. 2002

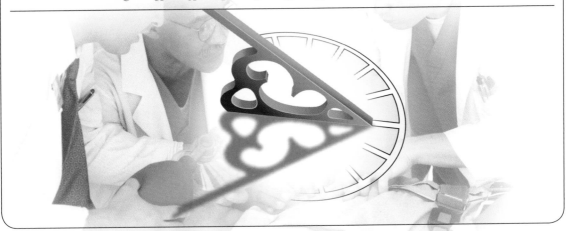

CREATION OF A NOVEL CLASS:

THE USE OF LINEZOLID
IN CRITICAL CARE MEDICINE

EDITOR

Marin H. Kollef, MD

LEARNING OBJECTIVES

After completion of this chapter, readers should be able to:

1. Understand the key issues facing critical care physicians, particularly, the rise of resistant pathogens in recent years.

2. Describe the pathogens most often implicated in pneumonia and bacteremia.

3. Identify key differences between community-, hospital-, and ventilator-associated pneumonia.

4. Discuss the importance of methicillin-resistant *Staphylococcus aureus* infections in critical care patients and the role linezolid may play in combating these infections.

THE OXAZOLIDINONE ANTIBIOTICS

Clinicians specializing in critical care medicine treat seriously ill patients with severe community-acquired pneumonia (CAP), acute renal failure, ischemic or hemorrhagic stroke, myocardial infarction, organ transplantation, traumatic wounds, and burns. Many of these patients are at increased risk of infection because of their underlying disease or injury; others are at increased risk because of medical interventions such as intravenous lines, central venous catheters, urinary catheters, and mechanical ventilation. Furthermore, hospitals in general, and intensive care units in particular, are major sources of resistant pathogens, such as vancomycin-resistant *Enterococcus faecium* and *Enterococcus faecalis*, methicillin-resistant *Staphylococcus aureus* (MRSA) and *Staphylococcus epidermidis*, and penicillin-resistant *Streptococcus pneumoniae*.[1,2] Some bacterial strains have developed resistance to multiple agents. Critically ill patients are at risk for nosocomial pneumonia, ventilator-associated pneumonia (VAP), bacteremia and sepsis, and serious urinary tract infections.

Treating infections in seriously ill patients presents a considerable clinical challenge. The continuing rise in resistant pathogens over the last decades has left clinicians with few therapeutic options, particularly for nosocomial infections. Older agents, such as the fluoroquinolones and vancomycin, remain effective in most, but not all, infections.[3] Moreover, evidence that early adequate treatment is critical to good clinical outcomes complicates this matter.[4-6] Newer agents, such as quinupristin-dalfopristin and linezolid, present hope for the treatment of infections that have proven resistant to other antibiotics.

Against the background of rising resistance, the approval of these newer agents to treat infections common to critical care medicine is welcome. Linezolid is approved by the US Food and Drug Administration for the treatment of vancomycin-resistant *E faecium* infections, including cases with concurrent bacteremia; nosocomial pneumonia caused by methicillin-susceptible and -resistant strains of *Staphylococcus aureus*, or penicillin-susceptible strains of *S pneumoniae*; CAP caused by *S pneumoniae* (penicillin-susceptible strains only), including cases with concurrent bacteremia, or *S aureus* (methicillin-susceptible strains only); uncomplicated skin and skin structure infections caused by *S aureus* (methicillin-susceptible strains only) or *Streptococcus pyogenes*; and complicated skin and skin structure infections caused by *S aureus* (methicillin-

susceptible and methicillin-resistant strains), *S pyogenes*, or *Streptococcus agalactiae*.[7] Quinupristin-dalfopristin is approved for treatment of patients with serious or life-threatening infections associated with bacteremia caused by vancomycin-resistant *E faecium* and for complicated skin and skin structure infections caused by methicillin-susceptible *S aureus* or *S pyogenes*.[8]

Pneumonia

Pneumonia is a leading cause of morbidity and mortality in the United States and is responsible for more than 63,000 deaths and 1.3 million hospital discharges a year. This disease is a major concern in critical care medicine.[9] The etiology and clinical outcomes of pneumonia vary according to the type—CAP, VAP, or hospital-acquired pneumonia (HAP)—as well as a number of host factors, including underlying comorbidities, alcoholism, or nursing home residency.[10] The 2001 American Thoracic Society[10] (ATS) guidelines list linezolid, the ketolides, the newer antipneumococcal fluoroquinolones (gatifloxacin, gemifloxacin, levofloxacin, moxifloxacin, trovafloxacin, and sparfloxacin), and vancomycin as agents active against drug-resistant *S pneumoniae*. Linezolid also has shown good activity against both methicillin-resistant and methicillin-susceptible staphylococcal, streptococcal, and enterococcal pathogens, including vancomycin-resistant enterococci (VRE) in patients with pneumonia.[11,12] Moreover, evidence from an intrapulmonary pharmacokinetics study in human volunteers indicates that penetration of the plasma and epithelial lining fluid (ELF) by linezolid is excellent, with the percentage of time the drug remains above the minimal inhibitory concentration (MIC) of 100% for the 12-hour dosing interval for enterococci and *S pneumoniae* organisms.[13] Mean concentrations of the agent in alveolar cells did not reach levels above the minimum concentration required to inhibit 90% of organisms (MIC_{90}) for *S aureus* and remained above the MIC_{90} for *Enterococcus* species for less than half the dosing interval and above the MIC_{90} for 12 hours for *S pneumoniae*.[13] However, the very high levels achieved in the ELF (range from 64.3±33.1 µg/mL at 4 hours to 0.7±0.8 µg/mL at 48 hours) suggested that linezolid was likely to be an effective agent in the treatment of pulmonary infections. In addition, in rat and mice models, linezolid had the highest time for the area under the time-concentration curve (AUC) compared with the MIC for MRSA[14] and for pneumococcal pneumonia.[15]

In contrast, vancomycin does not appear to penetrate lung tissue as well as linezolid. A study by Cruciani et al[16] evaluated 30 patients following a 1-hour intravenous infusion of vancomycin 1 g. It was found that mean concentrations in lung tissue were 9.6 mg/kg at hour 1, 5.7 mg/kg at hour 2, and 4.2 mg/kg at 3 to 4 hours after administration. The mean concentrations had fallen to 2.4 mg/kg and 2.8 mg/kg by hours 6 and 12, respectively. At the 6-hour interval, one of 6 patients did not have detectable levels of vancomycin in lung tissue, and 3 of 7 at hour 12 did not. The investigators concluded that a 1-hour infusion did not achieve sustained concentrations of vancomycin above the MIC for susceptible staphylococci over a 12-hour dosing interval and felt that continuous infusion should be considered if this agent was to be used to treat pulmonary infections. In another study, Lamer et al[17] found that mean vancomycin levels in ELF ranged from 0.4 µg/mL to 8.1 µg/mL, with a mean of 4.5±2.3 µg/mL, whereas Conte et al[13] found that mean levels of linezolid ranged from 64.3±33.1 µg/mL at 4 hours after administration to 7.6±6.0 µg/mL at 24 hours after administration.

Community-Acquired Pneumonia

The most likely pathogen involved in CAP, S pneumoniae, is becoming more difficult to treat with such first-line agents as the β-lactams and the macrolides.[10,18] Drug-resistant strains are more likely to occur in patients who have undergone recent antimicrobial therapy.[10] In severe CAP, the frequency of S aureus as a causative pathogen ranges from 1% to 22%. Other factors, such as underlying structural lung disease (eg, cystic fibrosis or bronchiectasis), intravenous drug use, and nursing home residency, increase the likelihood of S aureus involvement in pneumonia. Structural lung disease and prior antibiotic therapy also have been associated with pneumonia caused by Pseudomonas aeruginosa. Severe CAP requires admission to the ICU, but its definition has been a point of disagreement since the ATS first published guidelines.[10] In the 2001 guidelines, the ATS suggested that the presence of 1 of 2 major criteria (ie, need for mechanical ventilation, septic shock), or 2 of 3 minor criteria (ie, systolic blood pressure ≤90 mm Hg, multilobar disease, PAO_2/FIO_2 ratio <250) indicates a diagnosis of severe CAP, and ICU admission is advisable.

One of the phase III linezolid trials was conducted in 747 adults hospitalized with demonstrated or presump-

tive S pneumoniae CAP at 110 sites in North America, Latin America, Europe, and Asia.[12] Patients were included in the study if they were older than 13 years, expected to survive at least 60 days, and had 2 or more of the following symptoms: cough, purulent sputum, rales, signs of consolidation, dyspnea, tachypnea, and hypoxemia, and at least 1 of the following: fever; white blood cell count greater than 10,000/mL or less than 4500/mL, or greater than 15% left shift; and chest radiograph consistent with pneumonia.[12] Among the exclusion criteria were serious comorbid lung diseases, such as tuberculosis, cystic fibrosis, or malignancy, or recent antibiotic therapy of greater than 24 hours unless treatment was failing or the organism was known to be resistant. This comparator-controlled trial randomized 381 patients to receive linezolid (600 mg IV BID) followed by 7 to 14 days of oral linezolid therapy, and 366 patients to ceftriaxone (1 g IV BID) followed by a switch to oral cefpodoxime proxetil (200 mg BID). The transition to oral medication was made at the discretion of the investigator if the patient appeared to respond after receiving at least one intravenous dose. Patients in the linezolid group received concomitant aztreonam (1 g TID) if a polymicrobial infection with a gram-negative pathogen was suspected or likely.[12,19] The mean duration of therapy in all patients in the linezolid group was 10.9±4.1 days, including a mean of 4.6±2.5 days with the intravenous formulation and 8.0±3.0 days with oral linezolid.[12] The mean duration among clinically evaluable patients in the ceftriaxone-cefpodoxime group was 10.8±4.1 days, including 5.0±2.8 days with intravenous ceftriaxone and 7.9±3.0 days with oral cefpodoxime. In the intent-to-treat (ITT) population, the clinical cure rate was 83% (268/323) in the linezolid group and 76.4% (240/314) in the ceftriaxone-cefpodoxime group (P=.040; 95% confidence interval [CI], 0.3-12.8).[19] The microbiologically evaluable S pneumoniae CAP population demonstrated cure rates of 86.6% (71/82) in the linezolid group and 81.2% (69/85) in the ceftriaxone cefpodoxime group were found (P=.343; 95% CI, −5.7 to 16.5).

An analysis of cure rates by pathogen indicated that in evaluable S pneumoniae infections, 88.7% (63/71) in the linezolid group and 89.9% (62/69) in the ceftriaxone-cefpodoxime group were eradicated (P=.830; 95% CI, −11.4 to 9.1). Cure rates were higher with linezolid when S aureus was implicated.[12] S aureus was eradicated in 90.0% (18/20) of evaluable patients with CAP caused by S aureus in the linezolid group, compared with 76.5% (13/17) in the ceftriaxone-cefpodoxime group (P=.266; 95% CI, −10.5 to 37.6).[19] MRSA was isolated in only one patient at baseline. After a course of linezolid therapy, this patient had a negative culture. No treatment failures were attributed to the development of resistance to either linezolid or ceftriaxone-cefpodoxime. Patients treated with linezolid in whom *Moraxella catarrhalis* or *Haemophilus influenzae* were isolated at baseline received concomitant aztreonam, and nearly 50% of patients in the linezolid arm were taking aztreonam to provide coverage for gram-negative bacteria during the course of the trial. However, the lack of coverage for atypical pathogens in the ceftriaxone-cefpodoxime arm could be considered a drawback of this study. The authors stated that CAP due to atypical bacteria has a relatively mild course, making routine coverage for these pathogens controversial; however, the ATS guidelines appear to disagree with this statement.[20]

The overall study showed that the 2 regimens were comparable for the treatment of uncomplicated CAP caused by *S pneumoniae* in hospitalized patients.[12,19] However, in pneumonia caused by *S aureus* or complicated by bacteremia, higher cure rates were achieved with the administration of linezolid.[19]

Bacteremia is a serious complication of CAP. Fifty-one hospitalized patients who had CAP with bacteremia were investigated in a subanalysis of this study.[19] Twenty-nine patients were randomized to the linezolid intravenous/oral regimen and 22 to the ceftriaxone intravenous/cefpodoxime oral regimen. In patients with bacteremia caused by *S pneumoniae*, the clinical cure rate was 93% in the linezolid cohort versus 68% for those given the ceftriaxone intravenous/cefpodoxime oral regimen (P=.021). The investigators concluded that in patients with pneumonia complicated by bacteremia, linezolid demonstrated superior efficacy.

Hospital-Acquired Pneumonia

Nosocomial pneumonia is defined as pneumonia that develops 48 hours or more after hospital admission.[21] Although both CAP and HAP are serious, different spectra of pathogens are often involved in these 2 types of pneumonia. Community-acquired pneumonia is often caused by *S pneumoniae* and *H influenzae*,[10,18] whereas *S aureus* (MRSA), *P aeruginosa*, and *Acinetobacter* species are more likely to be implicated in HAP.[21-23] Nosocomial pathogens

also are more likely to be resistant, and patients in the ICU are therefore at higher risk for infection with drug-resistant bacteria.[23]

Until recently, vancomycin was the standard and the only option available for the treatment of MRSA infection, but limited data from large comparator-controlled trials were available to substantiate its efficacy over other antimicrobials. With the completion of the large phase III, double-blind, comparator-controlled trial on nosocomial pneumonia by Rubinstein et al[11] and a continuation of that trial by Wunderink et al,[24] enough data were available on the subset of patients with pneumonia caused by MRSA to support an analysis. The results of the overall trial showed equivalence for vancomycin and linezolid in the treatment of nosocomial pneumonia, but a survival difference favoring linezolid was noted when patients were stratified by acute physiology and chronic health evaluation (APACHE II) scores.[24,25]

A subgroup analysis of 2 double-blind comparator studies of the treatment of nosocomial pneumonia caused by MRSA was recently completed.[24] Although the 2 larger studies did not show any statistically significant differences between linezolid and the comparator, the subanalysis did. The larger trial, which was conducted with 1019 patients with suspected gram-positive nosocomial pneumonia, included 339 patients with documented pneumonia caused by *S aureus*. Documented MRSA organisms were found in 160 of these patients. Of this MRSA subset, 75 patients were randomized to receive linezolid (600 mg BID) and 85 were treated with vancomycin (1 g BID). Both groups were treated with concomitant aztreonam to provide coverage for gram-negative pathogens.

Kaplan-Meier survival rates from the ITT population for the overall trial were 81% (424/524) for linezolid and 78% (385/495) for vancomycin (P=.21).[24] In the subset of patients with nosocomial pneumonia caused by *S aureus*, the survival rates were 78% (131/168) for linezolid versus 71% (121/171) for vancomycin (P=.13). Additionally, in the MRSA subset, the survival rate for those treated with linezolid was 80% (60/75) versus 64% (54/85) for those treated with vancomycin (P=.03). Of the 44 patients (13%) with nosocomial pneumonia caused by *S aureus* who also had bacteremia, 82% (18/22) of those treated with linezolid survived, whereas 73% (16/22) treated with vancomycin survived (P=.47). Of patients with bacteremia caused by MRSA, 88% (7/8) and 64% (9/14) of those treated with linezolid and vancomycin, respectively, survived (P=.24). Clinical cure rates were nearly identical for the overall trial—53% for linezolid and 52% for vancomycin.[24] But when the S aureus subset was analyzed, important differences were observed. The clinical cure rates were 52% (70/136) for linezolid therapy compared with 43% (59/136) for vancomycin (P=.18) for all patients with S aureus. In the MRSA population, the figures were 59% (36/61) versus 36% (22/62) (P<.01).

This analysis demonstrated a statistically significant survival advantage and clinical cure rate in patients with nosocomial pneumonia caused by MRSA who were treated with linezolid, and it is the first trial to demonstrate the survival advantage of one antibiotic over another in the treatment of this population.[24] In another randomized, comparator-controlled clinical trial, quinupristin-dalfopristin and vancomycin had statistically equivalent cure rates across all subgroups of patients, including those with pneumonia caused by MRSA, but no statistically significant differences were found.[26] The investigators suggested that poor penetration of vancomycin into the lungs, as seen in pharmacokinetic studies,[16,17] may have had an effect on clinical cure and survival.[24] The 2 previously mentioned studies on the pulmonary tissue penetration of vancomycin and linezolid corroborate that view. Although Lamer et al[17] reported that the mean vancomycin level in ELF was 4.5±2.3 μg/mL over the entire dosing period, the study by Conte et al[13] showed the mean concentration of linezolid in ELF was 64.3±33.1 μg/mL at 4 hours after administration, 31.4±33.0 μg/mL at 8 hours after administration, 24.3±13.3 μg/mL at 12 hours after administration, 7.6±6.0 μg/mL at 24 hours after administration, and 0.7±0.8 μg/mL 48 hours after administration. Thus, linezolid concentrations in lung ELF fell to the vancomycin mean concentration 24 hours after the last dose was administered. The collective results of these pharmacokinetic studies indicate that, although linezolid concentrations exceed the MIC breakpoints for S aureus (4 μg/mL) throughout the 12-hour dosing interval, vancomycin does not.

Although it is acknowledged that vancomycin is not optimal therapy for methicillin-susceptible S aureus (MSSA) infections, the results of a prospective study by Gonzalez et al[27] of bacteremic pneumonia caused by S aureus provide some interesting insight. This study compared the outcomes of 32 cases of MRSA infection to those of 54 cases of MSSA infection. Antibiotic therapy was determined by the treating clinician. Infection with MRSA was significantly associated with prior use of antibiotics, underlying lung or vascular disease, prior infection, and the presence of a urinary or central venous catheter. Mortality was high in both groups of patients. Of the 32 patients with pneumonia caused by MRSA, 56% died as a result of the infection, whereas 41% with MSSA infections died.

Among evaluable patients, vancomycin treatment was associated with a 50% mortality rate in the MRSA group and a 47% rate in the MSSA group.[27] Because the patients in the MRSA group were primarily treated with vancomycin (20/22), no comparison could be made. But among patients with MSSA infections, mortality was significantly higher for those treated with vancomycin than for those treated with cloxacillin (47% versus 0%; P<.01), as shown in Figure 1.

Studies suggest that the efficacy of initial antibiotic therapy has an effect on survival rates. Inadequate antibiotic therapy has been associated with a hospital mortality rate that is approximately 50% higher than the rates associated with adequate initial treatment.[28] Thus, Wunderink

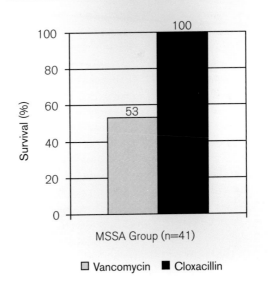

Figure 1. Survival rates among patients with bacteremic pneumonia caused by methicillin-susceptible *Staphylococcus aureus* (MSSA).[27] *P*<.01.

et al[24] stated in their recently published study that "the results of this retrospective analysis suggest that initial empiric therapy with linezolid should be considered in patients with suspected nosocomial pneumonia who are at risk for infection due to MRSA." However, empiric use of linezolid remains controversial, with others recommending more conservative use of the newer antibiotics.[29,30]

Ventilator-Associated Pneumonia

Occurring in 15% to 25% of mechanically-ventilated patients,[22,31] VAP has a mortality rate of 46%, significantly higher than the mortality rate observed in mechanically-ventilated patients who do not develop VAP (32%; $P=.004$).[31] Thus, VAP is a serious and all too common complication in critically ill patients in the ICU. Management of this illness is complicated by the diverse number of pathogens involved in its etiology. A 1999 study by Heyland et al[22] characterized the etiology of VAP. As indicated in the table, although gram-negative bacilli were isolated from 71% of patients, the most commonly isolated pathogen was S aureus, found in 37% of patients. Of the S aureus strains isolated, 6% were methicillin resistant. The next 2 most common pathogens were Haemophilus and Pseudomonas species (26% and 22%, respectively).

The prevalence of MRSA in VAP strongly suggests a role for linezolid in the treatment of this disease. The importance of prescribing the appropriate initial antibiotic therapy to patients with serious bacterial infections such as VAP is generally accepted.[32] A recent study by Kollef et al[32] on predictors of outcome in patients with VAP caused by gram-positive organisms showed a correlation between linezolid therapy and survival. This retrospective analysis of data from 2 large, randomized, double-blind studies examined data from 544 patients with VAP. Patients were randomized to treatment with linezolid 600 mg twice a day or vancomycin 1 g twice a day for 7 to 21 days. Aztreonam was given concomitantly to cover for gram-negative pathogens, such as P aeruginosa. Survival rates were higher in patients receiving linezolid (81%) than in those receiving vancomycin (77%) for all patients with VAP ($P=.342$). In those with S aureus infections, the survival rates were 81% for linezolid-treated patients and 75% for vancomycin-treated patients ($P=.291$).[32] In those with MRSA isolates, the survival rates were 84% for linezolid treatment and 70% for vancomycin treatment

($P=.131$). These differences were not statistically significant. The clinical cure rates for this study are presented in Figure 2.

Table 1. Organisms Associated With Ventilator-Associated Pneumonia in Study Patients*

Organism	No. of Patients (%)
Gram-negative bacilli	
Escherichia coli	17 (9.8)
Klebsiella	15 (8.7)
Enterobacter/Citrobacter	21 (12.1)
Serratia	5 (2.9)
Proteus/Providencia	9 (5.2)
Acinetobacter	6 (3.5)
Pseudomonas	38 (22.0)
Haemophilus	45 (26.0)
Other gram-negative bacilli	18 (10.4)
All gram-negative bacilli	123 (71.1)
Gram-positive cocci	
Streptococcus pneumoniae	14 (8.1)
Staphylococcus aureus†	64 (37.0)
Other gram-positive cocci	33 (19.1)
All gram-positive cocci	91 (52.6)
Gram-positive bacilli	5 (2.9)
Gram-negative cocci	13 (7.5)
Anaerobes	1 (0.6)
Candida/yeast	26 (15.0)
Mixed oropharyngeal	9 (5.2)
Other	12 (6.9)
No growth	5 (2.9)

*Organisms shown are those isolated from endotracheal aspirates, protected brush, or bronchoalveolar lavage from matched patients with adjudicated ventilator-associated pneumonia (n=173). The total number of organisms is more than the number of patients because several patients had more than one isolate.
† Four cases of S aureus were methicillin resistant.

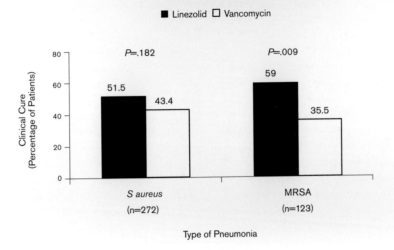

Figure 2. Clinical cure rates for linezolid and vancomycin therapy in patients with gram-positive, nosocomial pneumonia. Data from patients with indeterminate or missing clinical outcomes were excluded. MRSA = methicillin-resistant *Staphylococcus aureus* ventilator-associated pneumonia. Reprinted with permission from Wunderink RG, Rello J, Cammarata SK, Croos-Dabrera RV, Kollef MH. Linezolid vs vancomycin: analysis of two double-blind studies of patients with methicillin-resistant *Staphylococcus aureus* nosocomial pneumonia. *Chest.* 2003;124:1789-1797.

Nonetheless, logistic regression analysis identified 6 significant independent predictors of survival for all VAP-patients as follows[32] :

1. Linezolid therapy
2. APACHE II score ≤20
3. Single-lobe pneumonia
4. Age 65 years or less
5. Serum creatinine within 2 times the upper limit of normal
6. Absence of cardiac comorbidity

In patients with identified MRSA isolates, 2 additional significant predictors were observed: presence of pleural effusion and absence of bacteremia.

The investigators concluded by suggesting that patients with VAP caused by gram-positive organisms, particularly those at risk for developing MRSA infections, would benefit from therapy with linezolid, as use of this agent was associated with better clinical outcomes and higher survival rates than vancomycin therapy.[32]

Bacteremia

Bacteremia, or bloodstream infection, is one of the most serious complications encountered in critically ill pa-

tients. It occurs in approximately 10% of ICU patients and is associated with significant mortality—38%.[33] Coagulase-negative staphylococcal species, *S aureus*, and enterococci are the most common pathogens implicated in nosocomial bacteremia.[34] Mortality from bacteremia is associated with higher APACHE II scores, older age, lower serum albumin concentrations, use of dialysis, and therapy with vasopressors.[33] Patients who do not survive also are more likely to have received mechanical ventilation or to have required a central venous catheter. Longer duration of urinary tract catheterization or central venous catheterization is a risk factor for mortality as well. In fact, catheter-related bloodstream infections are the most common cause of nosocomial bacteremia[1,33] and are implicated in 24% of all incidents. Pneumonia is associated with 19% and urinary tract infection with 13% of cases.[33] Hospital-acquired bacteremia has a higher mortality rate (41%) than community-acquired bacteremia (34%).

In patients receiving inadequate antimicrobial treatment, the hospital mortality rate is 62%, and the bloodstream-infection–related mortality rate is 30%.[33] However, those receiving adequate therapy have a hospital mortality rate of 28% and a bloodstream-infection–related mortality rate of 12%. Patients who die are statistically less likely to have an infection attributed to coagulase-negative staphylococci or oxacillin-susceptible *S aureus* organisms. Pathogens associated with increased mortality include VRE and *Candida* species.

Linezolid is approved for the treatment of vancomycin-resistant *E faecium* infections, including those with concurrent bacteremia. Although the sample population of patients with bacteremia as the primary diagnosis in the VRE study was very small, all patients on the 600-mg twice-daily dose of linezolid were clinically (4/4) and microbiologically (3/3) cured at follow-up.[12] Furthermore, although FDA approval was received for vancomycin-resistant *E faecium* specifically, in vitro studies have indicated efficacy against *E faecalis*, including vancomycin-resistant strains, with the MIC_{90} (4 µg/mL) exceeding those of quinupristin-dalfopristin (16 µg/mL) and vancomycin (64 µg/mL).[35] Recent case studies also have indicated efficacy for linezolid in the treatment of bacteremia. In an account of septicemia caused by vancomycin-resistant *E faecalis* associated with burn injuries in 2 patients, Atkins et al[36] reported successful treatment of the bloodstream infection despite the serious nature of the burns and the immunocompromised condition of the patients. Successful treatment of persistent bacteremia caused by vancomycin-resistant *E faecium* with linezolid and gentamicin was noted in a report by Noskin et al.[37] Traditionally, bacteremia that occurs in individuals residing in the community has been defined as community-acquired, regardless of whether they have received health care in an outpatient facility.[38] Recently, it has been suggested that a third term, "health care-associated," be used in addition to "community acquired" and "nosocomial" to describe infections, particularly, bacteremia. In a prospective observational study, Friedman and colleagues[38] characterized bloodstream infections as either *health care-associated* (positive culture at the time of hospital admission or hospitalization of ≤48 hours, and in those who had received home, clinic, acute care hospitalization, or resided in a long-term facility); *community-acquired* (positive culture at the time of hospital admission or hospitalization of ≤48 hours, and in those who do not have the additional criteria under the health care-associated label); or *nosocomial* (positive culture after hospitalization for ≥48 hours). Analysis provided insight into a subset that until now, has been included with overall community-acquired infections. Of the 186 patients with health care-associated bacteremia, 16% resided in nursing homes, 34% received home health care, 42% received home-based or clinic-based intravenous therapy or dialysis, and 63% had been hospitalized in the 90 days preceding their bloodstream infection. Interestingly, the patients with health care-associated bacteremia shared more similarities with patients with nosocomial infections than with those with community-acquired infections. Both the health care-associated and nosocomial groups had similar frequencies of intravascular-device–related and gastrointestinal tract–related bacteremia, whereas those with community-acquired infection were more likely to have bacteremia secondary to urinary tract infection. The most likely pathogen in both nosocomial and health care-associated infections

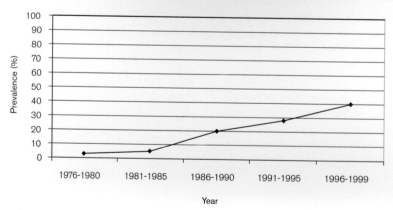

Figure 3. Estimated prevalence of methicillin-resistant *Staphylococcus aureus* in United States hospitals from 1976 to 1999. Adapted from Chambers HF. The changing epidemiology of *Staphylococcus aureus. Emerg Infect Dis.* 2001;7:178-182.

was *S aureus*, whereas in community-acquired infections, *Escherichia coli* and *S pneumoniae* were the most common pathogens.

Hospital length of stay (LOS), however, indicated a different pattern.[38] Patients with health care-associated infections had a median duration of stay closer to that of those with community-acquired infections (7 days versus 6 days), whereas patients with nosocomial infections had a median stay of 23 days. Mortality rates among the 3 groups were more stratified. The lowest death rate was found among those with community-acquired bacteremia (16%), followed by health care-associated bacteremia (29%); the highest rate—37%—was found in the group with nosocomial bacteremia.

Properly categorizing patients when considering the likely origin of infection can help determine the appropriate antibiotic therapy. The results of the study by Friedman[38] suggest that the likely pathogens and resistance patterns in patients with health care-associated infections such as bacteremia will more closely reflect those found in patients with nosocomial infections. In particular, MRSA should be suspected in these patients, since *S aureus* was the most commonly isolated pathogen.

The Importance of MRSA in Infections in Critical Care Patients

Because humans are a natural reservoir for *S aureus*, this pathogen often plays an important role in infection, particularly in critical care patients who often are compromised by underlying disease.[39] The rise of MRSA poses a great challenge to the clinicians who treat this population. Methicillin-resistant strains of *S aureus* have increased over the past 25 years from less than 5% of strains isolated in hospitals in 1976 to 1980 to more than 40% in 1996 to 1999 (Figure 3).[39] Increasingly, these infections have been reported in non–health care settings as well, including correctional facilities and among members of athletic teams.[40,41] Given the very high mortality rates found with serious MRSA infections such as pneumonia,[27] the presence of resistant strains in the community is alarming. In a Mississippi prison, 5% of the inmates were found to be carriers of MRSA.[41] However, there are no systematic surveys of MRSA in the community, so estimates of its prevalence are suspect.[39]

Summary

The approval of linezolid has provided critical care medicine with yet another bulwark against serious community-acquired and nosocomial infections. This is a welcome addition, particularly in light of the increasing prevalence of MRSA. Evidence from large, randomized, comparator-controlled clinical trials indicates that clinical cure and survival rates achieved with linezolid are comparable with those noted for vancomycin or ceftriaxone-cefpodoxime in the treatment of CAP, HAP, and VAP. Furthermore, a survival advantage was noted in patients with VAP treated with linezolid compared with those treated with vancomycin, although these differences did not reach statistical significance. Data also suggest that linezolid achieves higher concentrations in lung tissue than vancomycin, which may account for some of its advantage. In patients with CAP and bacteremia caused by *S pneumoniae*, significantly higher clinical cure rates were achieved with linezolid therapy than with ceftriaxone-cefpodoxime therapy. Given the importance of early, appropriate, and adequate antibiotic treatment to clinical outcomes in patients with serious infections caused by MRSA or other gram-positive organisms, linezolid is expected to play a major role in critical care medicine.

References

1. National Nosocomial Infections Surveillance System. National Nosocomial Infections Surveillance (NNIS) System report, data summary from January 1992-June 2001, issued August 2001. *Am J Infect Control*. 2001;29:404-421.
2. Doern GV, Heilmann KP, Huynh HK, Rhomberg PR, Coffman SL, Brueggemann AB. Antimicrobial resistance among clinical isolates of *Streptococcus pneumoniae* in the United States during 1999-2000, including a comparison of resistance rates since 1994-1995. *Antimicrob Agents Chemother*. 2001;45:1721-1729.
3. Khare M, Keady D. Antimicrobial therapy of methicillin resistant *Staphylococcus aureus* infection. *Pharmacotherapy*. 2003;4:165-177.
4. Wunderink RG, Cammarata SK, Oliphant TH, Kollef MH, for the Linezolid Nosocomial Pneumonia Study Group. Continuation of a randomized, double-blind, multicenter study of linezolid versus vancomycin in the treatment of patients with nosocomial pneumonia. *Clin Ther*. 2003;25:980-992.
5. Alvarez-Lerma F. Modification of empiric antibiotic treatment in patients with pneumonia acquired in the intensive care unit. ICU-Acquired Pneumonia Study Group. *Intensive Care Med*. 1996;22:387-394.
6. Kollef MH, Ward S. The influence of mini-BAL cultures on patient outcomes: implications for the antibiotic management of ventilator-associated pneumonia. *Chest*. 1998;113:412-420.
7. Zyvox [package insert]. Kalamazoo, Mich: Pharmacia & Upjohn Company; 2003.
8. Synercid IV [package insert]. Bristol, Tenn; Monarch Pharmaceuticals Inc; 2002.

9. Centers for Disease Control and Prevention, Department of Health and Human Services. Faststats: pneumonia. Available at: www.cdc.gov/nchs.fastats/pneumonia.htm. Accessed July 17, 2003.

10. Niederman MS, Mandell LA, Anzueto A, et al, for the American Thoracic Society. Guidelines for the management of adults with community-acquired pneumonia. Diagnosis, assessment of severity, antimicrobial therapy, and prevention. *Am J Respir Crit Care Med.* 2001;163:1730-1754.

11. Rubinstein E, Cammarata SK, Oliphant TH, Wunderink RG, and the Linezolid Nosocomial Pneumonia Study Group. Linezolid (PNU-100766) versus vancomycin in the treatment of hospitalized patients with nosocomial pneumonia: a randomized, double-blind, multicenter study. *Clin Infect Dis.* 2001;32:402-412.

12. Data on file. Pfizer Inc. New York, NY.

13. Conte JE Jr, Golden JA, Kipps J, Zurlinden E. Intrapulmonary pharmacokinetics of linezolid. *Antimicrob Agents Chemother.* 2002;46:1475-1480.

14. Yanagihara K, Kaneko Y, Sawai T, et al. Efficacy of linezolid against methicillin-resistant or vancomycin-insensitive *Staphylococcus aureus* in a model of hematogenous pulmonary infection. *Antimicrob Agents Chemother.* 2002;46:3288-3291.

15. Gentry-Nielsen MJ, Olsen KM, Preheim LC. Pharmacodynamic activity and efficacy of linezolid in a rat model of pneumococcal pneumonia. *Antimicrob Agents Chemother.* 2002;46:1345-1351.

16. Cruciani M, Gatti G, Lazzarini L, et al. Penetration of vancomycin into human lung tissue. *J Antimicrob Chemother.* 1996;38:865-869.

17. Lamer C, de Beco V, Soler P, et al. Analysis of vancomycin entry into pulmonary lining fluid by bronchoalveolar lavage in critically ill patients. *Antimicrob Agents Chemother.* 1993;37:281-286.

18. Ruiz M, Ewig S, Marcos MA, et al. Etiology of community-acquired pneumonia: impact of age, comorbidity, and severity. *Am J Respir Crit Care Med.* 1999;160:397-405.

19. San Pedro GS, Cammarata SK, Oliphant TH, Todisco T. Linezolid versus ceftriaxone/cefpodoxime in patients hospitalized for the treatment of *Streptococcus pneumoniae* pneumonia. *Scand J Infect Dis.* 2002;34:720-728.

20. Niederman MS, Bass JB Jr, Campbell GD, et al. Guidelines for the initial management of adults with community-acquired pneumonia: diagnosis, assessment of severity, and initial antimicrobial therapy. American Thoracic Society. Medical Section of the American Lung Association. *Am Rev Respir Dis.* 1993;148:1418-1426.

21. American Thoracic Society. Hospital-acquired pneumonia in adults: diagnosis, assessment of severity, initial antimicrobial therapy, and preventative strategies. A consensus statement, American Thoracic Society, November 1995. *Am J Respir Crit Care Med.* 1996;153:1711-1725.

22. Heyland DK, Cook DJ, Griffith L, Keenan SP, Brun-Buisson C. The attributable morbidity and mortality of ventilator-associated pneumonia in the critically ill patient. The Canadian Critical Trials Group. *Am J Respir Crit Care Med.* 1999;159(4 Pt 1):1249-1256.

23. Haddadin AS, Fappiano SA, Lipsett PA. Methicillin resistant *Staphylococcus aureus* (MRSA) in the intensive care unit. *Postgrad Med J.* 2002;78:385-392.

24. Wunderink RG, Rello J, Cammarata SK, Croos-Dabrera RV, Kollef MH. Linezolid vs vancomycin: analysis of two double blind studies of patients with methicillin-resistant *Staphylococcus aureus* nosocomial pneumonia. *Chest.* 2003;124:1789-1791.

25. Cammarata SK, Wunderink RG, Hempsall K, Todd WM, Hafkin B. Efficacy of linezolid in patients with nosocomial pneumonia based on severity of illness as determined by baseline APACHE II score. Paper presented at: 40th Annual Interscience Conference on Antimicrobial Agents and Chemotherapy; September 17-20, 2000; Toronto, Ontario. Abstract 2234.

26. Fagon J-Y, Patrick H, Haas DW, et al. Treatment of gram-positive nosocomial pneumonia. Prospective randomized comparison of quinupristin/dalfopristin versus vancomycin. Nosocomial Pneumonia Group. *Am J Respir Crit Care Med.* 2000;161(3 Pt 1):753-762.

27. Gonzalez C, Rubio M, Romero-Vivas J, Gonzalez M, Picazo JJ. Bacteremic pneumonia due to *Staphylococcus aureus*: a comparison of disease caused by methicillin-resistant and methicillin-susceptible organisms. *Clin Infect Dis.* 1999;29:1171-1177.

28. Kollef MH, Sherman G, Ward S, Fraser VJ. Inadequate antimicrobial treatment of infections: a risk factor for hospital mortality among critically ill patients. *Chest.* 1999;115:462-474.

29. Tenover FC. Development and spread of bacterial resistance to antimicrobial agents: an overview. *Clin Infect Dis.* 2001;33(suppl 3):S108-S115.

30. Leviton I. Separating fact from fiction: the data behind allergies and side effects caused by penicillins, cephalosporins, and carbapenem antibiotics. *Curr Pharm Des.* 2003;9:983-938.

31. Ibrahim EH, Tracy L, Hill C, Fraser VJ, Kollef MH. The occurrence of ventilator-associated pneumonia in a community hospital: risk factors and clinical outcomes. *Chest.* 2001;120:555-561.

32. Kollef MH, Cammarata SK, Croos-Dabrera RV, Wunderink R. Predictors of outcome in patients with ventilator-associated Gram-positive pneumonia treated with linezolid or vancomycin. *Intensive Care Med.* 2003: in press.

33. Ibrahim EH, Sherman G, Ward S, Fraser VJ, Kollef MH. The influence of inadequate antimicrobial treatment of bloodstream infections on patient outcomes in the ICU setting. *Chest.* 2000;118:146-155.

34. Fridkin SK, Gaynes RP. Antimicrobial resistance in intensive care units. *Clin Chest Med.* 1999;20:303-316.

35. Rybak MJ, Hershberger E, Moldovan T, Grucz RG. In vitro activities of daptomycin, vancomycin, linezolid, and quinupristin-dalfopristin against staphylococci and enterococci, including vancomycin-intermediate and -resistant strains. *Antimicrob Agents Chemother.* 2000;44:1062-1066.

36. Atkins JL, Hidvegi N, Teare L, Dziewulski P. The use of linezolid in the treatment of vancomycin-resistant enterococcal septicaemia in two patients with burn injuries. *Burns.* 2002;28:185-188.

37. Noskin GA, Siddiqui F, Stosor V, Kruzynski J, Peterson LR. Successful treatment of persistent vancomycin-resistant *Enterococcus faecium* bacteremia with linezolid and gentamicin. *Clin Infect Dis.* 1999;28:689-690.

38. Friedman ND, Kaye KS, Stout JE, McGarry SA, et al. Health care–associated bloodstream infections in adults: a reason to change the accepted definition of community-acquired infections. *Ann Intern Med.* 2002;137:791-797.

39. Chambers HF. The changing epidemiology of *Staphylococcus aureus*? *Emerg Infect Dis.* 2001;7:178-182.

40. Centers for Disease Control and Prevention. Public health dispatch: outbreaks of community-associated methicillin-resistant *Staphylococcus aureus* skin infections—Los Angeles County, California, 2002-2003. *MMWR Morb Mortal Wkly Rep.* 2003;52:88.

41. Centers for Disease Control and Prevention. Methicillin-resistant *Staphylococcus aureus* skin or soft tissue infections in a state prison—Mississippi, 2000. *MMWR Morb Mortal Wkly Rep.* 2001;50:919-922.

1. Which of the following statements is true regarding the results of studies conducted by Conte et al and Cruciani et al?
   a. Linezolid and vancomycin have comparable penetration of lung tissue.
   b. Linezolid does not appear to penetrate lung tissue as well as vancomycin.
   c. Vancomycin does not appear to penetrate lung tissue as well as linezolid.
   d. The investigators were unable to determine how well linezolid penetrated lung tissue.

2. Pneumonia is a leading cause of morbidity and mortality in the United States. Which of the following statements regarding community-acquired pneumonia is true?
   a. Drug-resistant strains are less likely to be isolated from patients who have undergone recent antimicrobial therapy.
   b. *Streptococcus pneumoniae* is the most likely pathogen to be involved in community-acquired pneumonia.
   c. *Staphylococcus aureus* is the most likely pathogen to be involved in community-acquired pneumonia.
   d. In severe community-acquired pneumonia, the frequency of *Staphylococcus aureus* as a causative pathogen ranges from 10% to 37%.

3. In one phase III clinical trial, researchers compared linezolid with ceftriaxone-cefpodoxime in the treatment of adults with community-acquired pneumonia. What were the overall clinical cure rates?
   a. 56% and 53%, respectively
   b. 65% and 66%, respectively
   c. 76% and 79%, respectively
   d. 83% and 76%, respectively

4. What pathogens are most often implicated in nosocomial pneumonia?
   a. *Haemophilus influenzae*, methicillin-susceptible *Staphylococcus aureus*, and *Streptococcus pneumoniae*
   b. Methicillin-resistant *Staphylococcus aureus*, *Pseudomonas aeruginosa*, and *Acinetobacter* species
   c. Enterococcal species
   d. Staphylococcal species

5. True or False: Inadequate antibiotic therapy has been associated with a mortality rate that is approximately 50% higher than the rate associated with adequate initial treatment.

CREATION OF A NOVEL CLASS:

USING LINEZOLID FOR INFECTED WOUNDS

EDITOR

Benjamin A. Lipsky, MD, FACP, FIDSA

LEARNING OBJECTIVES

After completion of this chapter, readers should be able to:

1. Describe the role of linezolid in treating wound infections.

2. Explain how linezolid compares with other antibiotics in the treatment of both complicated and uncomplicated skin and soft tissue infections.

3. Discuss issues critical to the care and management of diabetic foot infections.

4. Describe the different pathogens likely to infect bite wounds and burns.

5. Summarize the appropriate strategy for the treatment of osteomyelitis.

THE OXAZOLIDINONE ANTIBIOTICS

Common types of wounds include ulcerations caused by arterial or venous insufficiency, diabetic neuropathy, or constant pressure to the skin and muscle (ie, pressure sores, bedsores). Trauma, burns, or surgery also may cause skin wounds. Wounds are initially colonized by skin flora or introduced organisms. In some cases, these organisms proliferate, causing a host inflammatory response defined as infection.[1] Skin and soft tissue infections (SSTIs) include superficial conditions, such as erysipelas, cellulitis, folliculitis and furuncles, as well as deeper infections, such as abscesses, necrotizing fasciitis, myositis, and gas gangrene.[2]

Diagnosing wound infection is an important step in the treatment process. Although all wounds require treatment, only infected lesions require antimicrobial therapy. Because all open wounds become colonized with microorganisms, diagnosing infection relies on the clinical characteristics of the wound.[3] Wounds with the classic signs of infection (purulent drainage or signs of inflammation [eg, erythema, warmth, induration, tenderness]) should be cultured.[4] Culture and sensitivity reports are needed to help select the most appropriate antibiotic agents.[5]

The organisms most commonly isolated from infected wounds include Staphylococcus, Streptococcus, and Pseudomonas species (Table 1); however, a study compilation by Bowler et al[4] found that anaerobes may constitute more than one third of microbial isolates. Antibiotic-resistant pathogens, especially methicillin-resistant Staphylococcus aureus (MRSA), are a growing problem in wound care.[5-8] The great variety of causative organisms and their often unpredictable antibiotic susceptibilities emphasize the need for culturing infected wounds.

Treating infected wounds often requires surgical procedures (eg, debridement), especially for deep or necrotic wounds, as well as other adjunctive treatments, including weight off-loading, topical agents, special dressings, control of edema, and occasionally revascularization.[4] In addition, virtually all infected wounds require antimicrobial therapy. For superficial lesions, topical therapy may be sufficient, but deeper wounds require systemic therapy. The results of a recent survey of wound care specialists by Bamberg et al[5] states that systemic antimicrobials, debridement, and topical antimicrobials are the top 3 treatments for infected wounds (Table 2). Unfortunately, this survey also found that 70% of wounds are treated without ever being cultured, and only 12% of clinicians routinely culture wounds before treatment. Yet when asked the results when they do culture, 79% of the clinicians said they received a positive lab culture report. Many researchers believe that misuse of antibiotics is a frequent and avoidable cause of antibiotic resistance. Furthermore, inadequate antibiotic treatment can prolong infections and increase the risk of serious complications, such as

Table 1. Pathogens Most Commonly Isolated From Infected Wounds, Based on a Survey of Wound Care Specialists

Pathogen	No. (%) of Respondents*
Pseudomonas species	174 (66.2)
Staphylococcus aureus	119 (45.2)
Staphylococcus species (unspecified)	94 (35.7)
Methicillin-resistant Staphylococcus aureus	83 (31.6)
Streptococcus species	82 (31.2)
Escherichia coli	69 (26.2)
Enterococcus species	38 (14.4)
Proteus species	17 (6.5)
Staphylococcus epidermidis	17 (6.5)
Fungi	14 (5.3)
Vancomycin-resistant enterococci	9 (3.4)
Other Enterobacteriaceae	8 (3.0)
Klebsiella species	5 (1.9)
Corynebacterium species	1 (0.4)

*N=263.

Adapted from Bamberg R, Sullivan PK, Conner-Kerr T. Diagnosis of wound infections: current culturing practices of US wound care professionals. *Wounds*. 2002;14:314-327, with permission from HMP Communications. Copyright © 2002, HMP Communications. All rights reserved.

Table 2. Treatment Methods Used for Infected Wounds, Based on a Survey of Wound Care Specialists

Treatment	No. (%) of Respondents* Reporting
Systemic antimicrobials	284 (94.0)
Debridement	196 (64.9)
Topical antimicrobials	193 (63.9)
Antiseptics	56 (18.5)
Vacuum-assisted closure therapy	22 (7.3)
Electrical stimulation	13 (4.3)
Ultraviolet C light	7 (2.3)
Miscellaneous†	12 (4.1)

*N=302. Most respondents listed at least 2 most frequent treatments.
†Miscellaneous includes silver nitrate application, compression, pulsatile lavage with suction, irrigation, increased dressing changes, and hyperbaric oxygen chamber. Adapted from Bamberg R, Sullivan PK, Conner-Kerr T. Diagnosis of wound infections: current culturing practices of US wound care professionals. *Wounds.* 2002;14:314-327, with permission from HMP Communications. Copyright © 2002, HMP Communications. All rights reserved.

endocarditis, osteomyelitis, brain abscess, meningitis, lung abscess, or pneumonia.[9]

The Role of Linezolid in Treating Wound Infections

It was evident from early in vitro and in vivo testing that linezolid had potent activity against the staphylococcal and streptococcal pathogens that frequently cause wound infections.[10-16] Several key investigators were instrumental in establishing the efficacy and safety of linezolid in the treatment of SSTIs. The leading medical expert at Pharmacia & Upjohn Company during the development of linezolid was Carl Norden, a respected infectious diseases physician with clinical and research experience, particularly in treating osteomyelitis and diabetic foot infections. He had been a member of the US Food and Drug Administration (FDA) advisory board for antibiotic therapy and was knowledgeable about writing guidelines and the regulatory process. His guidance was crucial in instituting appropriate and well-designed clinical trials (B.A. Lipsky, personal communication, May 2003).

Dennis L. Stevens, Professor of Medicine at the University of Washington School of Medicine, Seattle, and Chief of Infectious Diseases at the Veterans Administration Medical Center in Boise, Idaho, was the primary investigator on the large phase III clinical trial of linezolid in the treatment of SSTIs. Stevens also is current chair of the Infectious Diseases Society of America (IDSA) guidelines committee on the treatment of SSTIs. His leadership on SSTI and MRSA protocols during the phase III clinical

trials was critical (B.A. Lipsky, personal communication, May 2003). Benjamin A. Lipsky, Professor of Medicine at the University of Washington School of Medicine in Seattle and Director of the Antibiotic Research Clinic at the Veterans Administration Puget Sound Health Care System, was instrumental in writing the protocol for the diabetic foot infection study, for which he was the lead investigator. Lipsky currently is the chair of both IDSA and the International Consensus Working Group on Diabetic Foot Infections. For the diabetic foot study, he ensured that the protocol would include secondary outcomes of important academic interest; he met with North American and European investigators to explain the study and secure their commitment (B.A. Lipsky, personal communication, May 2003).

Treatment of SSTIs

The results of the major phase III clinical trial published by Stevens et al[9] demonstrated the efficacy and safety of linezolid for treating complicated SSTIs. Penicillinase-resistant penicillins are the first-line therapeutic agents used to treat these infections, but the decline of pathogen susceptibility has created a need for new antimicrobial agents. This study compared treatment of SSTIs with oxacillin-dicloxacillin to treatment with linezolid. The randomized, double-blind comparison design of this trial and the large patient population (intent-to-treat [ITT] population = 819) demonstrated the equivalence of these 2 agents in treating these serious infections. Among clinically evaluable patients, cure rates were 89% for linezolid and 86% for oxacillin-dicloxacillin (P=.300; 95% confidence interval [CI] −2.5 to 8.2); among microbiologically evaluable patients, cure rates were 88% for linezolid and 86% for oxacillin-dicloxacillin (P=.606; 95% CI −5.6 to 9.7). The trial provided outcomes for a number of different types of complicated SSTIs, the most common of which were cellulitis, skin abscess, and erysipelas. Microbiological outcomes demonstrated that linezolid was as effective as the comparator in eradicating Staphylococcus aureus, Streptococcus pyogenes, and Streptococcus agalactiae. The authors suggested that the high concentration of linezolid in the skin and the drug's ability to interfere with bacterial virulence factors and toxin production in S aureus and S pyogenes might have contributed to its efficacy.

Patients with infections caused by MRSA were excluded from the trial,[9] but this pathogen is an increasing problem throughout the world.[7,17] The percentage of MRSA isolates cultured from clinical specimens has increased dramatically over the past decade. In 2001, the National Nosocomial Infections Surveillance System reported that 55% of 5070 S aureus strains isolated from ICU patients with nosocomial infections were resistant to methicillin, a 29% increase for the period between 1995 and 2000.[18] A 2003 analysis by Dang et al[7] of wound swabs taken from infected foot ulcers in patients with diabetes reported that MRSA infections doubled between 1998 and 2001.

Although the glycopeptides (eg, vancomycin, teicoplanin) remain active against the vast majority of MRSA strains, they must be given parenterally and frequently cause adverse effects.[19] Furthermore, glycopeptide-intermediate-resistant Staphylococcus aureus (GISA) isolates were identified in Japan in 1996[20] and in the United States in 1997.[21] Vancomycin-resistant strains were isolated in 2002.[22]

The oxazolidinones were developed against this background of issues with the glycopeptides. The unique mechanism of action of linezolid, the first oxazolidinone, makes cross-resistance with other antibiotic classes highly unlikely.[23] Though several reports of isolated cases of linezolid-resistant MRSA have been noted and certainly bear watching,[24,25] to date there has been limited evidence of bacterial resistance to this compound. In light of the high levels of penetration of linezolid to soft tissue and bones,[26,27] and its excellent activity against both resistant and susceptible gram-positive pathogens,[28] it seemed likely to be useful in treating SSTIs.[9] The excellent pharmaco-

dynamic properties also make it a promising empiric treatment for other community-acquired or nosocomial infections, especially where MRSA infections are prevalent.

Currently, linezolid is FDA approved for the treatment of vancomycin-resistant Enterococcus faecium infections, including cases with concurrent bacteremia; nosocomial pneumonia caused by methicillin-susceptible and -resistant strains of S aureus, or penicillin-susceptible strains of Streptococcus pneumoniae; community-acquired pneumonia caused by S pneumoniae (penicillin-susceptible strains only), including cases with concurrent bacteremia, or S aureus (methicillin-susceptible strains only); uncomplicated skin and skin structure infections caused by S aureus (methicillin-susceptible strains only) or S pyogenes; and complicated skin and skin structure infections caused by S aureus (methicillin-susceptible and methicillin-resistant strains), S pyogenes, or S agalactiae.[29]

Another study by Stevens et al[30] corroborated these findings by comparing the efficacy of linezolid with that of vancomycin in treating MRSA infections. The patients enrolled in this trial were diagnosed with SSTIs, pneumonia, urinary tract infections, bacteremia, and other infections caused by MRSA; among 460 enrolled patients, 230 had SSTIs. The cure rate in the overall ITT population with SSTIs was 65% with linezolid and 62% with vancomycin. In the ITT population with confirmed MRSA infections at baseline (MRSA-ITT), the cure rate was 70% with linezolid and 74% with vancomycin. In the 64 evaluable patients with MRSA infections, the clinical cure rate was 79% (27/34) in the linezolid cohort compared with 73% (22/30) in the vancomycin cohort. The investigators concluded that therapy with linezolid (intravenous initially, then oral) was safe and comparable to intravenous vancomycin therapy for treating nosocomial infections caused by MRSA. They further suggested that linezolid was a suitable alternative to vancomycin for these infections and may thus allow a reduction in vancomycin use. In 2002 the Centers for Disease Control and Prevention (CDC) began an educational campaign on how to prevent antimicrobial resistance in healthcare settings.[31] Step 9, "Know When to Say 'No' to Vanco" instructed health care workers as follows: (1) presence of fever and an intravenous line are not routinely indications for vancomycin; (2) MRSA may be susceptible to other antimicrobials; and (3) treat staphylococcal infection, not contaminants or colonization.

Other Studies on the Treatment of Complicated SSTIs

It is reasonable to ask how linezolid compares with other antibiotics in treating SSTIs. A study by Siami et al[32] compared the fluoroquinolone clinafloxacin with piperacillin-tazobactam for treating patients with severe SSTIs (cellulitis, wound infections, or diabetic foot infections). The authors reported clinical cure rates of 69% and 65% (P=.423; 95% CI, –7.5 to 14.6%), respectively, and microbiological cure rates of 62% and 57% (P=.500; 95% CI, –4.4 to 13.0%), respectively. Although both agents exhibit activity against gram-positive bacteria, their activity against gram-positive pathogens may be less than that for the agents used in the SSTI study by Stevens et al. Whereas linezolid achieved eradication rates of 91% against S aureus (P=.139; 95% CI, –2.1 to 16.0 [6.9]),[9] the eradication rates with clinafloxacin and piperacillin-tazobactam were 62% (P=.097; 95% CI, –4.4 to 71.1 [33.3]) and 57% (P<.40), respectively.[32] In addition, for S agalactiae, linezolid demonstrated a 100% eradication rate, whereas clinafloxacin and piperacillin-tazobactam exhibited eradication rates of 63% and 57%, respectively. However, eradication rates for S pyogenes were higher overall (92%) with clinafloxacin, and oxacillin-dicloxacillin appeared to be more effective against S aureus (85% eradication) and S agalactiae (67%) than either clinafloxacin or piperacillin-tazobactam.

Graham et al[33] compared high-dose levofloxacin (750 mg) with intravenous ticarcillin-clavulanate (with a switch to amoxicillin-clavulanate at the investigator's discretion) in the treatment of complicated SSTIs. Clinical response rates were equivalent for both treatment groups, but microbiological eradication rates were significantly higher in the group treated with levofloxacin. The overall success rates (cure or improvement) for clinically evaluable patients were 84% for patients in the levofloxacin group and 80% for the ticarcillin-clavulanate/amoxicillin-clavulanate group (95% CI, 13.3-5.8). Although these rates are comparable to those reported by Stevens et al,[9] cure rates for the clinically evaluable group were actually slightly higher for both linezolid (89%) and oxacillin-dicloxacillin (86%) in that study (P=.300; 95% CI, –2.5 to 8.2 [2.8]).

The study by Graham et al[33] also provided interesting data on clinical success rate by type of SSTI. Clinical success rates were higher in the ticarcillin-clavulanate group for infected nondiabetic ulcers (73% ticarcillin-clavulanate versus 63% levofloxacin) and unspecified (other) SSTIs (100% ticarcillin-clavulanate versus 91% levofloxacin). Conversely, cure rates were higher in the levofloxacin group for infected diabetic ulcers (69% levofloxacin versus 57% ticarcillin-clavulanate) and wound infection, (89% levofloxacin versus 85% ticarcillin-clavulanate). Success

Table 3. Clinical Success Rates in Complicated SSTIs (Evaluable Patients)[9,32,33]

Study and Agent	n/N (%)	P
Stevens 2000		
Linezolid (IV/PO)	264/298 (88.6)	.300 (95% CI, –2.5 to 8.2 [2.8])
Oxacillin (IV)-dicloxacillin (PO)	259/302 (85.8)	
Siami 2001		
Clinafoxacin (IV/PO)	99/144 (68.8)	.423 (95% CI, –7.5% to14.6%)
Piperacillin-tazobactam (IV)/ Amoxicillin-clavulanate (PO)	88/135 (65.2)	
Graham 2002		
Levofloxacin (IV/PO)	116/138 (84.1)*	95% CI, –13.3 to 5.8
Ticaracillin-clavulanate (IV)/ Amoxicillin-clavulanate (PO)	106/132 (80.3)*	

SSTIs= skin and soft tissue infections; CI = confidence interval.
*No P values given in study.

rates for treatment of major abscess were the same in both groups—90%.

Tables 3 and 4 list the clinical success and microbiological eradication rates, respectively, of all 3 studies. Although such observations are of interest, no determinations can be made from a comparison of these 3 studies, because inclusion criteria and study design differed.

Studies on the Treatment of Uncomplicated SSTIs

In a recent study, Wible et al[34] investigated the use of linezolid in the treatment of uncomplicated skin and skin structure infections in children. Patients aged 5 to 11 years were randomized to receive either linezolid oral suspension (10 mg/kg up to 600 mg BID) or cefadroxil suspension (15 mg/kg up to 500 mg BID), and patients aged 12 to 17 years received either linezolid tablets (600 mg BID) or cefadroxil capsules (500 mg BID) for 10 to 21 days. At the follow-up visit, cure rates in the ITT population were 89% for patients treated with linezolid and 86%

for those treated with cefadroxil (P=.405; 95% CI, –3.5 to 8.7), while in clinically evaluable patients, cure rates were 91% and 90% in the linezolid and cefadroxil groups, respectively (P=.737; 95% CI, –4.6 to 6.5). Among microbiologically evaluable patients, S aureus was eradicated in 90% of patients treated with linezolid and in 89% of those treated with cefadroxil. The investigators concluded that linezolid was as effective as cefadroxil in treating uncomplicated skin infections, including those caused by S aureus (including MRSA) and S pyogenes, in a pediatric population. Although differences in study design and patient population preclude definitive comparisons, it is instructive to discuss a study by Tarshis et al[35] on the treatment on uncomplicated SSTIs in adults with either once-daily oral gatifloxacin or oral levofloxacin. Clinical cure rates in clinically evaluable patients were 91% and 84% (95% CI, –2% to 15%) in the gatifloxacin and levofloxacin groups, respectively, and bacterial eradication in microbiologically evaluable patients was 92% in both groups. Clinical cure rates by infection diagnosis ranged from 80% for gatifloxacin and 78% for levofloxacin in the treatment of abscess to 100% for both regimens in the treatment of impetigo. These rates are comparable to

Table 4. Microbiological Eradication Rates of Select Pathogens–Complicated SSTIs[9,32,33]

Study and Agent	Eradication Rate n/N (%)			
	S aureus	MRSA	S pyogenes	S agalactiae
Stevens 2000				
Linezolid (IV/PO)	85/93 (91.4)*		23/29 (79.3)†	7/7 (100)‡
Oxacillin (IV)-dicloxacillin (PO)	87/103 (84.5)*		27/32 (84.4)†	4/6 (66.7)‡
Siami 2001				
Clinafloxacin (IV/PO)	38.61 (62.3)§	4/7 (57.1)§	11/12 (91.7)‖	5/8 (62.5)‖
Piperacillin-tazobactam (IV)/ Amoxicillin-clavulanate (PO)	32/54 (59.3)§	5/14 (35.7)§	7/10 (70.0)‖	8/14 (57.1)‖
Graham 2002				
Levofloxacin (IV/PO)		4/5 (80.0)¶	5/6 (83.3)¶	9/12 (75.0)#
Ticarcillin-clavulanate (IV)/ Amoxicillin-clavulanate (PO)		2/3 (66.7)¶	6/7 (85.7)¶	9/13 (69.2)#

SSTIs = skin and soft tissue infections; MRSA = methicillin-resistant *Staphylococcus aureus;* CI = confidence interval.
*P=.139 (95% CI, –2.1 to 16.0 [6.9]).
†P=.607 (95% CI, 124.4 to 14.3 [5.1]).
‡P=.097 (95% CI, –4.4 to 71.1 [33.3]).
§P<.40. Confidence interval not given in study.
‖P=nonsignificant.
¶P value and confidence interval not given.
#P value not given (95% CI, –45.0 to 33.5.)

those reported by Wible et al[34] for linezolid in the treatment of uncomplicated SSTIs.

Treatment Regimen and Length of Hospitalization

The costliest aspect of treating most infections is hospitalization. Li and colleagues[36] conducted a study to explore the effect of therapy with either linezolid or vancomycin on the duration of hospital stay in patients with complicated SSTIs caused by known or suspected MRSA. Complicated infections include those that involve the deep (subcutaneous) tissues (eg, fascia, skeletal muscles), and often require surgical intervention, hospitalization, and therapy with potent antibiotics. The standard treatment for infections caused by MRSA has been vancomycin; however, because this agent can be administered only intravenously, patients must be hospitalized. The 100% bioavailability of linezolid and its excellent tissue penetration characteristics make oral and intravenous dosing for this drug essentially equivalent. Although home intravenous treatment and outpatient parenteral therapy centers may be available, these alternatives are less convenient, more costly, and involve risks associated with intravenous line–related complications.

In this study, 122 patients with complicated SSTIs were randomized to receive linezolid, whereas 108 patients received vancomycin.[36] The patients in the linezolid arm of the study had more adverse prognostic features: The patients treated with linezolid were older (mean age 63.0 years versus 55.6 for vancomycin, P=.003), had more current medical conditions (mean of 4.5 versus 3.7 for vancomycin, P=.04), and were more likely to begin treatment while in an ICU or step-down unit than the patients treated with vancomycin (10.7% versus 5.6%). Despite these discrepancies, patients in the linezolid group had a much shorter duration of intravenous antibiotic treatment (mean of 5.8 days versus 12.6 days for those on vancomycin, P<.0001), and a shorter length of hospital stay (mean of 16 days versus 20 days in the vancomycin group; median of 12 versus 15 days, respectively; P=.009).

The results of a recent study of complicated SSTIs caused by MRSA corroborate these findings regarding length of stay (J. Weigelt, unpublished data, 2003). The open-label, multicenter trial compared oral or intravenous linezolid (600 mg BID) with intravenous vancomycin (1 g BID) given to 1200 hospitalized patients with complicated SSTIs caused by suspected or proven MRSA. In the ITT population, Investigator's Assessment Clinical Outcomes (IACO) cure rates were 96% with linezolid therapy and 94% with vancomycin therapy at the end of treatment, and 93% with linezolid and 89% with vancomycin at the test of cure 7 days after therapy. These results suggest equivalence of the 2 treatments. However, among clinically evaluable patients, linezolid exhibited statistical superiority over the comparator. In the clinically evaluable population, IACO cure rates at the end of treatment were 98% with linezolid and 95% with the comparator (P=.0422); at the test of cure, they were 95% with linezolid and 91% with the comparator. (P=.0125).

Statistical superiority for linezolid was also found in the Sponsor's Assessment Clinical Outcomes (SACO) cure rates among the microbiological ITT population (patients with a culture-proven staphylococcal infection), clinically evaluable, and microbiologically evaluable populations (J. Weigelt, unpublished data, 2003). The SACO cure rates ranged from 92% in the ITT population to 95% in the microbiologically evaluable population for linezolid; for the vancomycin group, SACO cure rates ranged from 89% in the ITT population to 90% in the clinically evaluable population.

Linezolid also was significantly more effective than vancomycin in treating major skin abscesses (J. Weigelt, unpublished data, 2003). In the clinically evaluable population, the SACO cure rate was 98% for linezolid therapy compared with 91% for vancomycin (P=.0256), and in the microbiologically evaluable population, it was 98% for linezolid and 90% for the vancomycin (P=.0277). For other diagnoses, outcomes were comparable for both study drugs.

For infections caused by MRSA, linezolid was more effective than vancomycin (89% linezolid versus 67% vancomycin, P<.0001), but the 2 agents demonstrated equivalence against infections caused by methicillin-susceptible *Staphylococcus aureus* (MSSA) (85% linezolid versus 75% comparator) and coagulase negative staphylococcal infections (93% linezolid versus 77% comparator) (J. Weigelt, unpublished data, 2003).

In a separate analysis of these trial data, Weigelt et al examined the effect of the 2 study regimens on the duration of hospital stay and intravenous treatment (J. Weigelt, unpublished data, 2003). Confirming the results of the smaller study by Li et al, the investigators found that the length of hospital stay for patients treated with linezolid was at least 2 days shorter than it was for patients treated with vancomycin. The difference in the duration of intravenous treatment for patients treated with linezolid versus vancomycin ranged from 7 days less in the ITT population to 11 days less for patients with confirmed MRSA infections.

limb amputations in the United States occur in individuals with diabetes.[40] Diabetic foot ulcers precede approximately 85% of these amputations, and infection is often the proximate cause.

Although many diabetic foot infections are polymicrobial, the most important pathogens are the aerobic gram-positive cocci, especially staphylococci and streptococci.[1,3,38,39,41] Patients who recently received antibiotic therapy, or who have chronic or necrotic wounds,

Table 5. Efficacy in the Clinically and Microbiologically Evaluable Population[47]

Parameter	No.	Linezolid	Comparator	95% CI
Clinically evaluable population	317	83%	73%	−0.006 to 0.197
Microbiologically evaluable population	212	72%	63%	−0.055 to 0.238

CI = confidence interval.

Risk Factors Associated With Treatment Failure in SSTIs

An analysis of phase III study data on the use of linezolid therapy for the treatment of SSTIs has provided valuable data on the risk factors associated with poorer outcomes. Wilson and colleagues[25] developed a severity scoring system to assess patient risk and found that cure rates were lower in patients with 1 or more comorbid conditions. Elevated blood urea nitrogen, hyponatremia, anemia, lesion size, and surgical wound infection were independent predictors of treatment failure, whereas therapy with linezolid was an independent predictor of cure ($P<.01$).

Treating Diabetic Foot Infections

The neurological and vascular complications of diabetes mellitus predispose patients to ulcerations of the foot. An estimated 10% to 17% of individuals with diabetes develop a foot ulcer at some point in their lives.[37] Once the protective barrier of the skin is broken, bacteria can colonize and infect the wound; infection may then extend deeper into the subcutaneous tissue or bone, resulting in osteomyelitis.[38,39] In addition, some patients with diabetes have reduced phagocytic and cell-mediated immune responses.[39] The importance of diabetic foot lesions is demonstrated by the fact that more than half of all lower

often have anaerobic organisms isolated along with the gram-positive cocci.[38] Numerous studies have shown that *Staphylococcus* and *Streptococcus* species constitute the majority of clinical isolates in acute, mild-to-moderate infections, whereas gram-negative and anaerobic pathogens, along with gram-positive cocci, are more likely to be isolated in chronic and severe infections.[1,4,38,39,42] Strains of MRSA have become predominant pathogens in diabetic foot infections[7,43] and are associated with prolonged healing periods.[43]

Treatment of diabetic foot infections may require surgical intervention, including drainage of pus, wound debridement, or revascularization. Antibiotic therapy for 1 to 2 weeks is usually sufficient to treat mild soft tissue infections, provided that debridement is performed and pressure off-loading has been achieved, but more severe infections may require longer treatment.[1] If osteomyelitis is involved, antibiotic treatment may be required for 6 weeks or longer.[44] Cure of chronic contiguous osteomyelitis usually also requires resection of the infected bone, but recent reports suggest prolonged antibiotic therapy alone may be successful in selected cases.[1,45]

The clinical efficacy of linezolid in treating complicated SSTIs (87% cure rate, $P=.3$) and MRSA infections (94% cure rate) makes this compound appropriate for treating diabetic foot infections.[46] The frequent presence of peripheral vascular disease in patients with diabetes hampers delivery of antibiotic to the infected site.[44] The high levels of linezolid in the exudate of induced blisters in human volunteers suggest that this agent penetrates infected skin and soft tissue and is thus especially valuable in treating these complex wounds.[26]

The efficacy of linezolid in treating various types of diabetic foot infections was studied in a trial conducted at 61 sites in 8 countries comparing the clinical and microbiological efficacy of linezolid (600 mg PO/IV BID) with either intravenous ampicillin-sulbactam (1.5-3 g every 6 hours) or oral amoxicillin-clavulanate (500-875 mg every 8 to 12 hours).[47,48] Patients were randomized on a 2-to-1 basis to linezolid. At the discretion of the investigator, patients in the aminopenicillin/β-lactamase inhibitor arm could receive supplemental intravenous vancomycin for suspected or proven MRSA infections. Patients in either arm could be given supplemental intravenous aztreonam for documented or suspected gram-negative pathogens. Patients received from 7 to 28 days of therapy and were either hospitalized or treated as outpatients. All types of foot infections were acceptable, with a few exclusions. Those with suspected osteomyelitis could be enrolled if the investigator believed 4 weeks of therapy would be sufficient. Patients with critical limb ischemia were excluded, but those with less severe arterial disease could be enrolled. A total of 371 evaluable patients were enrolled from April 2001 until March 2002.

Specimens for cultures were taken from wounds at baseline to document initial infections.[47] Cultures were then repeated 48 to 72 hours after treatment was initiated if wound material was available or bacteremia was documented, at the end of treatment, and at follow-up. Patients were withdrawn from the study if a culture grew a pathogen resistant to the study medication and the infection was not clinically improving; the infection was not responding; the patient failed to comply with the study regimen; the absolute neutrophil count was <500 cells/mm[3]; or persistent bacteremia developed.[49]

Clinical cure rates for patients treated with linezolid and aminopenicillin/β-lactam were comparable in both the ITT (81% linezolid; 71% aminopenicillin/β-lactam [95% CI, 1.9-25.2]) and clinically evaluable (83% linezolid; 73% aminopenicillin/β-lactam [95% CI, −.006 to .197]) popu-

lations.[47] In the largest subset of patients (78%), those with an infected ulcer, significantly more patients treated with linezolid than those treated with aminopenicillin/β-lactam were clinically cured (81% versus 68%; 95% CI, 1.9-25.2) (Table 5).[47] Similarly, a significantly higher clinical cure rate was also observed for patients without osteomyelitis who were treated with linezolid (86% linezolid versus 71% aminopenicillin/β-lactam; 95% CI, 4.5-25.7). These results were surprising in light of the fact that the number of patients enrolled was considered sufficient only to demonstrate equivalence. In patients with osteomyelitis, clinical cure rates were comparable (61% for linezolid versus 69% for aminopenicillin/β-lactam). Patients treated with aminopenicillin/β-lactamase inhibitor received concomitant therapy with vancomycin in 9.6% of cases. Only 2.5% of patients treated with an aminopenicillin/β-lactamase inhibitor and 5.0% of patients treated with linezolid received aztreonam. Eighty percent of those in the linezolid group who received aztreonam achieved a clinical cure, whereas none in the aminopenicillin/β-lactamase inhibitor did so.[49]

Drug-related adverse events occurred more frequently in the group receiving linezolid, but most events were mild to moderate in intensity and of limited duration.[47] Thrombocytopenia, reported in 3.7% of patients taking linezolid, usually occurred with treatment of more than 14 days.

The excellent outcome observed with linezolid monotherapy demonstrates the significance of gram-positive pathogens in diabetic foot infections. Linezolid can be considered an appropriate choice for treatment of diabetic foot infections when antibiotic-resistant gram-positive organisms (especially MRSA) are suspected or proven to be the causative pathogens.

Burns

Serious burn wounds pose some of the most difficult clinical challenges in the care and management of SSTIs.[50] Because burns destroy the skin barrier that normally prevents invasion of bacteria, burn victims are especially susceptible to nosocomial infection, including by resistant strains.[4,5,51] Although linezolid therapy for these infections has yet to be explored in clinical trials, the efficacy of this drug against virtually all antibiotic-resistant gram-positive pathogens suggests that it may have a role in this area. An in vitro study of gram-positive pathogens isolated from pediatric patients' burn wounds found that among 22 MRSA and 77 methicillin-resistant *Staphylococcus epidermidis* (MRSE) isolates, 96% were susceptible to linezolid; 100% were also susceptible to vancomycin.[52] However, among 21 *Enterococcus* isolates, only 38% were susceptible, a rate that is lower than has been reported in other studies.[52-54] The investigators concluded that linezolid may be an excellent adjunctive antibiotic in the treatment of burn patients, particularly those with infections caused by GISA.[52]

Bite Wounds

Bite wounds, whether inflicted by humans or animals, can lead to serious infections and related complications.[55] These infections often penetrate to tendons, joints, and bones. Numerous bacterial pathogens have been isolated from such wounds, including *Pasteurella, Actinobacillus, Haemophilus, Moraxella, Neisseria, Staphylococcus,* and *Streptococcus* species, as well as the anaerobic species *Bacteroides, Fusobacterium, Peptostreptococcus, Porphyromonas,* and *Prevotella*.[56] Linezolid exhibits activity against virtually all of the aerobic gram-positive organisms listed as well as many anaerobes, and, as shown in the Lovering et al[27] study, linezolid penetrates rapidly to bone, fat, and muscle. Thus, it may be a valuable agent in treating these infections, although most often it should be combined with an agent active against gram-negative bacilli.

Goldstein et al[56] compared the activity of linezolid with that of selected macrolides, amoxicillin-clavulanate, vancomycin, teicoplanin, and clindamycin against aerobic and anaerobic pathogens isolated from soft tissue bite infections in humans. The minimum concentrations needed to inhibit 90% of organisms (MIC_{90s}) of linezolid against many gram-negative bite wound pathogens were 8 µg/mL or greater. However, linezolid was active against *Pasteurella multocida* species at an MIC_{90} of 2 µg/mL or less and against *Pasteurella canis* at an MIC_{90} of 2 µg/mL. Only azithromycin and amoxicillin-clavulanate had lower MIC_{90s} for these pathogens (1 µg/mL and 0.25 µg/mL, respectively). The MIC_{90s} for vancomycin, teicoplanin, and clindamycin against all *Pasteurella* isolates were 32 µg/mL or higher. Consistent with in vitro and in vivo findings reported elsewhere, *Staphylococcus* and *Streptococcus* isolates were all susceptible to 2 µg of linezolid per mL or less.[11,12,56] Against *Staphylococcus* species, only amoxicillin-clavulanate had a lower MIC_{90} (0.5 µg/mL). The

authors concluded that linezolid appeared to be more active against common bite wound pathogens than the macrolides and warranted further clinical evaluation.

Osteomyelitis

Contiguous microbial invasion of bone is a serious complication of many wound infections and SSTIs.[30] Most cases of chronic contiguous osteomyelitis require surgical debridement, but antibiotic therapy is also needed. Choosing an appropriate antibiotic regimen for this type of complication can be difficult. A study of antibiotic concentrations achieved in bone in patients undergoing hip replacement revealed poorer penetration for vancomycin than either cefazolin or clindamycin.[57]

There are limited clinical data on using linezolid for treating osteomyelitis. The excellent penetration of linezolid in bone suggests it may be effective for treating osteomyelitis.[27] One concern about using linezolid for treating osteomyelitis is the long duration of therapy needed (at least 6 weeks).[44] Interpreting studies of bone penetration of antibiotics is fraught with difficult confounding issues. Results from an in vivo study of linezolid for treating experimental osteomyelitis in rats showed that the rats treated with linezolid fared no better than those that received no treatment and that cefazolin was significantly more effective.[58] However, results from case studies and the compassionate use program have shown efficacy for linezolid in treating osteomyelitis in humans. One case study described a patient undergoing hemodialysis who developed a catheter-related infection caused by vancomycin-resistant enterococci and MRSA.[59] An MRI scan revealed progressive destruction of the L3-L4 intervertebral disc. After failing to respond to other antibiotics, he was switched to intravenous linezolid (600 mg BID). Three weeks later, the patient underwent surgical debridement of necrotic bone and a bone graft. High levels of linezolid were detected in the debrided bone. Treatment with linezolid was continued for 3 more weeks, and despite the patient's renal failure, linezolid was well-tolerated without dose adjustment and effective in resolving the infection.

Finally, Rao et al[60] reported a series of 6 adult women who were treated with linezolid for chronic osteomyelitis involving lower extremity bones. Half the patients had diabetic foot infections; the other half had post-traumatic infections. Methicillin-resistant *S aureus* organisms were isolated from 4 patients, and methicillin-resistant coagulase-negative staphylococci were isolated from 2 others. Linezolid was administered for 6 to 15 weeks (mean 11 weeks), and all patients had a clinical and microbiological cure during the mean follow-up period of 37 weeks. One patient developed mild, reversible thrombocytopenia after 6 weeks of therapy.

Antimicrobial Resistance Among SSTI Pathogens

A major concern in the treatment of any bacterial infection is the susceptibility patterns of the likely causative pathogens. Some of the more common organisms that cause SSTIs, such as *S aureus*, have developed resistance to many of the antibiotics used to treat these infections. The North American SENTRY Antimicrobial Surveillance Program Group, which monitors resistance patterns in Canada and the United States, recently published a study report on susceptibility of bacterial isolates recovered from SSTIs in hospitalized patients.[42] Of the 1404 bacterial isolates studied, 46% were *S aureus*, 11% *Pseudomonas aeruginosa*, 8% *Enterococcus* species, 7% *Escherichia coli*, 6% *Enterobacter* species, and 5% *Klebsiella* species. Approximately 30% of *S aureus* isolates were resistant to oxacillin. This is particularly alarming because oxacillin and dicloxacillin are first-line therapeutic agents for SSTIs in many cases. On the other hand, vancomycin resistance among enterococci was only 8%, a marked decrease from earlier SENTRY program reports, and amikacin, cefepime, and the carbapenems remained effective against *P aeruginosa* and Enterobacteriaceae isolates, with more than 95% of isolates demonstrating susceptibility. Cefepime also was active against ceftazidime-resistant isolates of *Enterobacter* species. However, production of extended-spectrum β-lactamase was noted in 7% of *E coli* and 11% of *Klebsiella* species. These findings should be considered when choosing empiric treatment for SSTIs.

Summary

Linezolid has shown efficacy in treating various types of complicated and uncomplicated wounds and SSTIs caused by both antibiotic-resistant and susceptible strains of gram-positive cocci. It is highly active against many common skin and soft tissue pathogens. The excellent penetration of linezolid into most body tissues provides therapeutic levels at the site of wounds and SSTIs. With both intravenous and oral administration available, patients can make the transition from the hospital to home more easily. Furthermore, the drug's relatively narrow spectrum of activity means it can be used for targeted indications and may be less likely to provoke resistance across a wide variety of bacteria. Other key advantages of treating SSTIs with linezolid include the lack of interactions with most other medications, the twice-a-day dosing schedule, and the ability to use this agent in most patients with renal or hepatic dysfunction.

Clearly, more data are necessary to evaluate the compound's effectiveness in treating such complex infections as infected burn wounds, bite wounds, and osteomyelitis. However, indications are that linezolid is effective in such diverse infections as diabetic foot infections, wound infections, cellulitis, skin abscesses, and erysipelas caused by aerobic gram-positive pathogens.

References

1. Lipsky BA, Berendt AR. Principles and practice of antibiotic therapy of diabetic foot infections. *Diabetes Metab Res Rev.* 2000;16(suppl 1): S42-S46.
2. Lipsky BA. Cellulitis, erysipelas, and necrotizing soft-tissue infections. Best Practice of Medicine Web site. July 1, 2003. Available at: http://merck.micromedex.com/index.asp?page=bpm_brief&article_id=BPMO1ID08. Accessed July 8, 2003.
3. Lipsky BA. Infectious problems of the foot in diabetic patients. In: Bowker JH, Pfeifer MA, eds. *Levin and O'Neal's The Diabetic Foot.* 6th ed. St. Louis, Mo: Mosby, Inc.; 2001:467-480.
4. Bowler PG, Duerden BI, Armstrong DG. Wound microbiology and associated approaches to wound management. *Clin Microbiol Rev.* 2001;14:244-269.
5. Bamberg R, Sullivan PK, Conner-Kerr T. Diagnosis of wound infections: current culturing practices of US wound care professionals. *Wounds.* 2002;14:314-327.
6. Oncul O, Yuksel F, Altunay H, Acikel C, Celikoz B, Cavuslu S. The evaluation of nosocomial infection during 1-year-period in the burn unit of a training hospital in Istanbul, Turkey. *Burns.* 2002;28: 738-744.
7. Dang CN, Prasad YD, Boulton AJ, Jude EB. Methicillin-resistant *Staphylococcus aureus* in the diabetic foot clinic: a worsening problem. *Diabet Med.* 2003;20:159-161.
8. Grimble SA, Magee TR, Galland RB. Methicillin resistant *Staphylococcus aureus* in patients undergoing major amputation. *Eur J Vasc Endovasc Surg.* 2001;22:215-218.
9. Stevens DL, Smith LG, Bruss JB, et al. Randomized comparison of linezolid (PNU-100766) versus oxacillin-dicloxacillin for treatment of complicated skin and soft tissue infections. *Antimicrob Agents Chemother.* 2000;44:3408-3413.
10. Ford CW, Hamel JC, Wilson DM, et al. In vivo activities of U-100592 and U-100766, novel oxazolidinone antimicrobial agents, against experimental bacterial infections. *Antimicrob Agents Chemother.* 1996;40:1508-1513.
11. Jones RN, Johnson DM, Erwin ME. In vitro antimicrobial activities and spectra of U-100592 and U-100766, two novel fluorinated oxa-

zolidinones. *Antimicrob Agents Chemother.* 1996;40:720-726.

12. Jorgensen JH, McElmeel ML, Trippy CW. In vitro activities of the oxazolidinone antibiotics U-100592 and U-100766 against *Staphylococcus aureus* and coagulase-negative *Staphylococcus* species. *Antimicrob Agents Chemother.* 1997;41:465-467.

13. Mason EO Jr, Lamberth LB, Kaplan SL. In vitro activities of oxazolidinones U-100592 and U-100766 against penicillin-resistant and cephalosporin-resistant strains of *Streptococcus pneumoniae*. *Antimicrob Agents Chemother.* 1996;40:1039-1040.

14. Kaatz GW, Seo SM. In vitro activities of oxazolidinone compounds U100592 and U100766 against *Staphylococcus aureus* and *Staphylococcus epidermidis*. *Antimicrob Agents Chemother.* 1996;40:799-801.

15. Zurenko GE, Yagi BH, Schaadt RD, et al. In vitro activities of U-100592 and U-100766, novel oxazolidinone antibacterial agents. *Antimicrob Agents Chemother.* 1996;40:839-845.

16. Eliopoulos GM, Wennersten CB, Gold HS, Moellering RC Jr. In vitro activities in new oxazolidinone antimicrobial agents against enterococci. *Antimicrob Agents Chemother.* 1996;40:1745-1747.

17. Mylotte JM, Graham R, Kahler L, Young L, Goodnough S. Epidemiology of nosocomial infection and resistant organisms in patients admitted for the first time to an acute rehabilitation unit. *Clin Infect Dis.* 2000;30:425-432.

18. National Nosocomial Infections Surveillance System. National Nosocomial Infections Surveillance (NNIS) System report, data summary from January 1992-June 2001, issued August 2001. *Am J Infect Control.* 2001;29:404-421.

19. Khare M, Keady D. Antimicrobial therapy of methicillin resistant *Staphylococcus aureus* infection. *Pharmacotherapy.* 2003;4:165-177.

20. Centers for Disease Control and Prevention. Reduced susceptibility of *Staphylococcus aureus* to vancomycin—Japan, 1996. *MMWR Morb Mortal Wkly Rep.* 1997;46:624-626.

21. Centers for Disease Control and Prevention. *Staphylococcus aureus* with reduced susceptibility to vancomycin—United States, 1997. *MMWR Morb Mortal Wkly Rep.* 1997;46:765-766.

22. Centers for Disease Control and Prevention. *Staphylococcus aureus* resistant to vancomycin—United States, 2002. *MMWR Morb Mortal Wkly Rep.* 2002;51:565-567.

23. Fines M, Leclercq R. Activity of linezolid against Gram-positive cocci possessing genes conferring resistance to protein synthesis inhibitors. *J Antimicrob Chemother.* 2000;45:797-802.

24. Tsiodras S, Gold HS, Sakoulas G, et al. Linezolid resistance in a clinical isolate of *Staphylococcus aureus*. *Lancet.* 2001;358:207-208.

25. Wilson SE, Solomkin JS, Le V, Cammarata SK, Bruss JB. A severity score for complicated skin and soft tissue infections derived from phase III studies of linezolid. *Am J Surg.* 2003;185:369-375.

26. Gee T, Ellis R, Marshall G, Andrews J, Ashby J, Wise R. Pharmacokinetics and tissue penetration of linezolid following multiple oral doses. *Antimicrob Agents Chemother.* 2001;45:1843-1846.

27. Lovering AM, Zhang J, Bannister GC, et al. Penetration of linezolid into bone, fat, muscle and haematoma of patients undergoing routine hip replacement. *J Antimicrob Chemother.* 2002;50:73-77.

28. Yagi BH, Zurenko GE. In vitro activity of linezolid and eperezolid, two novel oxazolidinone antimicrobial agents, against anaerobic bacteria. *Anaerobe.* 1997;3:301-306.

29. Zyvox [package insert]. Kalamazoo, Mich: Pharmacia & Upjohn Company; 2003.

30. Stevens DL, Herr D, Lampiris H, et al, and the Linezolid MRSA Study Group. Linezolid versus vancomycin for the treatment of methicillin-resistant *Staphylococcus aureus* infections. *Clin Infect Dis.* 2002;34:1481-1490.

31. Centers for Disease Control and Prevention. Fact sheet: 12 steps to prevent antimicrobial resistance among hospitalized adults. Available at: http://www.cdc.gov/drugresistance/healthcare/ha/12 steps_HA.htm. Accessed August 3, 2003.

32. Siami G, Christou N, Eiseman I, Tack KJ, and the Clinafloxacin Severe Skin and Soft Tissue Infections Study Group. Clinafloxacin versus piperacillin-tazobactam in treatment of patients with severe skin and soft tissue infections. *Antimicrob Agents Chemother.* 2001;45: 525-531.

33. Graham DR, Talan DA, Nichols RL, et al. Once-daily, high-dose levofloxacin versus ticarcillin-clavulanate alone or followed by amoxicillin-clavulanate for complicated skin and skin-structure infections: a randomized, open-label trial. *Clin Infect Dis.* 2002;35:381-389.

34. Wible K, Tregnaghi M, Bruss J, Fleishaker D, Naberhuis-Stehouwer S, Hilty M. Linezolid versus cefadroxil in the treatment of skin and skin structure infections in children. *Pediatr Infect Dis J.* 2003;22:315-323.

35. Tarshis GA, Miskin BM, Jones TM, et al. Once-daily oral gatifloxacin versus oral levofloxacin in treatment of uncomplicated skin and soft tissue infections: double-blind, multicenter, randomized study. *Antimicrob Agents Chemother.* 2001;45:2358-2362.

36. Li JZ, Willke RJ, Rittenhouse BE, Rybak MJ. Effect of linezolid versus vancomycin on length of hospital stay in patients with complicated skin and soft tissue infections caused by known or suspected methicillin-resistant staphylococci: results from a randomized clinical trial. *Surg Infect [Larchmt].* 2003;4:45-58.

37. Palumbo P, Melton J III. Peripheral vascular disease and diabetes. In: Harris MI, Cowie CC, Stern MP, Boyko EJ, Reiber GE, Bennett PH, eds. *Diabetes in America.* 2nd ed. Bethesda, Md: National Institutes of Health; 1995:401-408.

38. Reiber GE, Lipsky BA, Gibbons GW. The burden of diabetic foot ulcers. *Am J Surg.* 1998;176(suppl 2A):5S-10S.

39. Lipsky BA, Pecoraro RE, Wheat LJ. The diabetic foot: soft tissue and bone infection. *Infect Dis Clin North Am.* 1990;4:409-432.

40. Reiber GE, Boyko EJ, Smith DG. Lower extremity foot ulcers and amputations in diabetes. In: Harris MI, Cowie CC, Stern MP, Boyko EJ, Reiber GE, Bennett PH, eds. *Diabetes in America.* 2nd ed. Bethesda, Md: National Institutes of Health; 1995:409-427.

41. Pathare NA, Bal A, Talvalkar GV, Antani DU. Diabetic foot infections: a study of microorganisms associated with the different Wagner grades. *Indian J Pathol Microbiol.* 1998;41:437-441.

42. Rennie RP, Jones RN, Mutnick AH, and SENTRY Program Study Group (North America). Occurrence and antimicrobial susceptibility patterns of pathogens isolated from skin and soft tissue infections: report from the SENTRY Antimicrobial Surveillance Program (United States and Canada, 2000). *Diagn Microbiol Infect Dis.* 2003;45:287-293.

43. Tentolouris N, Jude EB, Smirnof I, Knowles EA, Boulton AJ. Methicillin-resistant *Staphylococcus aureus*: an increasing problem in a diabetic foot clinic. *Diabet Med.* 1999;16:767-771.

44. Lipsky BA. Osteomyelitis of the foot in diabetic patients. *Clin Infect Dis.* 1997;25:1318-1326.

45. Pittet D, Wyssa B, Herter-Clavel C, Kursteiner K, Vaucher J, Lew PD. Outcome of diabetic foot infections treated conservatively: a retrospective cohort study with long-term follow-up. *Arch Intern Med.* 1999;159:851-856.

46. Data on file. Pfizer Inc. New York, NY.

47. Lipsky BA, Armstrong D, Acin F, Blume P, Kivitz A, Norden C, and the Linezolid DFI Study Group. Treating diabetic foot infections with linezolid vs aminopenicillins: a randomized international multicenter trial. Paper presented at: Infectious Diseases Society of America 40th Annual Meeting; October 24-27, 2002; Chicago, Ill. Abstract 189.

48. Lipsky BA, Norden C, Tang T, Patel D. A new antibiotic agent for diabetic foot infections: design of a randomized controlled trial of IV or oral linezolid vs aminopenicillins. Paper presented at: European Association for the Study of Diabetes–Diabetic Foot Study Group; August 29-September 1, 2002; Lake Balaton, Hungary. Abstract A24.

49. Lipsky BA, Itani K, Norden CT, and the Linezolid Diabetic Foot Infection Study Group. Treating diabetic foot infections with linezolid vs aminopenicillins: a randomized, international multicenter trial.

Clin Infect Dis. in press.

50. Zhou YP, Ren JL, Zhou WM, et al. Experience in the treatment of patients with burns covering more than 90% TBSA and full-thickness burns exceeding 70% TBSA. *Asian J Surg.* 2002;25:154-156.

51. Cook N. Methicillin-resistant *Staphylococcus aureus* versus the burn patient. *Burns.* 1998;24:91-98.

52. Heggers JP, Goodheart R, McCoy L, et al. Is linezolid an alternative to vancomycin in the treatment of burns? *J Burns Surg Wound Care [serial online].* 2002;1:13.

53. Jones RN, Ballow CH, Biedenbach DJ, ZAPS Study Group Medical Centers. Multi-laboratory assessment of the linezolid spectrum of activity using the Kirby-Bauer disk diffusion method: report of the Zyvox Antimicrobial Potency Study (ZAPS) in the United States. *Diagn Microbiol Infect Dis.* 2001;40:59-66.

54. Henwood CJ, Livermore DM, Johnson AP, James D, Warner M, Gardiner A. Susceptibility of gram-positive cocci from 25 UK hospitals to antimicrobial agents including linezolid. *J Antimicrob Chemother.* 2000;46:931-940.

55. Goldstein EJ. Bite wounds and infection. *Clin Infect Dis.* 1992;14:633-638.

56. Goldstein EJ, Citron DM, Merriam CV. Linezolid activity compared to those of selected macrolides and other agents against aerobic and anaerobic pathogens isolated from soft tissue bite infections in humans. *Antimicrob Agents Chemother.* 1999;43:1469-1474.

57. Graziani AL, Lawson LA, Gibson GA, Steinberg MA, MacGregor RR. Vancomycin concentrations in infected and noninfected human bone. *Antimicrob Agents Chemother.* 1988;32:1320-1322.

58. Patel R, Piper KE, Rouse MS, Steckelberg JM. Linezolid therapy of *Staphylococcus aureus* experimental osteomyelitis. *Antimicrob Agents Chemother.* 2000;44:3438-3440.

59. Melzer M, Goldsmith D, Gransden W. Successful treatment of vertebral osteomyelitis with linezolid in a patient receiving hemodialysis and with persistent methicillin-resistant *Staphylococcus aureus* and vancomycin-resistant *Enterococcus* bacteremias. *Clin Infect Dis.* 2000;31:208-209.

60. Rao N, Ziran BH, Santa ER. Treatment of chronic osteomyelitis with linezolid. Paper presented at: Infectious Diseases Society of America 40th Annual Meeting; October 24-27, 2002; Chicago, Ill. Abstract 195.

CHAPTER SEVEN CME QUESTIONS

1. A recent survey of wound care specialists found that only 12% of clinicians routinely culture wounds. What percentage of wounds are treated without ever being cultured?

   a. 20%

   b. 45%

   c. 70%

   d. 83%

2. The results of a large phase III clinical trial of the safety and efficacy of linezolid versus oxacillin-dicloxacillin in the treatment of complicated skin and soft tissue infections found that, among clinically evaluable patients, cure rates were:

   a. 63% for linezolid and 74% for oxacillin-dicloxacillin

   b. 74% for linezolid and 86% for oxacillin-dicloxacillin

   c. 65% for linezolid and 63% for oxacillin-dicloxacillin

   d. 89% for linezolid and 86% for oxacillin-dicloxacillin

3. True or False: Switching a patient from intravenous linezolid to an oral form requires a dosage adjustment.

4. The ability to switch from intravenous to oral medication with linezolid might allow for a shorter hospital stay. What was the mean length of hospital stay for linezolid versus vancomycin as reported by Li et al?

   a. 8.4 days with linezolid versus 10.5 days with vancomycin

   b. 13.5 days with linezolid versus 14.6 days with vancomycin

   c. 16.4 days with linezolid versus 19.5 days with vancomycin

   d. 21.2 days with linezolid versus 23.1 days with vancomycin

5. Oxacillin and dicloxacillin are often first-line therapy for skin and soft tissue infections; however, a recent SENTRY Antimicrobial Surveillance Program report found what percentage of *Staphylococcus aureus* isolates to be resistant to oxacillin?

   a. 25%

   b. 30%

   c. 40%

   d. 45%

CREATION OF A NOVEL CLASS:

THE USE OF LINEZOLID IN SURGICAL MEDICINE

EDITOR

John A. Weigelt, MD, DVM

LEARNING OBJECTIVES

After completion of this chapter, readers should be able to:

1. Describe those pathogens most likely to be involved in surgical site infections.

2. Discuss the importance of methicillin-resistant *Staphylococcus aureus* (MRSA) as a pathogen in surgical site infections.

3. Recognize the importance of antimicrobial prophylaxis in surgery as a method to reduce surgical wound infection.

4. Review the data on the efficacy and safety of linezolid in the treatment of surgical wound infections.

THE OXAZOLIDINONE ANTIBIOTICS

Surgery involves the intentional creation of a wound, which incurs the risk of infection inherent to any wound. Wounds caused by hospital procedures—either surgical or engendered through the use of intravenous medical devices—are among the leading causes of nosocomial infection.[1] Surgical wounds are categorized from class I/clean to class IV/dirty-infected (Table 1).[2] Many of the aerobic pathogens involved in these infections are the same as those implicated in skin and soft tissue infections (SSTIs)—gram-positive bacteria such as *Staphylococcus aureus* and *Staphylococcus epidermidis*, and gram-negative bacteria such as *Pseudomonas aeruginosa*.[1] The rate of infection depends on the type of surgery, varying from relatively low rates with clean surgery (eg, thoracic or orthopedic surgery) to much higher rates with surgical procedures that carry a greater risk of contamination (eg, intra-abdominal surgery).[3] Table 2 lists surgical site infection rates by operative procedure and risk index category.

Microbial Epidemiology of Surgical Site Infections

An epidemiological and microbiological study of surgical wound infections by Giacometti et al[1] in 2000 found that 28% of pathogens isolated from infected wounds were *S aureus*, 25% were *P aeruginosa*, 8% were *Escherichia coli*, 7% were *S epidermidis*, and 6% were *Enterococcus faecalis*. Although pure cultures were most likely to produce *S aureus*, *P aeruginosa*, and Enterobacteriaceae, polymicrobial infections often involved both gram-positive and gram-negative microbes. *S aureus* was the most frequent cause of surgical wound infections in this study, and 54% of the total *S aureus* isolates were methicillin resistant. Most interesting was the frequent coinfection with *S aureus* and *P aeruginosa*, the incidence of which increased over the 2-year period from 1997 to 1999. In this population, methicillin resistance was documented in 74% of the *S aureus* isolates.

The authors performed a retrospective analysis of the records of 676 patients who had surgery, including abdominal, vascular, orthopedic, and reparative, and tracked the increasing resistance found in wound pathogens over a 6-year period (1993 to 1999).[1] Susceptibility data collected indicated that some antibiotics commonly prescribed for surgical prophylaxis had only limited activity against the major surgical wound pathogens. These data, if confirmed, suggest that antimicrobial agents or drug combinations with wider spectra and less susceptibility to the enzymatic degradation by bacterial pathogens should be used as

---

Table 1. Surgical Wound Classification

Class I/clean	An uninfected operative wound in which no inflammation is encountered and the respiratory, alimentary, genital, or uninfected urinary tract is not entered. In addition, clean wounds are primarily closed and, if necessary, drained with closed drainage. Operative incisional wounds that follow nonpenetrating (blunt) trauma should be included in this category if they meet the criteria.
Class II/clean-contaminated	An operative wound in which the respiratory, alimentary, genital, or urinary tract is entered under controlled conditions and without unusual contamination. Specifically, operations involving the biliary tract, appendix, vagina, and oropharynx are included in this category, provided no evidence of infection or major break in technique is encountered.
Class III/contaminated	Open, fresh, accidental wounds. In addition, operations with major breaks in sterile technique (eg, open cardiac massage) or gross spillage from the gastrointestinal tract, and incisions in which acute, nonpurulent inflammation is encountered are included in this category.
Class IV/dirty-infected	Old traumatic wounds with retained devitalized tissue and those that involve existing clinical infection or perforated viscera. This definition suggests that the organisms causing postoperative infection were present in the operative field before the operation.

Table 2. Surgical Site Infection Rates per 100 Operations, by Operative Procedure and Risk Index Category, January 1992-June 2001

Operative Procedure	Duration Cutpoint (h)	Risk Index Category	N	Rate
Cardiac surgery	5	0	1510	0.66
CABG-chest and donor site	5	0	1836	1.20
CABG-chest only	4	0,1	11278	2.13
Other cardiovascular surgery	2	0,1	7680	0.65
Other respiratory surgery	2	0,1,2,3	1522	2.69
Thoracic surgery	3	0	1178	0.34
Liver/pancreas	4	0	362	3.04
Other digestive surgery	3	0	1128	2.30
Small bowel surgery	3	0	1230	5.20
Laparotomy	2	0	5192	1.71
Nephrectomy	4	0,1,2,3	2657	1.13
Other genitourinary surgery	2	0	11226	0.37
Prostatectomy	4	0	2207	0.91
Head and neck surgery	7	0	523	2.49
Other ENT surgery	2	0,1	3371	0.21
Herniorrhaphy	2	0	9292	0.77
Mastectomy	3	0	11330	1.80
Craniotomy	4	0	3546	0.90
Other nervous system	4	0,1,2,3	1980	1.62
Ventricular shunt	2	0	2619	4.35
Cesarean section	1	0	111335	2.86
Abdominal hysterectomy	2	0	29936	1.46
Other obstetrical surgery	1	0,1,2,3	1063	0.47
Vaginal hysterectomy	2	0,1,2,3	20342	1.29
Limb amputation	1	0,1,2,3	8465	3.71
Spinal fusion	4	0	28484	1.16
Open reduction fracture	2	0	12696	0.73
Hip prosthesis	2	0	21451	0.89
Knee prosthesis	2	0	30533	0.84
Laminectomy	2	0	46821	0.93
Other musculoskeletal	3	0	13841	0.65
Other prosthesis	3	0,1,2,3	2238	0.67
Other hematologic/lymphatic system	3	0,1,2,3	932	1.93
Other endrocrine system	3	0	1894	0.16
Other eye surgery	2	0,1,2,3	506	0.79
Other integumentary system	2	0,1,2,3	7039	1.25
Skin graft	3	0	925	0.86
Splenectomy	2	0	317	0.95
Organ transplant	6	0,1	3323	4.44
Vascular surgery	3	0	6099	0.89

CABG = coronary artery bypass graft; ENT = ear, nose, and throat.
Adapted from National Nosocomial Infections Surveillance System. National Nosocomial Infections Surveillance (NNIS) System report, data summary from January 1992-June 2001, issued August 2001. *Am J Infect Control.* 2001;29:404-421.

prophylaxis. However, this therapeutic strategy may or may not be associated with lower wound infection rates.

Likely pathogens causing surgical wound infections differ according to surgical site.[4] In clean surgical procedures, *S aureus* organisms from the patient's skin or surround-ing environment are most often implicated in infection, whereas in contaminated procedures, pathogens more often resemble the normal microflora of the surgical site.[4,5] Table 3 lists the pathogens most likely to cause infection after various surgical procedures.

Table 3. Surgeries and Likely Surgical Site Infection Pathogens

Surgeries	Likely Pathogens*†
Placement of all grafts, prostheses, or implants	*S aureus*; coagulase-negative staphylococci
Cardiac	*S aureus*; coagulase-negative staphylococci
Neurosurgery	*S aureus*; coagulase-negative staphylococci
Breast	*S aureus*; coagulase-negative staphylococci
Ophthalmic	*S aureus*; coagulase-negative staphylococci; streptococci; gram-negative bacilli
Orthopedic • Total joint replacement • Closed fractures/use of nails, bone plates, other internal fixation devices • Functional repair without implant/device • Trauma	*S aureus*; coagulase-negative staphylococci; gram-negative bacilli
Noncardiac thoracic • Thoracic (lobectomy, pneumonectomy, wedge resection, other noncardiac mediastinal procedures) • Closed tube thoracostomy	*S aureus*; coagulase-negative staphylococci; *S pneumoniae*; gram-negative bacilli
Vascular	*S aureus*; coagulase-negative staphylococci
Appendectomy	Gram-negative bacilli; anaerobes
Biliary tract	Gram-negative bacilli; anaerobes
Colorectal	Gram-negative bacilli; anaerobes
Gastroduodenal	Gram-negative bacilli; streptococci; oropharyngeal anaerobes (eg, peptostreptococci)
Head and neck (major procedures with incision through oropharyngeal mucosa)	*S aureus*; streptococci; oropharyngeal anaerobes (eg, peptostreptococci)
Obstetric and gynecologic	Gram-negative bacilli; enterococci; group B streptococci; anaerobes
Urologic	Gram-negative bacilli

*Likely pathogens from both endogenous and exogenous sources.
†Staphylococci will be associated with surgical site infection after all types of operations.
Adapted from Mangram AJ, Horan TC, Pearson ML, Silver LC, Jarvis WR, Hospital Infection Control Practices Advisory Committee. Guideline for prevention of surgical site infection, 1999. *Infect Control Hosp Epidemiol.* 1999;20:247-278, with permission. Copyright © 1999, The Society for Healthcare Epidemiology of America, Inc. All rights reserved.

Antimicrobial Prophylaxis and Surgery

Prevention of surgical site infection is a primary concern and must be taken into account before surgery. The Centers for Disease Control and Prevention (CDC) Hospital Infection Control Practices Advisory Committee[2] guidelines recommend treating and resolving any remote infection before surgery or postponing surgery until the infection is treated. Removal of hair from the operative site should be done only if needed to facilitate the surgery itself, and, if needed, should be done immediately before surgery. The patient's serum blood glucose should be controlled in the perioperative period, tobacco use should be stopped 30 days before surgery, and the patient should shower or bathe the night before the procedure, preferably using an antiseptic soap. These recommendations are supported by evidence from experimental, clinical, and epidemiologic studies.

Other suggestions to reduce the risk of surgical wound infections include applying preoperative antiseptic skin preparation in concentric circles from the incision site toward the periphery and keeping the preoperative stay in the hospital as short as possible.[2] Some of these suggestions are based on theoretical rationale and less rigorous data but appear to be valid nonetheless. The application of mupirocin in nares, improved patient nutritional status, and discontinuation or tapering of systemic steroid use before elective surgery are issues that remain unsubstantiated by clinical data.[2] Another unresolved issue is whether to increase oxygenation of the wound.[2,6] However, the results of a trial by Greif et al[7] suggest that perioperative administration of supplemental oxygen may reduce surgical site infection. In a patient population of 500, those who received 80% oxygen during surgery and for 2 hours afterward had a 5% infection rate, compared with an 11% rate for patients who received 30% oxygen.

Antimicrobial prophylaxis is recommended for procedures with high infection rates, including procedures involving implants, and where a wound infection would have severe or life-threatening consequences.[8] The value of perioperative or prophylactic antibiotics is a marked reduction in the risk of surgical site infection, according to a meta-analysis and systematic review.[9] When the antimicrobial agent is selected for its effect on expected pathogens associated with the type of surgery, a lower rate of surgical wound infection is seen.[2] Broad-spectrum agents are more

appropriate in surgery involving a higher risk of contamination, such as intra-abdominal or gynecological surgery, whereas first-generation cephalosporins can be used when susceptible staphylococci are suspected.[2,9] A single dose of antibiotic for prophylaxis is at least as effective as multiple-dose regimens in many surgical procedures. However, when the duration of an operation exceeds the half-life of the drug, redosing should be considered.[8] Short-term use poses less of a risk to the patient in terms of adverse events and is less likely to provoke bacterial resistance.[9]

Timing of antibiotic administration is crucial to achieve the best results from perioperative antibiotics as measured by the prevention of postoperative surgical site infection. Administration of initial antibiotic prophylaxis must be timed to ensure that adequate tissue levels are achieved in the skin when the incision is made.[2] Common clinical practice is to administer the drug 30 minutes before the incision.[8] The CDC guidelines recommend choosing an antimicrobial agent with efficacy against the expected pathogens and using intravenous administration to maintain adequate serum levels during the operation and for a maximum of a few hours after the incision is closed.[2] The chosen agent should be safe, inexpensive, bactericidal, and able to achieve therapeutic serum levels as well as tissue levels, because fibrin-enmeshed bacteria may be present in the clotted blood inherent to all surgical wounds. In the case of colorectal operations, the colon should be mechanically prepared before surgery through the use of enemas and cathartics. Antibiotic use in these cases can include nonabsorbable oral antimicrobial agents, perioperative broad-spectrum antibiotics, or both. Recently, the need for mechanical bowel preparation has been challenged[10]; however, sufficient data are not available at this time to change the current recommendations.

Cephalosporins are widely used in surgical prophylaxis because they are effective against many gram-positive and gram-negative bacteria.[2] For adequate coverage of anaerobic organisms, another drug may be needed to supplement the cephalosporin regimen. In patients with a penicillin allergy, clindamycin or vancomycin can be used. Although vancomycin may be necessary in cases where infections with methicillin-resistant *Staphylococcus aureus* (MRSA) or methicillin-resistant coagulase-negative staphylococci are probable, it is not recommended for routine antimicrobial prophylaxis.

Therapeutic Use of Antibiotics in Treating Surgical Site Infection

Surgical site infection surveillance of hospitalized patients may be done either directly by trained personnel observing the surgical site for signs of inflammation and infection or indirectly by reviewing patients' medical records.[2] The trend toward decreased hospital length of stay (LOS) creates a greater need for postdischarge surveillance. Often it is performed at a follow-up visit, but it is sometimes done via phone surveys or home nursing surveillance. It has been shown to be the most effective on postsurgical day 21 because this is the point where 90% of infections have occurred.[11] Once detected, a surgical site infection demands prompt attention, which may include simple opening of the wound without antibiotic treatment, antibiotic treatment alone, opening the wound and treatment with antibiotics, or wound debridement and antibiotic treatment.[5]

Surgical site infections are considered SSTIs in most cases, and treatment should be directed at the suspected pathogens until culture results identify the cause. Because staphylococci, particularly *S aureus*, are commonly isolated, treatment regimens should include drugs with gram-positive coverage. The problem in selecting gram-positive coverage is the growing concern about resistant gram-positive organisms, including staphylococci and en-

Table 4. Susceptibility Patterns of the Most Frequently Isolated Bacteria From Surgical Wound Infections

Organism(s)	Agent	% of Strains Showing Resistance		
		1993-1995	1995-1997	1997-1999
Enterobacteriaceae	Ampicillin	53.1	56.1	57.1
	AMX-CLV	16.3	18.4	18.1
	Piperacillin	10.2	11.2	12.4
	Cefazolin	51.0	53.1	53.3
	Ceftriaxone	10.2	15.3	17.1
	Imipenem	6.1	7.1	9.5
	Ciprofloxacin	16.3	20.4	24.8
	Netilmicin	14.3	13.3	17.6
	TMP-SMX	36.7	35.7	40.9
Pseudomonas aeruginosa	AMX-CLV	56.1	52.9	57.7
	Piperacillin	12.2	17.6	23.1
	Cefazolin	100.0	100.0	100.0
	Ceftazidime	14.6	13.7	20.5
	Ceftriaxone	56.1	58.8	64.1
	Imipenem	9.7	15.7	21.8
	Ciprofloxacin	19.5	31.4	39.7
	Netilmicin	12.2	15.7	17.9
	TMP-SMX	87.8	94.1	96.1
Staphylococcus aureus[*]	Methicillin	55.3	47.0	60.2
	AMX-CLV	21.3	19.7	26.9
	Piperacillin	42.5	36.4	46.1
	Cefazolin	25.5	24.2	28.2
	Imipenem	14.9	13.6	21.8
	Clarithromycin	19.1	19.7	27.0
	Ciprofloxacin	25.5	24.2	33.3
	Netilmicin	12.8	15.1	20.5
	Teicoplanin	0.0	1.5	1.3
	Vancomycin	0.0	1.5	1.3

Organism(s)	Agent	% of Strains Showing Resistance		
		1993-1995	1995-1997	1997-1999
Coagulase-negative staphylococci	Methicillin	42.4	47.9	59.6
	AMX-CLV	18.2	20.8	26.3
	Piperacillin	33.3	39.6	47.4
	Cefazolin	24.2	20.8	29.8
	Imipenem	12.1	14.6	22.8
	Clarithromycin	21.2	25.0	28.1
	Ciprofloxacin	24.2	29.2	35.1
	Netilmicin	9.1	12.5	17.5
	Teicoplanin	0.0	2.1	1.7
	Vancomycin	0.0	2.1	1.7
Streptococcus species	AMX-CLV	7.1	8.6	6.6
	Piperacillin	7.1	11.4	10.0
	Cefazolin	10.7	14.3	13.3
	Imipenem	0.0	0.0	0.0
	Clarithromycin	10.7	14.3	13.3
	Ciprofloxacin	17.8	20.0	23.3
	Netilmicin	14.3	22.8	20.0
	Teicoplanin	0.0	0.0	0.0
	Vancomycin	0.0	0.0	0.0
Enterococcus species	AMX-CLV	9.1	7.1	13.0
	Piperacillin	18.2	14.3	13.0
	Cefazolin	36.4	35.7	34.8
	Imipenem	9.1	7.1	8.7
	Clarithromycin	36.4	42.8	39.1
	Ciprofloxacin	54.5	50.0	56.5
	Netilmicin	45.4	42.8	43.5
	Teicoplanin	0.0	0.0	4.3
	Vancomycin	0.0	7.1	4.3

AMX-CLV = amoxicillin-clavulanate; TMP-SMX = trimethoprim-sulfamethoxazole.

* In this study, *S aureus* was the most common cause of surgical wound infections. Methicillin resistance was documented in 104 (54.4%) of 191 *S aureus* isolates. Although amoxicillin-clavulanate, cefazolin, and imipenem were shown to be active in vitro against more than 60% of the isolates, according to National Committee for Clinical Laboratory Standards recommendations, the methicillin-resistant staphylococci were considered resistant to all β-lactams, including penicillins, cephalosporins, β-lactam–β-lactamase inhibitor combinations, and carbapenems, since these agents may be clinically ineffective against such organisms.

Adapted from Giacometti A, Cirioni O, Schimizzi AM, et al. Epidemiology and microbiology of surgical wound infections. *J Clin Microbiol.* 2000;38:918-922, with permission from the American Society for Microbiology. Copyright © 2000, the American Society for Microbiology. All rights reserved.

terococci. The prevalence of MRSA is increasing worldwide and has been observed in up to 39% of wound or skin isolates.[12] The incidence of MRSA in surgical wound infection depends on a number of factors, but it has been rising over the last decade. Between 1995 and 2000, the National Nosocomial Infections Surveillance System[3] reported that nearly 30% of enterococcal isolates were resistant to vancomycin, and the CDC reported the presence of vancomycin-intermediate-resistant *Staphylococcus aureus* in Japan[13] in 1996 and in the United States[14] in 1997. Giacometti et al[1] found that nearly one third of *S aureus*

and coagulase-negative *Staphylococcus* isolates, nearly one quarter of *Streptococcus* isolates, and more than half of *Enterococcus* isolates were resistant to ciprofloxacin (Table 4). Although vancomycin resistance remained low in that study, it was noted for *S aureus*, coagulase-negative staphylococci, and enterococci species.

The Role of Linezolid in Treating SSTIs

As the first member of a novel class of antibiotics (the oxazolidinones), linezolid has shown efficacy equal or superior to that of standard antibiotic therapy in the treatment of SSTI, wound infection, nosocomial pneumonia, and bacteremia.[15-18]

The most likely pathogens involved in surgical site infections are listed in Table 3.[2] One of the most common surgical site pathogens is S aureus. Linezolid is efficacious in treating SSTIs caused by S aureus, suggesting that it may be a valuable therapeutic option in treating surgical site infections as well.[16] Two comparator-controlled studies of linezolid provided data on clinical cure rates achieved with linezolid versus oxacillin-dicloxacillin and vancomycin.[16,17] In the first study, which was part of the submission to the US Food and Drug Administration (FDA) for approval of the drug and investigated the use of linezolid for the treatment of complicated SSTIs, 400 patients were randomized to the linezolid group and 419 to the oxacillin-dicloxacillin group.[16] A subset of 25 patients (6%) randomized to the linezolid group and 26 patients (6%) to the oxacillin-dicloxacillin group had infected surgical incisions. The cure rate in the clinically evaluable patient population was 89% for the linezolid group and 86% for the oxacillin-dicloxacillin group (P=.300; 95% CI, −2.5 to 8.2 [point estimate 2.8]). Although there was no breakdown by diagnosis and thus no separate cure rate given for the surgical group, the authors stated that no statistically significant differences were observed between treatment groups when analyzed according to diagnosis. Similar efficacy also was demonstrated for all 3 major pathogens selected: S aureus, Streptococcus pyogenes, and Streptococcus agalactiae (S aureus P=.139; 95% CI, −2.1 to 16.0 [point estimate 6.9]; S pyogenes P=.607; 95% CI, −24.2 to 14.3 [point estimate 5.1]; S agalactiae P=.097; 95% CI, −4.4 to 71.1 [point estimate 33.3]).

In the second study, Stevens et al[17] examined the efficacy of linezolid versus vancomycin in the treatment of infections caused by MRSA, including skin infection, skin infection with bacteremia, pneumonia, pneumonia with bacteremia, urinary tract infection, urinary tract infection with bacteremia, and bacteremia of unknown origin. This study covered a number of diagnoses, but results concerning SSTIs, which constituted half of the infections, can be examined separately. Approximately half the SSTIs in both the linezolid group (49/92; 53%) and the vancomycin group (45/83; 54%) were either infected surgical incisions or wounds. The clinical cure rates for SSTIs treated with linezolid were similar to those achieved

with vancomycin. In the intent-to-treat (ITT) population, clinical cure was achieved in 64 of 99 patients (65%) in the linezolid group and in 54 of 87 (62%) patients in the vancomycin group. In the MRSA-ITT population, the cure rates for linezolid and vancomycin were 70% (37/53) and 74% (32/43), respectively. However, among evaluable patients with SSTIs caused by MRSA, a cure rate of 79% (27/34) was achieved with linezolid, and a cure rate of 73% (22/30) was observed for vancomycin. Linezolid was found to be safe, well tolerated, and as effective as vancomycin for the treatment of nosocomial infections due to MRSA and was recommended as a suitable alternative to vancomycin.

Use of Linezolid in Treating Nosocomial Pneumonia

Nosocomial pneumonia may occur in surgical patients as a result of mechanical ventilation or an underlying debilitated state. A study by Ibrahim et al[19] evaluated 3171 patients admitted consecutively to medical and surgical ICUs over a 22-month period. Of the total 880 patients who received mechanical ventilation, 43% (375) had undergone surgery before ICU admission. Sixty-five (17%) of the surgical patients developed ventilator-associated pneumonia (VAP) during the course of their stay in the ICU, compared with an overall rate of 15% for the total population, including both medical and surgical patients. The survival rate for all mechanically ventilated patients was 66% (579/880), whereas the survival rate among patients who had undergone surgical procedures was 78% (293/375). Although surgical patients seemed slightly more likely to develop VAP, they also appeared more likely to survive. The most commonly isolated pathogens among microbiologically evaluable patients were P aeruginosa, which occurred in 33% of survivors and 42% of nonsurvivors (P=.324), and S aureus, which was found in 19% of survivors and 37% of nonsurvivors (P=.027).[19] Among S aureus isolates, 72% were oxacillin resistant.

Surgical patients were not evaluated as a subgroup in the large phase III clinical trial of linezolid versus vancomycin in the treatment of nosocomial pneumonia[17]; however, the results of that trial indicate that this agent may have an important role in treating nosocomial pneumonia, including VAP occurring during the postoperative period. Given the high levels of oxacillin resistance detected in the study by Ibrahim[19] and the increasing incidence of

MRSA infections, empiric therapy often involves vancomycin. However, strains with intermediate resistance to vancomycin have been observed as well.[13,14] Thus, newer agents such as linezolid and quinupristin-dalfopristin may constitute the next line of defense against the pathogens causing nosocomial infections.

Furthermore, although the overall phase III linezolid trial showed therapeutic equivalence for vancomycin and linezolid,[17] Wunderink et al[18] performed a retrospective analysis of 2 studies and found a survival advantage in patients with pneumonia caused by MRSA treated with linezolid compared with those treated with vancomycin. Patients in the linezolid group had significantly better survival rates (80% versus 64%, P=.03) and clinical cure rates (59% versus 36%, P<.01) than those in the vancomycin group. Even after adjusting for baseline differences between the 2 patient groups, the survival advantage was significantly better with linezolid therapy.

A comparator-controlled study of quinupristin-dalfopristin versus vancomycin conducted in patients with nosocomial pneumonia found equivalence for clinical success rates for both agents (43% versus 45%, respectively; 95% CI, −13.2 to 9.3) in the overall population, as well as equivalent clinical success rates in the subset of patients with pneumonia caused by MRSA (19% versus 40%; 95% CI, −46.2 to 4.9).[20] Wunderink et al[18] postulated that the poor penetration of vancomycin into the lungs, as seen in pharmacokinetic studies,[21,22] may have accounted for some of the survivor advantage conferred by linezolid,[18] because the oxazolidinone has achieved high concentration levels in lung tissue.[23]

Use of Linezolid in Treating Surgical Infections—Experience From the Compassionate Use Program

A small study that comprised part of the compassionate use program, which made linezolid available to patients diagnosed with serious gram-positive infections who were unable to tolerate available agents, examined the use of linezolid in infections caused by multidrug-resistant gram-positive organisms.[24] Seventeen patients were treated; 15 had infections caused by vancomycin-resistant enterococci (VRE). The other 2 patients had infections caused by methicillin-resistant staphylococci and had adverse reactions when treated with vancomycin. Five of

the patients with VRE infections were orthotopic liver transplant recipients and 6 had abdominal or thoracic surgery before developing the infection. Of these 11 surgical patients, 5 had developed wound infections with VRE—2 with concurrent VRE peritonitis and 2 with concurrent VRE bacteremia. Peritonitis infection with VRE had developed in 4 of the 5 liver transplant recipients, and 3 also had bacteremia caused by VRE. Four had an intra-abdominal abscess from which VRE was isolated, and 2 had concurrent bacteremia caused by VRE. Multiple attempts were made to surgically drain or debride the abscesses and peritoneal infections, yet infection persisted after all conventional therapeutic options had been exhausted. Linezolid therapy was ultimately required in all patients. It must be emphasized that the transplant recipients in this study were on immunosuppressive therapy; therefore, the results of this study cannot be considered for all types of surgical patients.

The mean duration of linezolid therapy was 20.5 days ± 3.5 days (range, 5 days to 42 days).[24] The longest duration of intravenous therapy (42 days) occurred in a patient with VRE endocarditis, but ultimately, a clinical and microbiological cure was achieved. The mortality rate among the study population was very high (53%), but it must be kept in mind that this was a critically ill patient population.

Among surgical patients, 4 of the 5 liver transplant recipients survived to the long-term follow-up, 15 to 30 days after the completion of therapy.[24] The fifth patient died during therapy for pneumonia caused by Aspergillus. Two other surgical patients died of cancer, and a gastric resection patient died from overwhelming sepsis and multiple organ failure during therapy. A patient who had undergone a recent valve replacement and aortic graft placement and developed S aureus prosthetic aortic valve endocarditis with aortic abscess and bacteremia died of multiple organ failure before the short-term follow-up. Of the 2 surviving surgical patients, 1 developed an abdominal wound after an exploratory laparotomy for trauma wound infection, and the other had a recent abdominal aortic repair. Microbiological and clinical cure was achieved in both these patients as well as in the 4 liver transplant survivors.

Despite the high mortality rate in this cohort, the investigators noted that without therapy, all of these patients would have died.[24] The results suggested that in surgical patients with serious multidrug-resistant infections, linezolid could be an effective therapy.

Use of Linezolid in Treating Complicated SSTIs

Recently an open-label, comparator-controlled, multi-center study was conducted in 1200 hospitalized patients with complicated SSTIs and suspected or proven MRSA infection.[25] Patients were randomized to receive either linezolid (600 mg IV/PO BID), or vancomycin (1 g IV BID or dosed to therapeutic levels) for 7 to 21 days. If cultures revealed methicillin-susceptible *Staphylococcus aureus* (MSSA) organisms in patients randomized to vancomycin, they could be switched to an antistaphylo-coccal penicillin. Efficacy was assessed at the test-of-cure visit 7 days after the completion of therapy. Cellulitis was the most common diagnosis (45%), followed by major skin abscess (26%) and infected surgical incision (11%). Methicillin-resistant *S aureus* constituted 42% of the pathogens isolated; MSSA and coagulase-negative staphylococci made up 29% and 8%, respectively.

The results of this study were very encouraging, particularly considering the large population involved.[25] The clinical cure rate was significantly better with linezolid than with the comparators for clinically evaluable patients (*P*=.0234), modified ITT patients (*P*=.0326), and microbiologically evaluable patients (*P*=.0218); the cure rate was more than 92% in each of those populations. The cure rate also was significantly better with linezolid

(94%) than with vancomycin (84%) in treating infections caused by MRSA in the microbiologically evaluable group (*P*=.0108) (Figure 1).

Length of stay data also were analyzed for this patient population in a second study.[26] Patient locations were tracked for 35 days during and after treatment. Statistically significant differences were observed between LOS for those treated with linezolid and for those treated with either vancomycin or antistaphylococcal penicillin. The mean duration of stay was at least 2 days shorter for the linezolid group than for patients treated with the comparator drugs (*P*<.05). The largest difference in intravenous drug duration occurred in the population infected with MRSA. Patients in the linezolid cohort were on intravenous medication for a mean of 2 days, compared with 13 days in the vancomycin group. In the overall clinically evaluable population, the mean duration of intravenous administration was 2 days for linezolid and 9 days for vancomycin. These differences were statistically significant (*P*<.0001). The mean LOS was 7 days in the linezolid group and 9 days in the vancomycin group among clinically evaluable patients (*P*<.0001) and 8 days and 11 days, respectively, in patients with MRSA infections (*P*=.0026).

Although only approximately 11% of these infections involved infected surgical incisions,[25,26] results from this and other studies of SSTIs indicate equal or superior cure rates in patients treated with linezolid versus those treated with vancomycin or oxacillin-dicloxacillin.[16,17,25,26]

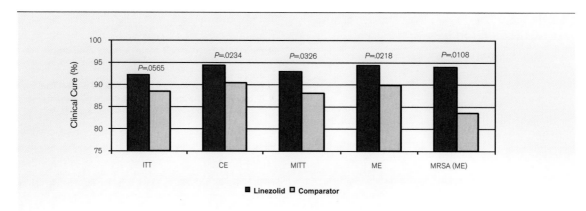

Figure 1. Clinical outcome–cure rate (indeterminate assessment not included).[25] ITT = intent-to-treat (received at least 1 dose of study medicine, n=1180); CE = clinically evaluable (n=963); MITT = modified intent-to-treat (ITT with a gram-positive baseline culture, n=840); ME = microbiologically evaluable (n=683); MRSA = methicillin-resistant *Staphylococcus aureus*.

The intravenous-to-oral equivalency possible with linezolid allows for a shorter length of hospital stay,[26,27] which not only decreases the considerable costs associated with these infections but also decreases the risk of the patient contracting another nosocomial infection.

Summary

Surgical site infections are a recognized complication of surgery. Prophylaxis may prevent many of them, and antibiotic prophylaxis before surgery is strongly recommended. Antiseptic technique must be maintained, and proper management of the surgical site can help keep infection rates low. However, despite the most stringent precautions, infections will occur in some patients. The rate of infection depends on the type of surgery, varying from relatively low rates with clean surgery to much higher rates with surgical procedures that carry a greater risk of contamination. The most commonly isolated pathogen in surgical site infections is S aureus.

The results of major clinical trials studying SSTIs have indicated that linezolid is safe, well tolerated, and comparable to vancomycin in the treatment of these infections. In some studies, linezolid has demonstrated superior efficacy. The ability to switch patients from intravenous to oral administration without changing dose or decreasing therapeutic effect is an obvious advantage of this agent and may shorten the LOS for patients hospitalized with surgical infections. Although no data suggest that linezolid should be used prophylactically in surgery, it should be considered a viable treatment option for all SSTIs in which a gram-positive organism is suspected. In particular, linezolid should be considered if the suspicion of MRSA organisms is high.

References

1. Giacometti A, Cirioni O, Schimizzi AM, et al. Epidemiology and microbiology of surgical wound infections. J Clin Microbiol. 2000;38:918-922.
2. Mangram AJ, Horan TC, Pearson ML, Silver LC, Jarvis WR. Guideline for prevention of surgical site infection, 1999. Hospital Infection Control Practices Advisory Committee. Infect Control Hosp Epidemiol. 1999;20:250-278.
3. National Nosocomial Infections Surveillance System. National Nosocomial Infections Surveillance (NNIS) System report, data summary from January 1992-June 2001, issued August 2001. Am J Infect Control. 2001;29:404-421.
4. Nichols RL. Preventing surgical site infections: a surgeon's perspective. Emerg Infect Dis. 2001;7:220-224.
5. Nichols RL. Prevention of infection in high risk gastrointestinal surgery. Am J Med. 1984;76(5A):111-119.
6. Gottrup F, Firmin R, Hunt TK, Mathes SJ. The dynamic properties of tissue oxygen in healing flaps. Surgery. 1984;95:527-536.
7. Greif R, Akca O, Horn EP, Kurz A, Sessler DI, for the Outcomes Research Group. Supplemental perioperative oxygen to reduce the incidence of surgical-wound infection. N Engl J Med. 2000;342:161-167.
8. Antimicrobial prophylaxis in surgery. Med Lett. 2001;43:92-97.
9. Auerbach A. Prevention of surgical site infections. In: Markowitz AJ, Shojania KG, Duncan BW, McDonald KM, Wachter RM, eds. Evidence Report/Technology Assessment No. 43, Making Health Care Safer: A Critical Analysis of Patient Safety Practices. San Francisco, Calif: Agency for Healthcare Research and Quality. 2003:221-243.
10. Zmora O, Mahajna A, Bar-Zakai B, et al. Colon and rectal surgery without mechanical bowel preparation: a randomized prospective trial. Ann Surg. 2003;237:363-367.
11. Weigelt JA, Dryer D, Haley RW. The necessity and efficiency of wound surveillance after discharge. Arch Surg. 1992;127:77-81; discussion 81-72.
12. Mylotte JM, Graham R, Kahler L, Young L, Goodnough S. Epidemiology of nosocomial infection and resistant organisms in patients admitted for the first time to an acute rehabilitation unit. Clin Infect Dis. 2000;30:425-432.
13. Centers for Disease Control and Prevention. Reduced susceptibility of Staphylococcus aureus to vancomycin—Japan, 1996. MMWR Morb Mortal Wkly Rep. 1997;46:624-626.
14. Centers for Disease Control and Prevention. Staphylococcus aureus with reduced susceptibility to vancomycin—United States, 1997. MMWR Morb Mortal Wkly Rep. 1997;46:765-766.
15. Rubinstein E, Cammarata SK, Oliphant TH, Wunderink RG, the Linezolid Nosocomial Pneumonia Study Group. Linezolid (PNU-100766) versus vancomycin in the treatment of hospitalized patients with nosocomial pneumonia: a randomized, double-blind, multicenter study. Clin Infect Dis. 2001;32:402-412.
16. Stevens DL, Smith LG, Bruss JB, et al, for the Linezolid Skin and Soft Tissue Infections Study Group. Randomized comparison of linezolid (PNU-100766) versus oxacillin-dicloxacillin for treatment of complicated skin and soft tissue infections. Antimicrob Agents Chemother. 2000;44:3408-3413.
17. Stevens DL, Herr D, Lampiris H, et al, for the Linezolid MRSA Study Group. Linezolid versus vancomycin for the treatment of methicillin-resistant Staphylococcus aureus infections. Clin Infect Dis. 2002;34:1481-1490.
18. Wunderink RG, Rello J, Cammarata SK, Croos-Dabrera RV, Kollef MH. Linezolid vs vancomycin: analysis of two double blind studies of patients with methicillin-resistant Staphylococcus aureus nosocomial pneumonia. Chest. 2003;124:1789-1797.
19. Ibrahim EH, Tracy L, Hill C, Fraser VJ, Kollef MH. The occurrence of ventilator-associated pneumonia in a community hospital: risk factors and clinical outcomes. Chest. 2001;120:555-561.
20. Fagon J-Y, Patrick H, Haas DW, et al, and the Nosocomial Pneumonia Group. Treatment of gram-positive nosocomial pneumonia. Prospective randomized comparison of quinupristin/dalfopristin versus vancomycin. Am J Respir Crit Care Med. 2000;161(3 pt 1):753-762.
21. Lamer C, de Beco V, Soler P, et al. Analysis of vancomycin entry into pulmonary lining fluid by bronchoalveolar lavage in critically ill patients. Antimicrob Agents Chemother. 1993;37:281-286.
22. Cruciani M, Gatti G, Lazzarini L, et al. Penetration of vancomycin into human lung tissue. J Antimicrob Chemother. 1996;38:865-869.
23. Conte JE Jr, Golden JA, Kipps J, Zurlinden E. Intrapulmonary pharmacokinetics of linezolid. Antimicrob Agents Chemother. 2002;46:1475-1480.
24. Chien JW, Kucia ML, Salata RA. Use of linezolid, an oxazolidinone, in the treatment of multidrug-resistant gram-positive bacterial infections. Clin Infect Dis. 2000;30:146-151.

25. Weigelt JA, Itani KM, Lau WK, Somero M, Birmingham MC. Linezolid (LZD) vs vancomycin (vanco) in the treatment of complicated skin and soft tissue infections (cSSTI): clinically significant outcome differences. Paper presented at: The 41st Annual Meeting of the Infectious Diseases Society of America; October 9-12, 2003; San Diego, Calif. Abstract 314.

26. Weigelt JA, Itani KM, Li JZ. Linezolid (LZD) reduces LOS when compared to vancomycin (vanco) for complicated skin and soft tissue infections (cSSTI) due to suspected or proven MRSA: results from a randomized trial. Paper presented at: The 41st Annual Meeting of the Infectious Diseases Society of America; October 9-12, 2003; San Diego, Calif. Abstract 315.

27. Li JZ, Willke RJ, Rittenhouse BE, Rybak MJ. Effect of linezolid versus vancomycin on length of hospital stay in patients with complicated skin and soft tissue infections caused by known or suspected methicillin-resistant staphylococci: results from a randomized clinical trial. *Surg Infect [Larchmt]*. 2003;4:45-58.

CHAPTER EIGHT CME QUESTIONS

1. Pathogens likely to cause surgical wound infections differ depending on the surgical site. In clean surgical procedures, what pathogen is most often implicated in infection?
   a. *Pseudomonas aeruginosa*
   b. *Staphylococcus aureus*
   c. *Staphylococcus epidermidis*
   d. *Enterococcus* species

2. The prevalence of methicillin-resistant *Staphylococcus aureus* is increasing worldwide. These bacteria have been identified in up to what percentage of wound or skin isolates?
   a. 15%
   b. 18%
   c. 25%
   d. 39%

3. True or False: The efficacy of linezolid for treating skin and soft tissue infections suggests that this drug might be a valuable therapeutic option in surgical site infections.

4. In a large study comparing linezolid with vancomycin in the treatment of infections caused by methicillin-resistant *Staphylococcus aureus* (MRSA), nearly half of skin and soft tissue infections involved infected surgical incisions or wounds. What were the cure rates among evaluable patients with skin and soft tissue infections caused by MRSA?
   a. 55.7% for linezolid and 63.4% for vancomycin
   b. 79.4% for linezolid and 73.3% for vancomycin
   c. 76.2% for linezolid and 83.7% for vancomycin
   d. 67.9% for linezolid and 68.2% for vancomycin

5. A study conducted of intravenous/oral linezolid versus intravenous vancomycin in patients with complicated skin and soft tissue infections and suspected or proven methicillin-resistant *Staphylococcus aureus* infection found that:
   a. There was little difference between the 2 groups in the length of time patients spent on intravenous medication.
   b. Patients in the linezolid cohort were on intravenous medication for a much shorter period than those in the vancomycin group.
   c. Despite differences in the duration of intravenous administration, there was no difference in the overall length of hospital stay.
   d. None of these statements is correct.

CREATION OF A NOVEL CLASS:

LINEZOLID AND THE OXAZOLIDINONES
P R E S E N T   A N D   F U T U R E

EDITORS

Donald H. Batts, MD, FACP

Marin H. Kollef, MD

LEARNING OBJECTIVES

After completion of this chapter, readers should be able to:

1. Understand the issue of possible microbial resistance to linezolid.

2. Identify potential mechanisms of microbial resistance to linezolid.

3. Recognize the possibility of serious adverse events inherent to any antibiotic therapy and describe those most likely to occur with long-term linezolid therapy.

4. Discuss the economic factors involved in the use of linezolid—both its high initial cost and the cost advantage offered by the intravenous and oral formulations.

5. Discuss future directions for therapeutic exploration of linezolid and the oxazolidinones and review other promising antibiotic compounds on the horizon.

THE OXAZOLIDINONE ANTIBIOTICS

The 7 large-scale, phase III trials and data from the compassionate use program provided substantial evidence of the effectiveness of linezolid for treatment of a number of serious illnesses due to gram-positive pathogens, including community-acquired and nosocomial pneumonia, complicated and uncomplicated skin and soft tissue infections, and infections caused by vancomycin-resistant enterococci (VRE) and methicillin-resistant *Staphylococcus aureus* (MRSA).[1-3] Linezolid proved comparable to first-line agents such as vancomycin in the treatment of these illnesses and caused few serious adverse effects.[1] Since approval by the US Food and Drug Administration (FDA), linezolid has been used in an estimated 300,000 patients worldwide (D. Batts, personal communication, May 2003). The cumulative experience of these patients has been added to the body of knowledge gathered from clinical trials, providing additional insight into the efficacy, adverse events profile, pharmacokinetics, and pharmacodynamics of this first oxazolidinone compound.

However, isolated cases of linezolid resistance have been reported.[4-8] This is a disturbing but not unanticipated development. The microbial universe is eminently dynamic. Changes that require eons in the human world may take place over days in the microbial universe; microbial generations are measured in minutes, not years.

The Specter of Microbial Resistance to Linezolid

As has been evident with vancomycin, a correlation exists between increasing use of an antibiotic agent and the emergence of resistance to it in targeted bacterial populations. Worldwide use of vancomycin increased from less than 1000 kg per year in the United States and western Europe in 1981 to nearly 10,000 kg per year by 1990, the year VRE first appeared.[9] By 1996, annual use of vancomycin had grown to nearly 14,000 kg,[9] and the first instance of vancomycin-intermediate-resistant *Staphylococcus aureus* was reported.[10,11] By 1997, nearly 20% of enterococcal isolates were resistant to vancomycin.[12]

The first evidence of linezolid-resistant enterococcal strains in humans emerged during the phase III clinical trials and compassionate use program. Resistance developed in 6 patients infected with *Enterococcus faecium* during the VRE trial, 4 of whom had received the lower dose (200

mg every 12 hours) of linezolid.[1,13] Resistance also developed in 8 patients with *E faecium* and 1 with *Enterococcus faecalis* during the compassionate use program.[1,13] All of these patients had either indwelling prosthetic devices or undrained abscesses.[1] Resistance to linezolid was not observed in *S aureus*, *Staphylococcus* species, or *Streptococcus* species, including *Streptococcus pneumoniae*, during phase III clinical trials.[1]

Approximately 1 year after the FDA approval of linezolid for the treatment of selected gram-positive bacterial infections, Gonzales et al[5] reported linezolid resistance in 5 patients being treated for VRE infections. Of these patients, 4 were transplant recipients, and 1 had undergone repair of an aortic aneurysm before developing an abscess around the graft with bacteremia secondary to vancomycin-resistant *E faecium* infection. These patients were treated with linezolid for a period ranging from 21 to 42 days with an average treatment duration of 31.8 days and a median duration of 28 days. Two of the patients had received prior courses of antibiotics; the third received 14 days of treatment with quinupristin-dalfopristin; and the fourth received 4 weeks of treatment with broad-spectrum antibiotics. Two patients died—one of undetermined causes 9 weeks after the end of linezolid treatment, and the other of multiorgan failure after being switched to quinupristin-dalfopristin.

Interestingly, one patient, a 28-year-old man who received 4 weeks of treatment with linezolid, showed a good clinical response to the medication, but peritoneal washings before closure of his abdominal wound indicated the presence of vancomycin-resistant *E faecium* resistant to linezolid.[5] Four of the 5 patients had resistant strains as determined by diameter of disk test zone; the other isolate showed intermediate resistance. In all, 3 patients demonstrated an initial response to linezolid but were switched to quinupristin-dalfopristin after resistance was observed. The authors noted that in the compassionate use program, resistance occurred in patients on long courses of therapy[14]; this was found to be true in this group of patients as well. The incidence of resistance to linezolid in VRE in the overall patient population at the investigators' hospital was 1 in 45 patients, or 2.2%.[5] The investigators recommended that clinicians contemplating linezolid therapy for VRE infection measure the susceptibility of all isolates at the start of therapy. They further suggested that attention to proper dosing and prompt removal of infected devices whenever feasible could help to limit the emergence of resistance.

In 2001, Tsiodras et al[6] reported what may have been the first documented instance of an MRSA isolate resistant to linezolid in an 85-year-old man treated for dialysis-associated peritonitis. The patient, who had a hypersensitivity to vancomycin, was treated in the hospital with oral linezolid (600 mg BID) for 3 weeks, during which time cultures were intermittently positive for MRSA and susceptible to linezolid. One month after isolation of the original isolate and initiation of linezolid therapy, the patient was readmitted to the hospital with signs and symptoms of recurrent peritonitis. An MRSA isolate was recovered from his peritoneal fluid, but this time the strain proved resistant to linezolid. Restriction endonuclease testing showed that the resistant strain was different from the initial infecting strain. Linezolid therapy was discontinued, and the patient received ampicillin, azithromycin, gentamicin, levofloxacin, and quinupristin-dalfopristin for coverage against MRSA, E faecalis, and Pseudomonas aeruginosa, all of which were isolated from the peritoneal fluid. Within one week, all cultures were negative; however, the patient died 3 weeks later of the underlying disease.

The authors noted that no other linezolid-resistant S aureus isolates had been recovered from any patients at the institution and that the resistant strain was unrelated to the previously isolated linezolid-susceptible MRSA strains obtained from this patient.[6] All 3 resistant isolates showed mutations in DNA encoding the central loop of domain V of 23S rRNA, which also has been reported in linezolid-resistant clinical isolates of VRE.[6,15]

In December 2002, Potoski and colleagues[7] reported on linezolid resistance in 2 patients. The first was a 47-year-old man with a history of right ankle and subtalar arthritis who had several procedures on the ankle and subsequently developed a hematoma that required drainage. He was given cephalexin for 7 days; however, over the next several weeks, the area became swollen and erythematous, spontaneously draining purulent material. After irrigation and debridement, a sample was taken from the wound for culture, and the patient was discharged with a prescription for amoxicillin-clavulanate.

The culture grew S aureus organisms that were susceptible to vancomycin, trimethoprim-sulfamethoxazole (TMP-

SMX), and gentamicin, but it was resistant to all β-lactam antibiotics and clindamycin.[7] Susceptibility testing to linezolid was not performed. Because of the resistance to β-lactams, amoxicillin-clavulanate was discontinued, and the patient was started on linezolid 600 mg twice a day. He had a good clinical response and finished a 7-week course of the antibiotic. However, 2 days after completing therapy, he returned to the hospital because the infection had flared up again. Linezolid therapy was stopped, and intravenous vancomycin was started at 1 g twice a day. The pin that had been used to fuse the ankle was removed, samples for cultures were obtained, and the patient continued therapy with vancomycin. The cultures grew MRSA, which susceptibility testing found to be susceptible to linezolid and TMP-SMX. Vancomycin therapy was continued for 4 weeks, followed by 8 weeks of TMP-SMX. The patient remained asymptomatic 6 months after completion of therapy.

The second patient was a 41-year-old woman with refractory acute lymphocytic leukemia. She was admitted to the hospital for allogenic bone marrow transplantation.[7] She had received several prior courses of antibiotics, including imipenem, amikacin, piperacillin-tazobactam, vancomycin, amphotericin B lipid complex, fluconazole, ciprofloxacin, and tobramycin. While she was receiving vancomycin, a strain of E faecium that proved to be resistant to vancomycin and other antibiotics was isolated, and the patient was started on linezolid 600 mg twice a day. Susceptibility testing to linezolid was requested; however, before results could be obtained, the patient, who had been on the drug only 3 days, died. Subsequent test results revealed that the isolate was resistant to linezolid, with a minimal inhibitory concentration (MIC) of 32 μg/mL, but had intermediate susceptibility to quinupristin-dalfopristin.

Although the MRSA isolate from the first patient was susceptible to linezolid, the MIC was 4 μg/mL, which was 3 dilutions greater than that found in a patient who had undergone successful treatment of osteomyelitis.[7] The findings from this case report led the authors to suggest that linezolid and quinupristin-dalfopristin be included in the initial susceptibility testing routinely performed before treatment is initiated, particularly since inappropriate initial antibiotic therapy has been associated with a significant increase in morbidity, mortality, and cost.[7,16,17]

Possible Resistance Mechanism

Despite these case reports, no evidence indicates a rise in bacterial resistance to linezolid.[18] Results of the SENTRY Antimicrobial Surveillance Program published in 2002 found that linezolid was consistently active against all enterococci, with a minimum concentration at which 90% of organisms are inhibited (MIC_{90}) of 2 µg/mL, and against all streptococci with an MIC_{90} of 1 µg/mL. Quinupristin-dalfopristin also was active against all streptococci but against only 75% of VRE isolates. As for staphylococci, both linezolid and quinupristin-dalfopristin were active against all isolates regardless of the susceptibility patterns found for other antimicrobials. The MICs for linezolid were 4 µg/mL or lower against all gram-positive bacteria tested in the SENTRY program.

A Canadian study covering the years 1997 to 2002 reported similar findings with no resistance to either vancomycin or linezolid observed among S pneumoniae strains.[19] However, intermediate resistance was noted to quinupristin-dalfopristin, although the incidence was only 0.1%. This same study found that resistance to TMP-SMX was 19% among S pneumoniae isolates tested, whereas resistance to macrolides increased from 7.9% to 11.1% over the duration of the 5-year study. Fluoroquinolone resistance to S pneumoniae was noted as well, although rates ranged from 0.5% to 1.1%. This is in contrast to the SENTRY

Table 1. Activity of Linezolid Against Control Isolates and Isolates Resistant to Inhibitors of Protein Synthesis

Isolates	Resistance	Linezolid MIC (µg/mL)
MLS$_B$ Resistance (Target Modification)		
S aureus RN450 control isolate	None	1
S aureus HM290 wild type	ermA (inducible)	1
S aureus HM290-1 mutant	ermA (constitutive)	1
S aureus HM1054 control isolate	None	1
S aureus 1054/R transconjugant of HM1054	ermC (constitutive)	0.5
S aureus GUE wild type	ermC (inducible)	0.5
E faecalis JH2-2 control isolate	None	1
E faecalis JH2-2 (Tn1545) transconjugant of JH2-2	ermB (constitutive)	1
S pyogenes control isolate	None	0.5
S pyogenes CNN1 wild type	ermTR (inducible)	0.25
S pyogenes CNN1-1 mutant of CNN1	ermTR (constitutive)	0.25
Resistance to Macrolides by Efflux		
S aureus RN4220 control isolate	None	1
S aureus RN4220 (msrA) transconjugant of RN4220	msrA	1
S pneumoniae control isolate	None	0.5
S pneumoniae 02J1175 wild type	mefE	0.25
S pyogenes control isolate	None	0.5
S pyogenes UVC3 wild type	mefA	0.25
S agalactiae control isolate	None	0.5
S agalactiae COH31γ/δ wild type	mreA	0.5
Resistance to Lincosamides by Drug Modification		
S haemolyticus BM4610-1 cured derivative from BM4610	None	0.5
S haemolyticus BM4610 wild type	linA	0.5
S aureus BM4611-1 cured derivative from BM4611	None	0.5
S aureus BM4611 wild type	linA'	0.5
E faecalis JH2-2 control isolate	None	1
E faecalis JH2-2 (linB) transconjugant of JH2-2	linB	1
Resistance to Streptogramins by Efflux or Drug Modification		
E faecalis JH2-2 control isolate	None	1
E faecalis JH2-2 (satA) transconjugant of JH2-2	satA	1
S aureus RN450 control isolate	None	1
S aureus RN450 (pIP524) transductant of RN450	vgb-vat-vga	1

Isolates	Resistance	Linezolid MIC (µg/mL)
Resistance to Tetracyclines by Ribosomal Protection or by Efflux		
E faecalis JH2-2 control isolate	None	1
E faecalis JH2-2 (tetO) transconjugant of JH2-2	tetO	1
E faecalis JH2-2 (Tn1545-tetM) transconjugant of JH2-2	tetM	1
S aureus RN4220 control isolate	None	1
S aureus (tetM) wild type	tetM	1
E faecalis JH2-2 control isolate	None	1
E faecalis JH2-2 (tetK) transconjugant of JH2-2	tetK	1
Resistance to Chloramphenicol by Drug Modification		
E faecalis JH2-2 control isolate	None	1
E faecalis JH2-2 (pIP112) transconjugant of JH2-2	cat	1
Resistance to Aminoglycosides by Drug Modification		
E faecalis JH2-2 control isolate	None	1
E faecalis JH2-2 (pAT392) transconjugant of JH2-2	aac(5')-aph(2")	1
E faecalis JH2-2 (Tn1545) transconjugant of JH2-2	aphA-3	1
S aureus RN450 control isolate	None	1
S aureus RN450 (pIP524) transductant of RN450	ant(4') (4")-I	1

MIC = minimal inhibitory concentration; MLS$_B$ = macrolide, lincosamide, and streptogramin B antimicrobials. Adapted from Fines M, Leclercq R. Activity of linezolid against Gram-positive cocci possessing genes conferring resistance to protein synthesis inhibitors. *J Antimicrob Chemother.* 2000;45:797-802, with permission from Oxford University Press. Copyright © 2000 British Society for Antimicrobial Chemotherapy. All rights reserved.

program observations, which found that 18.4% to 25.6% of viridans group streptococci were ciprofloxacin resistant.[18]

Although linezolid resistance has yet to manifest itself to any great extent, it is necessary to be vigilant and anticipate its rise. Toward that end, a number of researchers have characterized possible bacterial resistance mechanisms to linezolid.

Most species of bacteria have multiple copies of rRNA genes. This makes the ribosome an excellent antibiotic target because multiple bacterial mutations are required to alter the antibiotic binding site effectively.[15] Xiong et al[15] used oxazolidinone-resistant *Escherichia coli* that contained a randomly mutated plasmid-borne rRNA operon to produce an oxazolidinone-resistant wild type *E coli* to identify the 23S rRNA binding site and better characterize the mechanism of action of the oxazolidinones. In doing so, they also identified a potential mechanism of bacterial resistance to linezolid—alteration of the central region of domain V of 23S rRNA.

Fines and Leclercq[20] examined the MICs of linezolid against strains of bacteria that exhibited resistance to other antibiotics to determine whether there was potential for cross-resistance. Bacterial resistance to antibiotics that inhibit protein synthesis depends on 3 mechanisms. The first is modification of the ribosomal target, which

has been found in isolates resistant to macrolides and related antibiotics. The second, enzymatic drug inactivation, is found in bacteria resistant to aminoglycosides, chloramphenicol, streptogramins, and lincosamides. The third mechanism is active transport across the cell membrane by an efflux pump, which can cause resistance to streptogramins A, tetracyclines, or macrolides. Fines and Leclercq indicated that despite the presence of numerous mechanisms of resistance against protein synthesis inhibitors, linezolid MICs against selected bacterial strains remained consistently low. Linezolid activity was unaffected by the presence of modifying enzymes, active efflux systems, or the modification or protection of the antimicrobial target (Table 1). In vitro studies and data from the compassionate use program have indicated that resistance to linezolid occurs as a result of point mutations in the 23S rRNA domain V in *S aureus*, *E faecalis*, and *E faecium*.

Work by Prystowsky et al[21] and Marshall et al[22] built upon these earlier studies and helped further characterize resistance to linezolid. The Prystowsky study demonstrated that it was more difficult to select for enterococcal resistance to linezolid than to quinupristin-dalfopristin.[21,23] Furthermore, the investigators found that even though linezolid resistance could be selected for in *E faecalis* with 3 passes, in vancomycin-resistant *E faecalis* isolates, resistance did not begin to develop until at least 10 passes, thus suggesting that resistance mechanisms for the 2 enterococci differ in some way.[21] In 2002, results of a study by Marshall et al[22] also indicated that the G2576U rRNA mutation conferred resistance and found a direct correlation between the number of mutated genes and the level of resistance. They also suggested that homologous recombination between mutated and wild type strains could promote resistance under persistent antimicrobial selective pressure.

to 4 µg/mL, with a mode of 2 and a geometric mean of 2.[24] Using the NCCLS-approved method of MH broth dilution and air incubation, the investigators found that linezolid MICs ranged from 2 µg/mL to 8 µg/mL with a mode of 4 and a geometric mean of 3.63. However, it cannot be assumed that the MH broth dilution would produce higher MICs in all cases. When 21 strains of E faecalis and 21 of E faecium were tested using these methods, the MH agar dilution produced linezolid MICs that ranged from

Table 2. Published Breakpoints for Linezolid

Agency	Breakpoints	Test Method
BSAC	All species: S≤4 µg/mL, R≥8 µg/mL	BSAC
EUCAST	All species: S≤4 µg/mL, R≥8 µg/mL	Not mandated
FDA, NCCLS	Staphylococci: S≤4 µg/mL, R≥8 µg/mL Streptococci and enterococci: S≤2 µg/mL, I 4 µg/mL, R≥8 µg/mL	NCCLS
MCA	All species: S≤2 µg/mL, R≥8 µg/mL Limited data to suggest that staphylococcal and enterococcal isolates for which the MIC of linezolid is 4 µg/mL may be successfully treated. Data are insufficient to determine whether streptococcal species for which the linezolid MIC is 4 µg/mL will respond to therapy.	Not mandated

S = susceptible; I = intermediate; R = resistant; BSAC = British Society for Antimicrobial Chemotherapy; EUCAST = European Committee on Antimicrobial Susceptibility; MCA = Medicines Control Agency; FDA = US Food and Drug Administration; NCCLS = National Committee for Clinical Laboratory Standards. Adapted from Livermore DM, Mushtaq S, Warner M. Susceptibility testing with linezolid by different methods, in relation to published 'general breakpoints.' *J Antimicrob Chemother.* 2001;48:452-454, with permission from Oxford University Press. Copyright © 2001 British Society for Antimicrobial Chemotherapy. All rights reserved.

Establishing Breakpoints

Breakpoints are established by several international committees, including the British Society for Antimicrobial Chemotherapy (BSAC), the European Committee on Antimicrobial Susceptibility (EUCAST), the Medicines Control Agency in Europe, and the National Committee for Clinical Laboratory Standards (NCCLS) in the United States. Breakpoints published for linezolid differ somewhat depending on the agency (Table 2).[24] However, some variations in the observed MICs may be considered artifactual, the result of differences in testing methods, which are not always specified. Livermore et al[24] tested the effects of different media, including those used by the BSAC and the NCCLS, to determine any effects the testing methods had on MICs.

The authors found considerable differences. For instance, when 42 S aureus isolates were tested using the NCCLS-approved method of Mueller-Hinton (MH) agar dilution and air incubation, linezolid MICs ranged from 1 µg/mL

2 µg/mL to 4 µg/mL for both, with modes of 2 and a geometric mean of 2.42 for E faecalis and 2.36 for E faecium. The MH broth dilution produced MICs that ranged from 0.25 µg/mL to 2 µg/mL, with a mode of 2 and a geometric mean of 1.25 for E faecalis and MICs that ranged from 0.06 µg/mL to 4.00 µg/mL, with a mode of 2 and a geometric mean of 1.00 for E faecium.

The authors concluded that the linezolid breakpoints of 4 µg/mL adopted by the BSAC and EUCAST seemed appropriate, given the pharmacodynamic data on this agent, which indicate that a 600-mg dose achieves serum drug concentrations above 4 µg/mL throughout the 12-hour dosing period.[24] They also noted that the resistant E faecium that emerged during therapy as reported by Gonzales et al[5] had MICs in the range of 32 µg/mL to 64 µg/mL, which is well above any of the published breakpoints.

The most frequently cited breakpoints are those set by the NCCLS. The NCCLS has established breakpoints for linezolid of 4 µg/mL or lower for susceptible strains and

8 µg/mL or higher for resistant strains for staphylococci, and of 2 µg/mL or lower for susceptible strains for both streptococci and enterococci.[25]

Adverse Events

Despite our familiarity with them, antibiotics are important medications and are the drug class for which adverse events are most often reported.[26] As a result of the frequent clinical success with antibiotic treatment, one may forget that the diseases these drugs treat are often deadly without therapy. Thus, the high incidence of adverse events is regrettable but not surprising. In general, linezolid is safe and well tolerated for up to 28 days.[1] The most common adverse events observed with linezolid therapy are diarrhea, nausea, and headache in adults and loose stools and vomiting in children. These events are mild to moderate in intensity and usually of limited duration. However, in phase III studies, 2.4% of patients on linezolid therapy and 1.5% of those on comparator drugs developed reversible thrombocytopenia.

Since approval, reversible myelosuppression has been reported in patients during therapy with linezolid.[27-29] Green et al[27] reported on 3 patients who developed myelosuppression with red cell hypoplasia after therapy with linezolid. The first was a 70-year-old man who had been on linezolid 600 mg twice a day for 4 months for an MRSA infection in a femoral-popliteal Gore-Tex® graft. During antibiotic treatment, the patient's platelet count decreased from 215 x 10³/µL to 60 x 10³/µL, and hemoglobin levels decreased from 14.3 g/dL to 7.0 g/dL with a reticulocyte count of 0%. Iron saturation levels were 95%. Within 10 days of discontinuing linezolid therapy, platelet counts and hemoglobin levels had returned to normal, iron saturation levels had fallen to 25%, and the reticulocyte count had risen to 5.8%.

Similar irregularities were noted in 2 other patients, 1 who had received linezolid 600 mg twice a day for 6 weeks for treatment of a chronic MRSA infection of a facial sinus and another who received linezolid for MRSA metatarsal osteomyelitis.[27] As with the first case, the second patient experienced declines in platelet count and hemoglobin levels and increases in iron saturation to 74%. In the third patient, reticulocyte counts declined from 1.4% to 0% during the first 2 weeks of therapy, and the drug was discontinued for 2 weeks. With the patient's consent,

therapy was continued for 4 more weeks. Reticulocytes again declined, this time from 4.5% to 0%, and decreases in hemoglobin and platelets were noted, as was an increase in iron saturation to 96%. After discontinuation of therapy, all values returned to normal levels. In the first 2 patients, vacuolated erythroblasts appeared. The authors noted that these effects were similar to those sometimes observed with chloramphenicol therapy and warranted monitoring of iron levels and reticulocyte counts in patients receiving linezolid for prolonged periods.

More recently, Monson et al[30] reported the case of a 52-year-old man with bullous emphysematous lung disease and sickle cell trait who was admitted to the hospital with fever, leukocytosis, and pneumonic infiltration with fluid in some of the bullae. The patient was treated with 6 different antibiotics but showed minimal clinical response; treatment was changed to vancomycin and imipenem. There was a gradual resolution of symptoms, therapy was changed to an oral regimen of linezolid and gatifloxacin with continued clinical improvement. Anemia and thrombocytosis were noted at hospital discharge, but they were attributed to chronic disease and nonspecific response to infection. However, 2 months after discharge and after a total of 8 weeks of therapy with linezolid, the patient's anemia continued to worsen. The hemoglobin level fell to 5.9 g/dL, and iron saturation levels reached 89.2%. Linezolid therapy was discontinued, and the hemoglobin level had increased to 12.1 g/dL 4 weeks later. As with the earlier report on 3 patients developing myelosuppression, the authors suggested close monitoring of patients on prolonged therapy and obtaining a baseline reticulocyte count at initiation of linezolid therapy.

An analysis of clinical trial data to determine the incidence of anemia, thrombocytopenia, and neutropenia in nearly 4000 patients treated with either linezolid or a comparator found downward shifts for hemoglobin in 6.6% of those treated with linezolid and 6.4% treated with a comparator.[31] Platelet count decreases occurred in 2.9% of patients treated with linezolid and 1.6% treated with a comparator, and absolute neutrophil counts decreased in 3.3% versus 3.4% of patients, respectively. Most shifts occurred in those treated for 2 weeks or longer, and most were mild, grade 1 or grade 2 changes. The more serious grade 3 or 4 shifts occurred in few patients and were similar in the linezolid and comparator groups.

Reticulocyte indices were evaluated in 637 patients in the linezolid group and 611 in the comparator group.[31] These indices were found to decrease significantly from baseline in linezolid-treated patients. In contrast, in those treated with comparators, reticulocyte indices increased significantly. Although mean reticulocyte indices differed significantly between the groups at the end of treatment ($P<.01$), differences were no longer significant at follow-up (Table 3).

A mild, reversible thrombocytopenia has been observed in some patients treated with linezolid for 2 weeks or longer.[31] Although the mechanism involved is unknown, there is no evidence of antiplatelet or antilinezolid antibodies or interference with platelet function.[13] Although decreased reticulocytes may be associated with anemia, no

osteomyelitis due to MRSA infection.[34] He had been treated with citalopram 20 mg twice a day for 3 weeks before being admitted to the hospital. The patient was also on a number of other medications, including low doses of prednisone and methotrexate, digoxin, torsemide, insulin, and oxazepam. After surgical debridement, the patient was treated with 600 mg of linezolid twice a day. Although the infection appeared to respond well, within a week the patient exhibited changes in mental status; by the third week, he developed thrombocytopenia, serotonin syndrome, and lactic acidosis. The patient died after several episodes of cardiac arrest. The authors suggest caution when prescribing linezolid for patients already receiving SSRIs, recommending that the SSRI be discontinued at least 2 weeks before the initiation of linezolid therapy.

Table 3. Mean Reticulocyte Count and Change From Baseline (±SD)

Time Point (Parameter)	Linezolid	Comparators	Adjusted Difference	95% Confidence Interval
Baseline				
Mean index	4.54±2.38	4.62±2.64	−0.06	−0.33 to 0.31
End of treatment				
Mean index	4.02±2.28	5.4±2.45	−1.43	−1.68 to −1.17
Change from baseline	-0.52±2.52*	0.8±2.54*	−1.36	−1.63 to −1.09
Follow-up				
Mean index	5.84±2.89	5.65±2.64	0.25	−0.045 to 0.55
Change from baseline	1.29±2.58*	1.03±2.64*	0.31	0.031 to 0.6

SD = standard deviation.

*Change from baseline within treatment group ($P<.01$). Adapted from Gerson SL, Kaplan SL, Bruss JB, et al. Hematologic effects of linezolid: summary of clinical experience. *Antimicrob Agents Chemother*. 2002;46:2723-2726, with permission from the American Society for Microbiology. Copyright © 2002 the American Society for Microbiology. All rights reserved.

clinical evidence was found of aplastic anemia in any patients. Given the serious nature of the infections treated with this agent and its efficacy against pathogens resistant to most other antibiotics, the benefits outweigh the risks in most cases. Nonetheless, patients with underlying hematologic abnormalities or lower baseline values appear to be more likely to experience hematologic effects and therefore should be monitored more closely.

Serotonin syndrome has been noted with the concomitant use of linezolid and selective serotonin reuptake inhibitors (SSRIs), albeit rarely.[32,33] A 2003 report describes the case of an 81-year-old man who developed

Economic Factors

The cost of any drug plays a role in clinical decisions. The patient's ability to pay, Medicaid, Medicare, and formulary rules are all factors that must be considered. However, the true cost of drug treatment must factor in not only the initial cost of the agent itself but also costs associated with drug administration and treatment failure.

A 1999 study of the economic impact of *S aureus* infections in New York City hospitals revealed that direct medical costs for methicillin-resistant infections averaged $34,000 per patient, compared with an average of

$31,500 for methicillin-susceptible infections in direct medical costs.[35] The differences in costs between MRSA and methicillin-susceptible *Staphylococcus aureus* infections ranged from $1700 to $5100, whereas the death rate from MRSA infections was 21%, more than 2.5 times the death rate for susceptible infections (8%). The increased cost was attributable to the higher cost of vancomycin, the first-line treatment for MRSA infections at that time, longer hospital stay, and the cost of patient isolation procedures.

Although one of the drawbacks of linezolid is its high cost, the ability to transition patients from intravenous therapy to oral therapy with linezolid more rapidly than is possible with vancomycin reduces the length of hospital stays significantly, as shown in the study by Li et al.[36] Despite the fact that patients in the linezolid group were older than those on vancomycin, they had a much shorter duration of intravenous antibiotic treatment, with a mean of 5.8 days versus 12.6 days for the vancomycin group (P<.0001). Most important, those treated with linezolid had a shorter hospital length of stay (LOS) and a higher likelihood of hospital discharge. The mean LOS in the linezolid group was 16.4 days versus 19.5 days in the vancomycin group.

Thus, despite the disadvantages of the cost of acquisition, reductions in associated costs and LOS as well as reductions in the risk for secondary infection inherent with intravenous administration may offset some of the cost. Although third-party payors may continue to balk at the initial high cost of acquisition of linezolid, it is hoped that insurers will realize the benefit of shortened hospital stays and improved patient outcomes.

Use of Linezolid in Other Infections

The FDA has approved linezolid for the treatment of the following infections caused by susceptible strains of designated organisms: vancomycin-resistant *E faecium* infections, including cases with concurrent bacteremia; nosocomial pneumonia caused by methicillin-susceptible and -resistant strains of *S aureus* or penicillin-susceptible strains of *S pneumoniae*; community-acquired pneumonia caused by *S pneumoniae* (penicillin-susceptible strains only), including cases with concurrent bacteremia, or *S aureus* (methicillin-susceptible strains only); uncomplicated skin and skin structure infections caused by *S aureus*

(methicillin-susceptible strains only) or *Streptococcus pyogenes*; and complicated skin and skin structure infections caused by *S aureus* (methicillin-susceptible and methicillin-resistant strains), *S pyogenes*, or *Streptococcus agalactiae*.

Linezolid has been used in the treatment of conditions other than those approved by the FDA. Data continue to accumulate on its efficacy in these diseases. Infections such as meningitis and endocarditis present some of the most complex clinical challenges physicians face. Achieving adequate concentration levels of antibiotics is difficult when treating these infections; penetration of cerebrospinal fluid (CSF) is particularly challenging.

Evidence of efficacy comes from case studies and in vivo experiments in animals. In 2001, Hachem and colleagues[37] reported the successful treatment of meningitis caused by VRE with linezolid. A 62-year-old man who had been treated for a cerebellar metastatic lesion with obstructive hydrocephalus secondary to earlier renal cell carcinoma developed progressive mental status changes and leakage of CSF from the suboccipital craniotomy incision. After insertion of a ventriculoperitoneal shunt, a routine CSF culture revealed leukocytosis and the presence of enterococci. The patient was started on high-dose ampicillin and gentamicin. When the organism was subsequently identified as vancomycin-resistant *E faecium*, he was given linezolid 600 mg intravenously every 12 hours in combination with 2 doses of gentamicin 5 mg. Within 48 hours of initiation of linezolid therapy, the patient was afebrile, his mental status had improved, and the leukocyte count in the CSF decreased from a baseline of 250/mm^3 to 8/mm^3.

By the fifth day of treatment, the patient's CSF cultures were negative, and follow-up at day 10 yielded a negative culture.[37] The patient continued to progress clinically. Gentamicin was continued for 5 days, and linezolid therapy was continued for 3 weeks until the patient died because of his underlying malignancy, renal failure, and gastrointestinal bleeding.

In another case report, a patient who developed vancomycin-resistant *E faecium* infection in conjunction with a *Strongyloides stercoralis* hyperinfection was initially treated with chloramphenicol after failing to improve with ampicillin, ceftazidime, and vancomycin.[38] The patient received chloramphenicol 750 mg intravenously every 6 hours along with a 7-day course of albendazole. After 2 days of chloramphenicol therapy, the patient's clinical condition had not improved, and linezolid 600 mg intravenously every 12 hours was begun. The patient had developed thrombocytopenia, which continued to worsen, and as a result chloramphenicol therapy was discontinued 4 days later. The patient's platelet count stabilized, and results of tests on CSF samples showed improvement, becoming negative; the patient showed marked clinical improvement. Intravenous linezolid was continued for a total of 28 days, and follow-up CSF analysis 10 days after linezolid was discontinued showed no evidence of vancomycin-resistant *E faecium* infection.

One week into the course of therapy, plasma and CSF samples were obtained 7 hours after the dose of linezolid to assay the levels of the agent in both.[38] Plasma levels were reported to be 7.32 μg/mL, and the level of linezolid in the CSF was 5.4 μg/mL, or 74% of the plasma concentration. Samples taken 3 weeks after the start of therapy with linezolid demonstrated levels of approximately 6 μg/mL in the CSF. These findings indicate that linezolid concentrations in both plasma and CSF are above the MIC.

The data showing good tissue penetration into the CSF are corroborated by findings from animal models of meningitis caused by penicillin-susceptible and penicillin-resistant pneumococci.[39] In rabbits with experimentally induced pneumococcal meningitis, levels of linezolid in the CSF remained above the MIC during the entire dosing period. Interestingly, ceftriaxone achieved better clinical efficacy. Although the reasons behind this poorer showing were unclear, the authors suggested that it may have been the result of the marginal bactericidal activity of linezolid against pneumococcal strains. Bactericidal activity is a well-documented prerequisite for the treatment of pneumococcal meningitis.

Finally, in 2002, Viale et al[40] reported on 5 neurosurgical patients treated for central nervous system infections. Of these, 3 were cases of meningitis, 1 was a case of ventriculitis, and 1 infection was due to an abscess. Of the cases involving meningitis, 1 was caused by methicillin-resistant *Staphylococcus epidermidis* (MRSE), 1 by MRSA, and 1 by gram-positive cocci. The patient with ventriculi-tis had an MRSE infection, and the abscess was caused by penicillin-susceptible *S pneumoniae*.

All patients had either failed to improve with prior treatment with vancomycin or had experienced serious adverse events while on therapy with that agent.[40] All 5 showed a clinical response when treated with linezolid for 13 to 28 days. A sustained response was observed at 3 months in 4 patients, although 1 died at 6 months without evidence of a relapse. Another patient died of acute heart failure on day 13.

The authors suggested further exploration of linezolid use for this indication because they thought that neither vancomycin nor ceftazidime achieved therapeutically active concentrations in the CSF.[40]

Infectious endocarditis is usually fatal without treatment. Even with intervention, 15% to 40% of patients die.[41] A number of the newer quinolones have been proposed as promising treatments in these complex infections, as has quinupristin-dalfopristin. However, the use of oxazolidinone compounds as treatment for endocarditis has been questioned because of their lack of bactericidal activity.

Despite this, a rabbit endocarditis model used to test linezolid versus vancomycin in treating *S aureus* infections showed efficacy for both agents. Linezolid reduced *S aureus* in aortic valve vegetations at 50- and 75-mg/kg doses given at 8-hour intervals, although not at the 25-mg/kg dose. Blood levels of linezolid were above the MIC at both peak and trough with the higher doses.[42] The investigators noted that in contrast to in vitro bacteriostatic effects, which produce less than 2-log reductions in bacterial counts at 24 hours, the in vivo study found 4-log to 5-log reductions in bacterial counts after 5 days of therapy, which they thought constituted more than a bacteriostatic effect.

In a second study of the efficacy of linezolid versus that of vancomycin in the treatment of experimental endocarditis, the investigators used MRSA to produce infection in rabbits. A high mortality rate was found in the group given 25 mg/kg/dose, and bacterial counts in the valve vegetations were similar to those in untreated controls.[43] But significant reductions were observed with either an intravenous dose of 50 mg/kg or 75 mg/kg of linezolid or intravenous vancomycin. The efficacy of the 75-mg/kg dose of linezolid was comparable to that of vancomycin given at 25 mg/kg. It was observed that in this model of infection, trough levels of linezolid in plasma must be above the MIC at the end of the final dosing period to have a clinically significant impact.

A third study examined the use of linezolid in the treatment of endocarditis caused by vancomycin-resistant E faecium in rats and found that its activity was similar to that of LY333328, an investigational glycopeptide that is bactericidal against enterococci.[44] Although the authors noted that E faecium endocarditis has been treated successfully in humans with quinupristin-dalfopristin, this agent is not active against E faecalis, and with few alternatives, resistance to quinupristin-dalfopristin is a concern.

Several investigators have reported their findings on linezolid therapy for bacterial endocarditis in humans. Chien et al[45] reported on the successful treatment of a patient with VRE endocarditis with linezolid during the compassionate use program. The patient achieved microbiological cure and was alive at the short-term follow-up evaluation.

Babcock et al[46] also reported the successful treatment of VRE endocarditis with linezolid. The patient was a 34-year-old woman with hypothyroidism, hyperlipidemia, congenital cyanotic heart disease (including a common atrium and a large ventricular septal defect), and end-stage renal disease requiring hemodialysis. The patient developed signs of vancomycin-resistant E faecium bacteremia and endocarditis and was treated with quinupristin-dalfopristin at 7.5 mg/kg intravenously every 8 hours. However, after 12 days of treatment, blood culture results were still positive for VRE and P aeruginosa.

Because the patient had been treated for VRE infection with chloramphenicol, the decision was made to initiate treatment with linezolid plus cefepime for the P aeruginosa infection.[46] After 2 intravenous doses of linezolid, blood culture results were negative for VRE. On the third day, the patient was switched to oral linezolid and oral ciprofloxacin to eradicate the P aeruginosa organisms. She continued to receive 600 mg of linezolid twice a day and 500 mg of ciprofloxacin twice a day for 6 weeks, and she tolerated the regimen well. Three months after the completion of therapy, blood culture results were negative for VRE, remaining so 9 months after treatment.

With the exception of the 3-day course of intravenous therapy, the entire treatment regimen was administered orally, and clinical and microbiological cure was achieved. Because this patient had a long history of intravenous line infections, the investigators noted that the ability to treat her infection with oral antibiotics, with the dialysis catheter as the only venous access, was especially advantageous.

Treatment failure in endocarditis has occurred with linezolid therapy as well. Zimmer et al[47] described a patient with endocarditis caused by E faecalis who did not respond to treatment with linezolid, and Ruiz and colleagues[48] noted treatment failures in endocarditis caused by MRSA in 2 patients. The first case occurred in a patient with chronic obstructive pulmonary disease who was treated with intravenous linezolid after transesophageal echocardiography revealed a vegetation on the mitral valve.[48] Despite 7 days of treatment, the patient remained bacteremic, and a regimen of TMP-SMX plus gentamicin was initiated. The bacteremia cleared within a day. A second patient was placed on linezolid after purulent discharge from an intravenous catheter tested positive for MRSA. The catheter was removed, and the patient was discharged on intravenous linezolid. However, blood culture results remained positive for MRSA, and an aortic valve vegetation was discovered 21 days later. The bacteremia resolved after vancomycin and rifampin therapy was begun.

In another instance, endocarditis developed during treatment with linezolid. A previously healthy 38-year-old man developed skin infections caused by MRSA and P aeruginosa after sustaining burns on more than 85% of his body.[49] Linezolid therapy was started, initially intravenously and then orally, at a dosage of 600 mg twice a day for 16 days. By the third day of treatment, MRSA had disappeared from burn wound samples. However, on the last day of linezolid therapy, the patient developed a fever and a subsequent blood culture again grew MRSA.

Vancomycin therapy was initiated.[49] At this time, a cardiac murmur was noted, and aortic endocarditis was diagnosed. Large vegetations were found on the aortic valve extending into the ventricular septum. Culture of the native valve grew linezolid-susceptible MRSA. The valve was replaced, the patient completed 4 weeks of vancomycin therapy and ultimately was discharged home.

These reports underscore not only the difficulty of treating infections such as endocarditis even when pathogens are susceptible to the antibiotics prescribed, but also the need to monitor closely those patients with serious infections. Linezolid has not been approved for use in endocarditis and may not be effective for this condition.

Continuing Rise of Resistant Pathogens

Given the growing prevalence of resistant pathogens, newer antibiotics such as linezolid are likely to play an increasingly important role in the antimicrobial armamentarium; MRSA in particular is a cause of concern. Recent reports from California have noted MRSA infections in various community settings, including correctional facilities, among members of athletic teams, and at health care facilities.[50] Among inmates, all those affected initially had skin infections; however, approximately 1% (10/928) developed invasive disease, including bacteremia, endocarditis, or osteomyelitis. An earlier report noted MRSA infections in a Mississippi state prison population; tests on samples obtained using swabs of the anterior nares revealed MRSA carriage in 4.9% of inmates.[51]

Methicillin-resistant S aureus infections are also on the rise globally.[52,53] In 2000, an extensive outbreak occurred in a hospital on the south coast of England,[54] and a prevalence survey of elderly patients performed 3 weeks after admission to another English hospital found that approximately 16% carried MRSA.[55] A dramatic increase of in MRSA strains was also found in the community.[56]

The Future of Linezolid and the Oxazolidinones

Much remains to be done in researching this compound and establishing its therapeutic role in bacterial infections. The possibility that protein synthesis inhibitors, including linezolid, target bacterial virulence factors and endotoxins needs to be explored further.[57,58] Recently published results, based on in vitro testing, indicate that linezolid may be synergistic with amoxicillin, erythromycin, imipenem, sparfloxacin, teicoplanin, or tetracycline. However, this must be explored in vivo to establish potency.[59] Another article indicates that linezolid in combination with either moxifloxacin or rifampin may provide a powerful therapeutic regimen.[60]

Reports also suggest possible efficacy against mycobacteria.[61-63] Early oxazolidinones exhibited in vitro activity against both Mycobacterium tuberculosis and nontubercular mycobacteria.[64,65] This observation was repeated later in a murine model by Cynamon et al[62] in 1999 with linezolid, eperezolid, and PNU-100480. More recently, Brown-Elliott et al[63] reported on the in vitro activity of linezolid against 15 species of nontuberculous mycobacteria, finding potential activity for most species.

Linezolid should be explored for treatment of osteomyelitis, prosthetic joint infection, and endocarditis (B.A. Lipsky, personal communication, May 2003), as well as bacteremia and catheter-related bacteremia (J.A. Weigelt, personal communication, May 2003). Although case reports have provided valuable insight into treatment of these infections with linezolid, use of this drug in these types of infections cannot be generally recommended without data from well-designed clinical trials.

Appropriate use of linezolid and other new antibiotics, such as quinupristin-dalfopristin, may help forestall the rise of bacterial resistance.[5] These powerful agents should be reserved for severe infections or those that have proved resistant to other antibiotics. Linezolid should be reserved for use in cases of documented or suspected gram-positive infection with resistant strains of staphylococci, enterococci, or streptococci (J.A. Weigelt, personal communication, May 2003). Avoidance of subtherapeutic doses, attention to proper dosing, and prompt removal of infected devices may limit the emergence of resistance.[5]

Other promising drugs on the horizon include newer fluoroquinolones, cyclic lipopeptides, glycylcyclines, novel glycopeptide derivatives, and fifth-generation cephalosporins. Other oxazolidinones are also in development.[66] Desirable features in newer oxazolidinones would include activity against gram-negative organisms, less bone marrow suppression, bactericidal activity, and once-daily dosing.

Linezolid offers several key advantages over its major competitors, vancomycin and quinupristin-dalfopristin. Its high bioavailability allows both intravenous and oral administration,[1] and its excellent tissue penetration permits high levels of the active compound to reach the site of infection.[67] Plus, it is better tolerated and less expensive than quinupristin-dalfopristin. (R. Owens, personal communication, May 2003).

Summary

Linezolid is a valuable new addition to the antibiotic armamentarium. Its unique mechanism of action demonstrates no cross-resistance with other classes of antibiotics. The presence of this trait suggests that resistance may develop slowly and, if this new agent is used judiciously, minimally. Its excellent pharmacokinetics and pharmacodynamics allow it to reach therapeutic levels in numerous infection sites, including lung tissue, skin and soft tissue, and possibly, bone and the central nervous system by either the oral or intravenous route. Its metabolic pathway allows for dosing in renally and hepatically impaired patients without fear of interaction with compounds metabolized by the cytochrome P-450 system. Data from large phase III clinical trials, the compassionate use program, postmarketing studies, and case studies have provided robust evidence of its efficacy and safety. Most adverse events are mild or moderate in nature and limited in duration, although myelosuppression can occur in patients treated for extended periods. Linezolid is active against VRE, MRSA, MRSE, and penicillin-resistant S pneumoniae. The ability to administer this agent either orally or intravenously with equivalent clinical outcomes offers a distinct advantage in the treatment of serious infections with gram-positive organisms and may reduce the length of hospital stay for many seriously ill patients.

References

1. Zyvox [package insert]. Kalamazoo, Mich: Pharmacia & Upjohn Company; 2003.
2. Rubinstein E, Cammarata SK, Oliphant TH, Wunderink RG, and the Linezolid Nosocomial Pneumonia Study Group. Linezolid (PNU-100766) versus vancomycin in the treatment of hospitalized patients with nosocomial pneumonia: a randomized, double-blind, multicenter study. Clin Infect Dis. 2001;32:402-412.
3. Stevens DL, Smith LG, Bruss JB, et al. Randomized comparison of linezolid (PNU-100766) versus oxacillin-dicloxacillin for treatment of complicated skin and soft tissue infections. Antimicrob Agents Chemother. 2000;44:3408-3413.
4. Herrero IA, Issa NC, Patel R. Nosocomial spread of linezolid-resistant, vancomycin-resistant Enterococcus faecium. N Engl J Med. 2002;346:867-869.
5. Gonzales RD, Schreckenberger PC, Graham MB, Kelkar S, DenBesten K, Quinn JP. Infections due to vancomycin-resistant Enterococcus faecium resistant to linezolid. [letter] Lancet. 2001;357:1179.
6. Tsiodras S, Gold HS, Sakoulas G, et al. Linezolid resistance in a clinical isolate of Staphylococcus aureus. [letter] Lancet. 2001;358:

207-208.
7. Potoski BA, Mangino JE, Goff DA. Clinical failures of linezolid and implications for the clinical microbiology laboratory. Emerg Infect Dis. 2002;8:1519-1520.
8. Duncan RA, Haas S, Craven DE, et al. Linezolid-resistant vancomycin-resistant Enterococcus faecium (LR-VREF) infection in a liver transplant recipient intolerant of dalfopristin/quinupristin and treated with daptomycin. Paper presented at: 39th Annual Meeting of the Infectious Diseases Society of America; October 25-28, 2001; San Francisco, Calif. Abstract 537.
9. Kirst HA, Thompson DG, Nicas TI. Historical yearly usage of vancomycin [letter]. Antimicrob Agents Chemother. 1998;42:1303-1304.
10. Centers for Disease Control and Prevention. Reduced susceptibility of Staphylococcus aureus to vancomycin—Japan, 1996. MMWR Morb Mortal Wkly Rep. 1997;46:624-626.
11. Hiramatsu K, Hanaki H, Ino T, Yabuta K, Oguri T, Tenover FC. Methicillin-resistant Staphylococcus aureus clinical strain with reduced vancomyin susceptibility [letter]. J Antimicrob Chemother. 1997;40:135-146.
12. Paladino JA. Economic justification of antimicrobial management programs: implications of antimicrobial resistance. Am J Health Syst Pharm. 2000;57:10-12.
13. Data on file. Pfizer Inc. New York, NY.
14. Zurenko GE, Todd WM, Hafkin B, et al. Development of linezolid-resistant Enterococcus faecium in two compassionate use program patients treated with linezolid. Paper presented at: 39th Interscience Conference on Antimicrobial Agents and Chemotherapy; September 26-29, 1999; San Francisco, Calif.
15. Xiong L, Kloss P, Douthwaite S, et al. Oxazolidinone resistance mutations in 23S rRNA of Escherichia coli reveal the central region of domain V as the primary site of drug action. J Bacteriol. 2000;182:5325-5331.
16. Ibrahim EH, Sherman G, Ward S, Fraser VJ, Kollef MH. The influence of inadequate antimicrobial treatment of bloodstream infections on patient outcomes in the ICU setting. Chest. 2000;118:146-155.
17. Kollef MH, Sherman G, Ward S, Fraser V. Inadequate antimicrobial treatment of infections: a risk factor of hospital mortality among critically ill patients. Chest. 1999;115:462-474.
18. Mutnik AH, Biedenbach DJ, Turnidge JD, Jones RN. Spectrum and potency evaluation of a new oxazolidinone, linezolid: report from the SENTRY Antimicrobial Surveillance Program, 1998-2000. Diagn Microbiol Infect Dis. 2002;43:65-73.
19. Zhanel GG, Palatnick L, Nihol KA, Bellyou T, Low DE, Hoban DJ. Antimicrobial resistance in respiratory tract Streptococcus pneumoniae isolates: results of the Canadian Respiratory Organism Susceptibility Study, 1997 to 2002. Antimicrob Agents Chemother. 2003;47:1867-1874.
20. Fines M, Leclercq R. Activity of linezolid against Gram-positive cocci possessing genes conferring resistance to protein synthesis inhibitors. J Antimicrob Chemother. 2000;45:797-802.
21. Prystowsky J, Siddiqui F, Chosay J, et al. Resistance to linezolid: characterization of mutations in rRNA and comparison of their occurrences in vancomycin-resistant enterococci. Antimicrob Agents Chemother. 2001;45:2154-2156.
22. Marshall SH, Donskey CJ, Hutton-Thomas R, Salata RA, Rice LB. Gene dosage and linezolid resistance in Enterococcus faecium and Enterococcus faecalis. Antimicrob Agents Chemother. 2002;46:3334-3336.
23. Millichap J, Ristow RA, Noskin GA, Peterson LR. Selection of Enterococcus faecium strains with stable and unstable resistance to the streptogramin RP 59500 using step-wise in vitro exposure. Diagn Microbiol Infect Dis. 1996;25:15-20.
24. Livermore DM, Mushtaq S, Warner M. Susceptibility testing with linezolid by different methods, in relation to published 'general breakpoints.' J Antimicrob Chemother. 2001;48:452-454.

25. User's Guide: Neo-Sensitabs Susceptibility Testing. Available at: http://www.aaconet.nl/manuals/neo-sensitabs15.pdf. Accessed December 28, 2003.

26. Leape LL, Brennan TA, Laird N, et al. The nature of adverse events in hospitalized patients. Results of the Harvard Medical Practice Study II. N Engl J Med. 1991;324:377-384.

27. Green SL, Maddox JC, Huttenbach ED. Linezolid and reversible myelosuppression. JAMA. 2001;285:1291.

28. Abena PA, Mathieux VG, Scheiff JM, Michaux LM, Vandercam BC. Linezolid and reversible myelosuppression. JAMA. 2001;286:1973.

29. Waldrep TW, Skiest DJ. Linezolid-induced anemia and thrombocytopenia. Pharmacotherapy. 2002;22:109-112.

30. Monson T, Schichman SA, Zent CS. Linezolid-induced pure red blood cell aplasia. Clin Infect Dis. 2002;35:E29-E31.

31. Gerson SL, Kaplan SL, Bruss JB, et al. Hematologic effects of linezolid: summary of clinical experience. Antimicrob Agents Chemother. 2002;46:2723-2726.

32. Lavery S, Ravi H, McDaniel WW, Pushkin YK. Linezolid and serotonin syndrome. Psychosomatics. 2001;42:432-434.

33. Wigen CI, Goetz MB. Serotonin syndrome and linezolid. Clin Infect Dis. 2002;34:1651-1652.

34. Bernard L, Stern R, Lew D, Hoffmeyer P. Serotonin syndrome after concomitant treatment with linezolid and citalopram. Clin Infect Dis. 2003;36:1197.

35. Rubin RJ, Harrington CA, Poon A, Dietrich K, Greene JA, Moiduddin A. The economic impact of Staphylococcus aureus infection in New York City hospitals. Emerg Infect Dis. 1999;5:9-17.

36. Li JZ, Willke RJ, Rittenhouse BE, Rybak MJ. Effect of linezolid versus vancomycin on length of hospital stay in patients with complicated skin and soft tissue infections caused by known or suspected methicillin-resistant staphylococci: results from a randomized clinical trial. Surg Infect. 2003;4:45-58.

37. Hachem R, Afif C, Gokaslan Z, Raad I. Successful treatment of vancomycin-resistant Enterococcus meningitis with linezolid. Eur J Clin Microbiol Infect Dis. 2001;20:432-434.

38. Zeana C, Kubin CJ, Della-Latta P, Hammer SM. Vancomycin-resistant Enterococcus faecium meningitis successfully managed with linezolid: case report and review of the literature. Clin Infect Dis. 2001;33:477-482.

39. Cottagnoud P, Gerber CM, Acosta F, Cottagnoud M, Neftel K, Tauber MG. Linezolid against penicillin-sensitive and -resistant pneumococci in the rabbit meningitis model. J Antimicrob Chemother. 2000;46:981-985.

40. Viale P, Pagani L, Cristini F, et al. Linezolid for the treatment of central nervous system infections in neurosurgical patients. Scand J Infect Dis. 2002;34:456-459.

41. Gutschik E. New developments in the treatment of infective endocarditis (infective cardiovasculitis). Int J Antimicrob Agents. 1999;13:79-92.

42. Oramas-Shirey MP, Buchanan LV, Dileto-Fang CL, et al. Efficacy of linezolid in a staphylococcal endocarditis rabbit model. J Antimicrob Chemother. 2001;47:349-352.

43. Dailey CF, Dileto-Fang CL, Buchanan LV, et al. Efficacy of linezolid in treatment of experimental endocarditis caused by methicillin-resistant Staphylococcus aureus. Antimicrob Agents Chemother. 2001;45:2304-2308.

44. Patel R, Rouse MS, Piper KE, Steckelberg JM. Linezolid therapy of vancomycin-resistant Enterococcus faecium experimental endocarditis. Antimicrob Agents Chemother. 2001;45:621-623.

45. Chien JW, Kucia ML, Salata RA. Use of linezolid, an oxazolidinone, in the treatment of multidrug-resistant gram-positive bacterial infections. Clin Infect Dis. 2000;30:146-151.

46. Babcock HM, Ritchie DJ, Christiansen E, Starlin R, Little R, Stanely S. Successful treatment of vancomycin-resistant Enterococcus endocarditis with oral linezolid. Clin Infect Dis. 2001;32:1373-1375.

47. Zimmer SM, Caliendo AM, Thigpen MC, Somani J. Failure of linezolid treatment for enterococcal endocarditis. Clin Infect Dis. 2003;37:E29-E30.

48. Ruiz ME, Guerrero IC, Tuazon CU. Endocarditis caused by methicillin-resistant Staphylococcus aureus: treatment failure with linezolid. Clin Infect Dis. 2002;15:1018-1020.

49. Ben Mansour EH, Jacob E, Monchi M, et al. Occurrence of MRSA endocarditis during linezolid treatment. Eur J Clin Microbiol Infect Dis. 2003;22:372-373.

50. Centers for Disease Control and Prevention. Public health dispatch: outbreaks of community-associated methicillin-resistant Staphylococcus aureus skin infections—Los Angeles County, California, 2002-2003. MMWR Morb Mortal Wkly Rep. 2002;52:88.

51. Centers for Disease Control and Prevention. Methicillin-resistant Staphylococcus aureus skin or soft tissue infections in a state prison—Mississippi, 2000. MMWR Morb Mortal Wkly Rep. 2001;40:919-922.

52. EARSS Annual Report 2002. Bilthoven, Netherlands: European Antimicrobial Resistance Surveillance System; August 2003.

53. Dikema DJ, Pfaller MA, Schmitz FJ, et al, SENTRY Participants Group. Survey of infections due to Staphylococcus species: frequency of occurrence and antimicrobial susceptibility of isolates collected in the United States, Canada, Latin America, Europe, and the Western Pacific Region of the SENTRY Antimicrobial Surveillance Program, 1997-1999. Clin Infect Dis. 2001;32(suppl 2):S114-S132.

54. Aucken HM, Ganner M, Murchan S, Cookson BD, Johnson AP. A new UK strain of epidemic methicillin-resistant Staphylococcus aureus (EMRSA-17) resistant to multiple antibiotics. J Antimicrob Chemother. 2002;50:171-175.

55. Hori S, Sunley R, Tami A, Grundmann H. The Nottingham Staphylococcus aureus population study: prevalence of MRSA among the elderly in a university hospital. J Hosp Infect. 2002;50:25-29.

56. Duckworth G. Controlling methicillin resistant Staphylococcus aureus: time to return to more stringent methods of control in the United Kingdom? [letter]. BMJ. 2003;327:1177-1178.

57. Coyle EA. Targeting bacterial virulence: the role of protein synthesis inhibitors in severe infections. Insights from the Society of Infectious Diseases Pharmacists. Pharmacotherapy. 2003;23:638-642.

58. Coyle EA, Cha R, Rybak MJ. Influences of linezolid, penicillin, and clindamycin, alone and in combination, on streptococcal pyrogenic exotoxin a release. Antimicrob Agents Chemother. 2003;47:1752-1755.

59. Sweeney MT, Zurenko GE. In vitro activities of linezolid combined with other antimicrobial agents against staphylococci, enterococci, pneumococci, and selected gram-negative organisms. Antimicrob Agents Chemother. 2003;47:1902-1906.

60. Cha R, Rybak M. Linezolid and vancomycin, alone and in combination with rifampin, compared with moxifloxacin against a multidrug-resistant and a vancomycin-tolerant Streptococcus pneumoniae strain in an in vitro pharmacodynamic model. Antimicrob Agents Chemother. 2003;47:1984-1987.

61. Wallace RJ Jr, Brown-Elliott BA, Ward SC, Crist CJ, Mann LB, Wilson RW. Activities of linezolid against rapidly growing mycobacteria. Antimicrob Agents Chemother. 2001;45:764-767.

62. Cynamon MH, Klemens SP, Sharpe CA, Chase S. Activities of several novel oxazolidinones against Mycobacterium tuberculosis in a murine model. Antimicrob Agents Chemother. 1999;43:1189-1191.

63. Brown-Elliott BA, Crist CJ, Mann LB, Wilson RW, Wallace RJ Jr. In vitro activity of linezolid against slowly growing nontuberculous mycobacteria. Antimicrob Agents Chemother. 2003;47:1736-1738.

64. Barbachyn MR, Hutchinson DK, Brickner SJ, et al. Identification of a novel oxazolidinone (U-100480) with potent antimycobacterial activity. J Med Chem. 1996;39:680-685.

65. Ashtekar DR, Costa-Periera R, Shrinivasan T, Iyyer R, Vishvanathan N, Rittel W. Oxazolidinones, a new class of synthetic antituberculosis agent. In vitro and in vivo activities of DuP-721 against Mycobacterium tuberculosis. Diagn Microbiol Infect Dis. 1991;14:465-471.

66. Tokuyama R, Takahashi Y, Tomita Y, et al. Structure-activity rela-
tionship (SAR) studies on oxazolidinone antibacterial agents. 3.
Synthesis and evaluation of 5-thiocarbamate oxazolidinones. *Chem
Pharm Bull [Tokyo].* 2001;49:361-367.

67. Livermore DM. Quinupristin/dalfopristin and linezolid: where, when,
which and whether to use. *J Antimicrob Chemother.* 2000;46:347-350.

CHAPTER NINE CME QUESTIONS

1. True or False: Bacterial resistance to linezolid
has not been reported in the literature.

2. Researchers have suggested which of the following as a potential mechanism of resistance to
linezolid?
  a. Modifying enzymes
  b. Active efflux systems
  c. Point mutations in the 23S rRNA domain V
  d. Modification or protection of the
  antimicrobial target

3. Linezolid is safe and well tolerated for up to:
  a. 2 weeks
  b. 21 days
  c. 28 days
  d. 42 days

4. True or False: Since approval, there have been
reports of reversible myelosuppression occurring
in patients during therapy with linezolid.

5. Which of the following is NOT a key advantage
of linezolid over many of its competitors?
  a. High bioavailability allows both intravenous
  and oral administration.
  b. Excellent tissue penetration permits high
  levels of the active compound to reach the
  site of infection.
  c. The drug is better tolerated and less expensive than quinupristin-dalfopristin.
  d. This agent exhibits bactericidal action for all
  susceptible pathogens.

UNIVERSITY OF KENTUCKY

CREATION OF A NOVEL CLASS:
THE OXAZOLIDINONE ANTIBIOTICS

Released: February 1, 2004 | Expires: January 31, 2005 |

A passing score of 70% or higher on the post-test awards the participant six (6) AMA PRA Category 1 or ACPE credit. To claim continuing education credit, individuals must complete the self-study activity, post-test, and evaluation and mail the form below postmarked by January 31, 2005 to:

Attn: Distance Education
Continuing Education Office
Colleges of Pharmacy and Medicine
University of Kentucky
One Quality Street, 6th Floor
Lexington, KY 40507-1428

TEST CODE: XDEHEF03

NAME:

CREDENTIALS: ___ SOC SEC #: ___ (FOR IDENTIFICATION PURPOSES ONLY)

ADDRESS:

CITY: ___ STATE: ___ ZIP: ___

DAYTIME PHONE: ___ FAX: ___

E-MAIL:

SIGNATURE: ___

EVALUATION	POOR		SATISFACTORY		EXCELLENT
1. EXTENT TO WHICH THE OBJECTIVES WERE ACHIEVED:	1	2	3	4	5
2. POTENTIAL IMPACT ON YOUR PRACTICE:	1	2	3	4	5
3. DETAIL OF INFORMATION PRESENTED:	1	2	3	4	5
4. OVERALL EVALUATION OF THIS CE ACTIVITY:	1	2	3	4	5

5. SUGGESTIONS FOR FUTURE CE TOPICS: ___

POST-TEST ANSWERS: *Circle the correct answer.*

Chapter 1
1. a b c d
2. a b c d
3. a b c d
4. a b c d
5. a b c d e

Chapter 2
1. T or F
2. a b c d
3. a b c d
4. a b c d
5. a b c d e f

Chapter 3
1. T or F
2. T or F
3. a b c
4. a b c d e
5. a b c d

Chapter 4
1. a b c d
2. T or F
3. a b c d
4. a b c d e
5. a b c d

Chapter 5
1. a b c d
2. a b c
3. T or F
4. a b c d
5. a b c d

Chapter 6
1. a b c d
2. a b c d
3. a b c d
4. a b c d
5. T or F

Chapter 7
1. a b c d
2. a b c d
3. T or F
4. a b c d
5. a b c d

Chapter 8
1. a b c d
2. a b c d
3. T or F
4. a b c d
5. a b c d

Chapter 9
1. T or F
2. a b c d
3. a b c d
4. T or F
5. a b c d